GRAMMAR AND BEYOND 2A

Second Edition

with Academic Writing

Randi Reppen

CAMBRIDGE
UNIVERSITY PRESS

Shaftesbury Road, Cambridge CB2 8EA, United Kingdom

One Liberty Plaza, 20th Floor, New York, NY 10006, USA

477 Williamstown Road, Port Melbourne, VIC 3207, Australia

314–321, 3rd Floor, Plot 3, Splendor Forum, Jasola District Centre, New Delhi – 110025, India

103 Penang Road, #05–06/07, Visioncrest Commercial, Singapore 238467

Cambridge University Press & Assessment is a department of the University of Cambridge.

We share the University's mission to contribute to society through the pursuit of
education, learning and research at the highest international levels of excellence.

www.cambridge.org
Information on this title: www.cambridge.org/9781108784917

© Cambridge University Press & Assessment 2021

First published 2013
Second edition 2021

20 19 18 17 16 15 14 13 12 11 10 9 8 7 6 5

Printed in Great Britain by Ashford Colour Limited

A catalogue record for this publication is available from the British Library

ISBN Student's Book 2A with Online Practice 978-1-108-78491-7

Additional resources for this publication at www.cambridge.org/grammarandbeyond

About the Author

Randi Reppen is Professor of Applied Linguistics and TESL at Northern Arizona University (NAU) in Flagstaff, Arizona. She has over 20 years' experience teaching ESL students and training ESL teachers, including 11 years as the Director of NAU's Program in Intensive English. Randi's research interests focus on the use of corpora for language teaching and materials development. In addition to numerous academic articles and books, she is the author of *Using Corpora in the Language Classroom* and a co-author of *Basic Vocabulary in Use*, 2nd edition, both published by Cambridge University Press.

Corpus Consultants

Michael McCarthy is Emeritus Professor of Applied Linguistics at the University of Nottingham, UK, and Adjunct Professor of Applied Linguistics at Pennsylvania State University. He is a co-author of the corpus-informed *Touchstone* series and the award-winning *Cambridge Grammar of English*, both published by Cambridge University Press, among many other titles, and is known throughout the world as an expert on grammar, vocabulary, and corpus linguistics.

Jeanne McCarten has over 30 years of experience in ELT/ESL as a teacher, publisher, and author. She has been closely involved in the development of the spoken English sections of the *Cambridge International Corpus*. Now a freelance writer, she is co-author of the corpus-informed *Touchstone* series and *Grammar for Business*, both published by Cambridge University Press.

Advisory Panel

The ESL advisory panel has helped to guide the development of this series and provided invaluable information about the needs of ESL students and teachers in high schools, colleges, universities, and private language schools throughout North America.

Neta Simpkins Cahill, Skagit Valley College, Mount Vernon, WA
Shelly Hedstrom, Palm Beach State College, Lake Worth, FL
Richard Morasci, Foothill College, Los Altos Hills, CA
Stacey Russo, East Hampton High School, East Hampton, NY
Alice Savage, Lone Star College-North Harris, Houston, TX

Scope and Sequence

Unit	Theme	Grammar	Topics
PART 1 The Present			
UNIT 1 page 2	Are You Often Online?	Simple Present	Simple Present (p. 4) Time Clauses and Factual Conditionals (p. 9)
UNIT 2 page 16	Brainpower	Present Progressive and Simple Present	Present Progressive (p. 18) Simple Present and Present Progressive Compared (p. 21)
UNIT 3 page 30	What's Appropriate?	Imperatives	Imperatives (p. 32) *Let's . . .* (p. 36)
PART 2 The Past			
UNIT 4 page 42	Entrepreneurs	Simple Past	Simple Past (p. 44) Simple Past of *Be* and *There Was / There Were* (p. 50)
UNIT 5 page 56	Science and Society	Simple Past, Time Clauses, *Used To*, and *Would*	Time Clauses and the Order of Past Events (p. 58) Past with *Used To* and *Would* (p. 61)
UNIT 6 page 70	Memorable Events	Past Progressive	Past Progressive (p. 72) Using *When* and *While* with Past Progressive (p. 76)
PART 3 Nouns, Determiners, and Pronouns			
UNIT 7 page 82	Privacy Matters	Count and Noncount Nouns	Count Nouns and Noncount Nouns (p. 84) Noncount Nouns: Determiners and Measurement Words (p. 89)

Avoid Common Mistakes	Academic Writing
Avoiding *amn't*; remembering a comma after a time clause at the beginning of a sentence	**Doing Research Online** • Find a reliable source • Evaluate an Internet source
Remembering a form of *be* with the present progressive; remembering *-ing* for the present progressive	**Opinion Writing** Writing prompt: *Should governments spend more money on space exploration?* • Identify purpose • Supporting details • Brainstorm
Avoiding *No* in imperatives; remembering an apostrophe in *Don't* and *Let's*	• Evaluate evidence • The imperative in academic writing
Avoiding the past form after *did not* and *didn't*; avoiding putting a time expression between the subject and the verb	• Organize an essay • Thesis statements • The simple past in academic writing
Remembering a subject in time clauses; remembering the *-d* in *used to* for affirmative statements	• Plan the essay • Write the first draft
Avoiding a time clause as a complete sentence; remembering a comma when the time clause comes first in a sentence	• Revise and edit
Remembering a determiner with a singular count noun; avoiding *a/an* with a noncount noun; avoiding plural noncount nouns	**Expository Writing** Writing prompt: *Choose a new area of technology or invention to analyze. Write a report about its advantages and disadvantages, and include a prediction in the conclusion.* • Use a T-chart to identify advantages and disadvantages • Brainstorm

Unit	Theme	Grammar	Topics
UNIT 8 page 98	The Media	Articles	Articles (p. 100) Generalizing: More about Articles (p. 104)
UNIT 9 page 108	Challenging Ourselves	Pronouns Direct and Indirect Objects	Pronouns (p. 110) Direct and Indirect Objects (p. 115)
PART 4 The Present Perfect			
UNIT 10 page 122	Discoveries	Present Perfect	Present Perfect (p. 124) Present Perfect or Simple Past? (p. 128)
UNIT 11 page 136	Unsolved Mysteries	Adverbs with Present Perfect *For* and *Since*	Adverbs with Present Perfect (p. 138) Present Perfect with *For* and *Since* (p. 142)
UNIT 12 page 148	Cities	Present Perfect Progressive	Present Perfect Progressive (p. 150) Present Perfect Progressive or Present Perfect? (p. 154)
PART 5 Adjectives, Adverbs, and Prepositions			
UNIT 13 page 160	A Good Workplace	Adjectives	Adjectives (p. 162) More About Adjectives (p. 165)
UNIT 14 page 174	Learn Quickly!	Adverbs of Manner and Degree	Adverbs of Manner (p. 176) Adverbs of Degree (p. 179)
UNIT 15 page 186	Food on the Table	Prepositions	Prepositions of Place and Time (p. 188) Prepositions of Direction and Manner (p. 192) Phrasal Prepositions and Prepositions After Adjectives (p. 196)

Avoid Common Mistakes	Academic Writing
Remembering *a/an* the first time you mention a new idea; avoiding *the* with generalizations	• Plan and write an introductory paragraph
Remembering *to* or *for* with certain verbs; avoiding double pronouns	• Introduce advantages and disadvantages • Complete the first draft • Revise and edit
Remembering when to use the simple past; remembering when to use the present perfect	**Comparison-and-Contrast Writing** Writing prompt: *Compare and contrast the whale shark and the tiger shark.* • Use Venn diagrams • Combine sentences
Avoiding *never* in negative statements; avoiding *ever* in affirmative statements	• Write topic sentences • Plan body paragraphs
Remembering *have* with the present perfect progressive; avoiding the present progressive with *for* and *since*	• Write the first draft • Revise and edit
Avoiding misspelling adjectives ending in *-ful*; remembering to put opinion adjectives first	**Argumentative Writing** Writing prompt: *Do you agree or disagree with the following statement? "The fashion industry is harmful to society and the environment." Use reasons and examples to support your answer.* • Identify strong arguments • Brainstorm and organize • Use descriptive adjectives
Remembering to use adverbs to describe how something happened; avoiding putting an adverb between the verb and the object; remembering that some adverbs have the same form as adjectives	• Introductory paragraphs in argumentative essays • Body paragraphs in argumentative essays • Use adverbs of degree
Using prepositions correctly	• Write with cohesion • Write the first draft • Revise and edit

Unit	Theme	Grammar	Topics
PART 6 The Future			
UNIT 16 page 204	Life Lists	Future (1)	*Be Going To*, Present Progressive, and Simple Present for Future Events (p. 206)
UNIT 17 page 216	Getting Older	Future (2)	Future with *Will* (p. 218) Future with *Will*, *Be Going To*, and Present Progressive (p. 222)
UNIT 18 page 230	Learning to Communicate	Future Time Clauses and Future Conditionals	Future Time Clauses (p. 232) Future Conditionals; Questions with Time Clauses and Conditional Clauses (p. 236)
PART 7 Modal Verbs and Modal-like Expressions			
UNIT 19 page 244	Amazing Science	Ability	Ability with *Can* and *Could* (p. 246) *Be Able To* (p. 250)
UNIT 20 page 260	Good Causes	Requests and Offers	Permission (p. 262) Requests and Offers (p. 266)
UNIT 21 page 274	The Right Job	Advice and Suggestions	Advice (p. 276) Suggestions (p. 280)
UNIT 22 page 286	How to Sell It	Necessity, Prohibition, and Preference	Necessity and Prohibition (p. 288) Preference (p. 292)
UNIT 23 page 298	Life Today, Life Tomorrow	Present and Future Probability	Present Probability (p. 300) Modals of Future Probability (p. 303)

Avoid Common Mistakes	Academic Writing
Remembering *be* with *going to*; remembering *be* before the subject in *Wh-* questions with *be going to*	**Opinion Writing** Writing prompt: *Should colleges and universities require students to take physical education classes?* • Brainstorm reasons and evaluate evidence • Plan an opinion essay
Remembering *will* before the main verb with the future; remembering the base form of the verb after *will*	• State opinions • Structure opinion essays
Avoiding *will* in the conditional clause; avoiding *will* in the time clause	• Use future conditionals • Write the first draft • Revise and edit
Remembering to spell *cannot* as one word; remembering the *be* and *to* in *be able to*	**Cause-and-Effect Writing** Writing prompt: *Describe the human causes of climate change and the effects climate change can have on the planet.* • Organize a cause-and-effect essay • Describe causes and effects • Brainstorm
Avoiding *could* in short answers to requests for permission; avoiding *could* or *would* in responses to requests to do things	• Describe causes and effects • Use causes and effects to express solutions or predictions • Make requests in academic writing
Remembering *had* in *had better*; avoiding *could not* in negative suggestions	• Maintain paragraph coherence • Choose strong supporting details • Use formal modals for advice and suggestions
Avoiding an infinitive with *would rather*; remembering *would* before *rather*	• Write an effective hook • Use modals of necessity and prohibition • Write the first draft
Avoiding *can* for present or future probability; avoiding *couldn't* for uncertainty	• Use modals to express future possibility • Revise and edit

Unit	Theme	Grammar	Topics
PART 8 Verbs + Prepositions and Phrasal Verbs			
UNIT 24 page 310	Getting Along at Work	Transitive and Intransitive Verbs Verbs and Prepositions	Transitive and Intransitive Verbs (p. 312) Verb + Object + Preposition Combinations (p. 314) Verb + Preposition Combinations (p. 316)
UNIT 25 page 324	Money, Money, Money	Phrasal Verbs	Intransitive Phrasal Verbs (p. 326) Transitive Phrasal Verbs (p. 329)
PART 9 Comparatives and Superlatives			
UNIT 26 page 336	We Are All Different	Comparatives	Comparative Adjectives and Adverbs (p. 338) Comparisons with *As . . . As* (p. 343)
UNIT 27 page 350	The Best and the Worst	Superlative Adjectives and Adverbs	Superlative Adjectives and Adverbs (p. 352)
PART 10 Gerunds and Infinitives			
UNIT 28 page 360	Managing Time	Gerunds and Infinitives (1)	Verbs Followed by Gerunds or Infinitives (p. 362) Verbs Followed by Gerunds and Infinitives (p. 365)
UNIT 29 page 374	Civil Rights	Gerunds and Infinitives (2)	More About Gerunds (p. 376) More About Infinitives (p. 379)
PART 11 Clauses and Conjunctions			
UNIT 30 page 386	Sleep	Subject Relative Clauses (Adjective Clauses with Subject Relative Pronouns)	Subject Relative Clauses (p. 388) More About Subject Relative Clauses (p. 392)
UNIT 31 page 400	Viruses	Object Relative Clauses (Adjective Clauses with Object Relative Pronouns)	Object Relative Clauses (p. 402) More About Object Relative Clauses (p. 406)
UNIT 32 page 414	Special Days	Conjunctions and Adverb Clauses	Conjunctions (p. 416) Adverb Clauses (p. 420)

Avoid Common Mistakes	Academic Writing
Remembering the object with a transitive verb; using prepositions with verbs	**Description and Analysis** Writing prompt: *Describe the trends in a multiple line graph, and analyze the data. Do some additional research to discuss the trends you identify.* • Understand and interpret line graphs • Use noun and verb phrases to describe graphs
Remembering a particle in phrasal verbs; avoiding putting an object pronoun after a particle	• Choose the important details from a graph • Write the concluding paragraph
Avoiding using *more* and *-er* together; remembering the second as in *as . . . as* comparisons	• Use comparatives to describe and analyze graphs • Write the first draft
Remembering irregular superlative forms; avoiding an object pronoun before a superlative	• Use superlatives in academic writing • Revise and edit
Using infinitives and gerunds after verbs; remembering *to* in infinitives	**Summary and Response** Writing prompt: *Write a summary paragraph of "Nontraditional Weddings." Then write a response paragraph giving your opinion about the changes in wedding traditions described in the article.* • Analyze a text • Summarize a text
Avoiding plural verbs with gerund subjects; avoiding infinitives after prepositions; remembering *It* and *to* in *It* sentences	• Paraphrase • Respond to a writer's ideas • Use gerunds and infinitives in academic writing
Avoiding a subject pronoun after a subject relative pronoun; remembering the relative pronoun in a subject relative clause	• Write a personal response • Use subject relative clauses in summary writing
Avoiding *who* in possessives; avoiding *whom* in subject relative clauses; avoiding an object pronoun at the end of an object relative clause	• Use object relative clauses in a personal response • Write the first draft
Remembering a comma after the adverb clause when it is first	• Revise and edit • Use adverb clauses to connect contrasting ideas

Appendices   A1

Glossary of Grammar Terms   G1

Index and Credits   I1

Grammar and Beyond is a research-based and content-rich grammar and academic writing series for beginning to advanced-level students. The series focuses on the most commonly used English grammar structures and practices all four skills in a variety of authentic and communicative contexts.

Grammar and Beyond is Research-Based

The grammar presented in this series is informed by years of research on the grammar of written and spoken English as it is used in college lectures, textbooks, academic essays, high school classrooms, and conversations between instructors and students. This research, and the analysis of over one billion words of authentic written and spoken language data known as the *Cambridge International Corpus*, has enabled the authors to:

- Present grammar rules that accurately represent how English is actually spoken and written

- Identify and teach differences between the grammar of written and spoken English

- Focus more attention on the structures that are commonly used, and less on those that are rarely used, in writing and speaking

- Help students avoid the most common mistakes that English language learners make

- Choose reading topics that will naturally elicit examples of the target grammar structure

- Introduce important vocabulary from the Academic Word List

Special Features of *Grammar and Beyond*

Realistic Grammar Presentations

Grammar is presented in clear and simple charts. The grammar points presented in these charts have been tested against real-world data from the *Cambridge International Corpus* to ensure that they are authentic representations of actual use of English.

Data from the Real World

Many of the grammar presentations and application sections include a feature called Data from the Real World. Concrete and useful points discovered through analysis of corpus data are presented and practiced in exercises that follow.

Avoid Common Mistakes

Every unit features an Avoid Common Mistakes section that develops students' awareness of the most common mistakes made by English language learners and gives them an opportunity to practice detecting and correcting these errors. This section helps students avoid these mistakes in their own work. The mistakes highlighted in this section are drawn from a body of authentic data on learner English known as the *Cambridge Learner Corpus*, a database of over 35 million words from student essays written by non-native speakers of English and information from experienced classroom teachers.

Academic Vocabulary

Every unit in *Grammar and Beyond* includes words from the Academic Word List (AWL), a research-based list of words and word families that appear with high frequency in English-language academic texts. These words are introduced in the opening text of the unit, recycled in the charts and exercises, and used to support the theme throughout the unit. By the time students finish each level, they will have been exposed several times to a carefully selected set of level-appropriate AWL words, as well as content words from a variety of academic disciplines.

Academic Writing

Every unit ends with an Academic Writing section. In Levels 1 through 3, this edition of *Grammar and Beyond* teaches students to write academically using writing cycles that span several units. Each writing cycle is organized around a writing prompt and focuses on a specific type of academic writing, such as descriptive, narrative, and process. Students move through the steps of the writing process - Brainstorm, Organize, Write, Edit - while learning and practicing new writing skills and ways to incorporate the unit grammar into their writing. In Level 4, the entire scope and sequence is organized around the types of essays students write in college, and focuses on the grammar rules, conventions, and structures needed to master them.

Series Levels

The following table provides a general idea of the difficulty of the material at each level of *Grammar and Beyond*. These are not meant to be interpreted as precise correlations.

	Description	TOEFL IBT	CEFR Levels
Level 1	Beginning	20 – 34	A1 – A2
Level 2	Low Intermediate to Intermediate	35 – 54	A2 – B1
Level 3	High Intermediate	55 – 74	B1 – B2
Level 4	Advanced	75 – 95	B2 – C1

Student Components

Student's Book with Online Practice

Each unit, based on a high-interest topic, teaches grammar points appropriate for each level in short, manageable cycles of presentation and practice. Academic Writing focuses on the structure of the academic essay in addition to the grammar rules, conventions, and structures that students need to master in order to be successful college writers. Students can access both the Digital Workbook and Writing Skills Interactive using their smartphones, tablets, or computers with single log-in. See pages xviii–xxiii for a Tour of a Unit.

Digital Workbook

The Digital Workbook provides additional online exercises to help master each grammar point. Automatically-graded exercises give immediate feedback for activities such as correcting errors highlighted in the Avoid Common Mistakes section in the Student's Book. Self-Assessment sections at the end of each unit allow students to test their mastery of what they learned. Look for [icon] in the Student's Book to see when to use the Digital Workbook.

Writing Skills Interactive

Writing Skills Interactive is a self-grading course to practice discrete writing skills, reinforce vocabulary, and give students an opportunity with additional writing practice. Each unit has:

- Vocabulary review
- Short text to check understanding of the context
- Animated presentation of target unit writing skill
- Practice activities
- Unit Quiz to assess progress

Teacher Resources

A variety of downloadable resources are available on Cambridge One (cambridgeone.org) to assist instructors, including the following:

Teacher's Manual

- Suggestions for applying the target grammar to all four major skill areas, helping instructors facilitate dynamic and comprehensive grammar classes
- An answer key and audio script for the Student's Book
- Teaching tips, to help instructors plan their lessons
- Communicative activity worksheets to add more in-class speaking practice

Assessment

- Placement Test
- Ready-made, easy-to-score Unit Tests, Midterm, and Final in .pdf and .doc formats
- Answer Key

Presentation Plus

Presentation Plus allows teachers to digitally project the contents of the Student's Books in front of the class for a livelier, interactive classroom. It is a complete solution for teachers because it includes easy-to-access answer keys and audio at point of use.

Acknowledgements

The publisher and author would like to thank these reviewers and consultants for their insights and participation:

Marty Attiyeh, The College of DuPage, Glen Ellyn, IL

Shannon Bailey, Austin Community College, Austin, TX

Jamila Barton, North Seattle Community College, Seattle, WA

Kim Bayer, Hunter College IELI, New York, NY

Linda Berendsen, Oakton Community College, Skokie, IL

Anita Biber, Tarrant County College Northwest, Fort Worth, TX

Jane Breaux, Community College of Aurora, Aurora, CO

Anna Budzinski, San Antonio College, San Antonio, TX

Britta Burton, Mission College, Santa Clara, CA

Jean Carroll, Fresno City College, Fresno, CA

Chris Cashman, Oak Park High School and Elmwood Park High School, Chicago, IL

Annette M. Charron, Bakersfield College, Bakersfield, CA

Patrick Colabucci, ALI at San Diego State University, San Diego, CA

Lin Cui, Harper College, Palatine, IL

Jennifer Duclos, Boston University CELOP, Boston, MA

Joy Durighello, San Francisco City College, San Francisco, CA

Kathleen Flynn, Glendale Community College, Glendale, CA

Raquel Fundora, Miami Dade College, Miami, FL

Patricia Gillie, New Trier Township High School District, Winnetka, IL

Laurie Gluck, LaGuardia Community College, Long Island City, NY

Kathleen Golata, Galileo Academy of Science & Technology, San Francisco, CA

Ellen Goldman, Mission College, Santa Clara, CA

Ekaterina Goussakova, Seminole Community College, Sanford, FL

Marianne Grayston, Prince George's Community College, Largo, MD

Mary Greiss Shipley, Georgia Gwinnett College, Lawrenceville, GA

Sudeepa Gulati, Long Beach City College, Long Beach, CA

Nicole Hammond Carrasquel, University of Central Florida, Orlando, FL

Vicki Hendricks, Broward College, Fort Lauderdale, FL

Kelly Hernandez, Miami Dade College, Miami, FL

Ann Johnston, Tidewater Community College, Virginia Beach, VA

Julia Karet, Chaffey College, Claremont, CA

Jeanne Lachowski, English Language Institute, University of Utah, Salt Lake City, UT

Noga Laor, Rennert, New York, NY

Min Lu, Central Florida Community College, Ocala, FL

Michael Luchuk, Kaplan International Centers, New York, NY

Craig Machado, Norwalk Community College, Norwalk, CT

Denise Maduli-Williams, City College of San Francisco, San Francisco, CA

Diane Mahin, University of Miami, Coral Gables, FL

Melanie Majeski, Naugatuck Valley Community College, Waterbury, CT

Jeanne Malcolm, University of North Carolina at Charlotte, Charlotte, NC

Lourdes Marx, Palm Beach State College, Boca Raton, FL

Susan G. McFalls, Maryville College, Maryville, TN

Nancy McKay, Cuyahoga Community College, Cleveland, OH

Dominika McPartland, Long Island Business Institute, Flushing, NY

Amy Metcalf, UNR/Intensive English Language Center, University of Nevada, Reno, NV

Robert Miller, EF International Language School San Francisco – Mills, San Francisco, CA

Marcie Pachino, Jordan High School, Durham, NC

Myshie Pagel, El Paso Community College, El Paso, TX

Bernadette Pedagno, University of San Francisco, San Francisco, CA

Tam Q Pham, Dallas Theological Seminary, Fort Smith, AR

Mary Beth Pickett, GlobalLT, Rochester, MI

Maria Reamore, Baltimore City Public Schools, Baltimore, MD

Alison M. Rice, Hunter College IELI, New York, NY

Sydney Rice, Imperial Valley College, Imperial, CA

Kathleen Romstedt, Ohio State University, Columbus, OH

Alexandra Rowe, University of South Carolina, Columbia, SC

Irma Sanders, Baldwin Park Adult and Community Education, Baldwin Park, CA

Caren Shoup, Lone Star College – CyFair, Cypress, TX

Karen Sid, Mission College, Foothill College, De Anza College, Santa Clara, CA

Michelle Thomas, Miami Dade College, Miami, FL

Sharon Van Houte, Lorain County Community College, Elyria, OH

Margi Wald, UC Berkeley, Berkeley, CA

Walli Weitz, Riverside County Office of Ed., Indio, CA

Bart Weyand, University of Southern Maine, Portland, ME

Donna Weyrich, Columbus State Community College, Columbus, OH

Marilyn Whitehorse, Santa Barbara City College, Ojai, CA

Jessica Wilson, Rutgers University – Newark, Newark, NJ

Sue Wilson, San Jose City College, San Jose, CA

Margaret Wilster, Mid-Florida Tech, Orlando, FL

Anne York-Herjeczki, Santa Monica College, Santa Monica, CA

Hoda Zaki, Camden County College, Camden, NJ

We would also like to thank these teachers and programs for allowing us to visit:

Richard Appelbaum, Broward College, Fort Lauderdale, FL

Carmela Arnoldt, Glendale Community College, Glendale, AZ

JaNae Barrow, Desert Vista High School, Phoenix, AZ

Ted Christensen, Mesa Community College, Mesa, AZ

Richard Ciriello, Lower East Side Preparatory High School, New York, NY

Virginia Edwards, Chandler-Gilbert Community College, Chandler, AZ

Nusia Frankel, Miami Dade College, Miami, FL

Raquel Fundora, Miami Dade College, Miami, FL

Vicki Hendricks, Broward College, Fort Lauderdale, FL

Kelly Hernandez, Miami Dade College, Miami, FL

Stephen Johnson, Miami Dade College, Miami, FL

Barbara Jordan, Mesa Community College, Mesa, AZ

Nancy Kersten, GateWay Community College, Phoenix, AZ

Lewis Levine, Hostos Community College, Bronx, NY

John Liffiton, Scottsdale Community College, Scottsdale, AZ

Cheryl Lira-Layne, Gilbert Public School District, Gilbert, AZ

Mary Livingston, Arizona State University, Tempe, AZ

Elizabeth Macdonald, Thunderbird School of Global Management, Glendale, AZ

Terri Martinez, Mesa Community College, Mesa, AZ

Lourdes Marx, Palm Beach State College, Boca Raton, FL

Paul Kei Matsuda, Arizona State University, Tempe, AZ

David Miller, Glendale Community College, Glendale, AZ

Martha Polin, Lower East Side Preparatory High School, New York, NY

Patricia Pullenza, Mesa Community College, Mesa, AZ

Victoria Rasinskaya, Lower East Side Preparatory High School, New York, NY

Vanda Salls, Tempe Union High School District, Tempe, AZ

Kim Sanabria, Hostos Community College, Bronx, NY

Cynthia Schuemann, Miami Dade College, Miami, FL

Michelle Thomas, Miami Dade College, Miami, FL

Dongmei Zeng, Borough of Manhattan Community College, New York, NY

Tour of a Unit

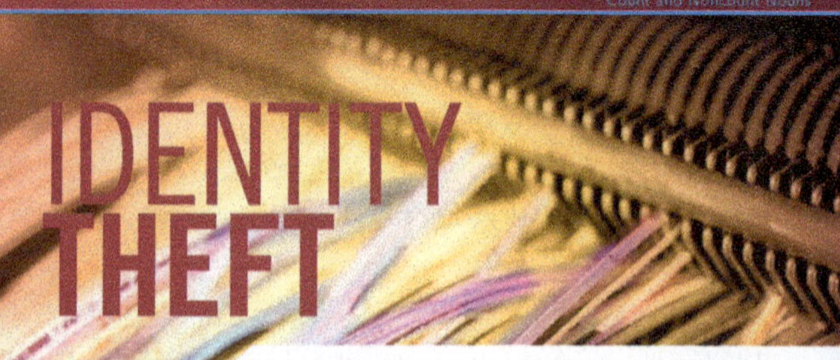

GRAMMAR PRESENTATION

begins with an overview that describes the grammar in an easy-to-understand summary.

THEME-RELATED EXERCISES

boost fluency by providing grammar practice in a variety of different contexts.

3 Noncount Nouns: Determiners and Measurement Words

Grammar Presentation

| You can use certain determiners and measurement words with noncount nouns. | Can you give me *some advice* about spyware programs?
She told me two interesting *pieces of news*. |

3.1 Noncount Nouns with Determiners

A Use *a lot of, some,* and *a little* with noncount nouns in affirmative statements.	There was *a lot of milk* in the refrigerator. I have *some* important *information* for you. Could I have *a little cream* in my coffee, please?
B Use *much, a lot of,* and *any* with noncount nouns in questions.	Was there *much furniture* in the apartment? Is there *a lot of traffic* at 5:00 p.m.? Are you making *any progress* with your English these days?
C Use *some* and *a little* for questions that are offers and requests.	Would you like *some tea*? Would you like *a little sugar* in your coffee?
D Use *not much, not a lot,* and *not any* with noncount nouns in negative statements.	There's *not much juice* left in your glass. She does*n't* earn *a lot of money* in her present job. We did*n't* do *any work* yesterday.
E Do not use *much* or *a little* with count nouns.	We don't have *much time* left. We don't have much *hours* left. There's *a little coffee* in the cup. There's *a little cups* on the table.

3.3 Noncount Nouns with Measurement Words *(continued)*

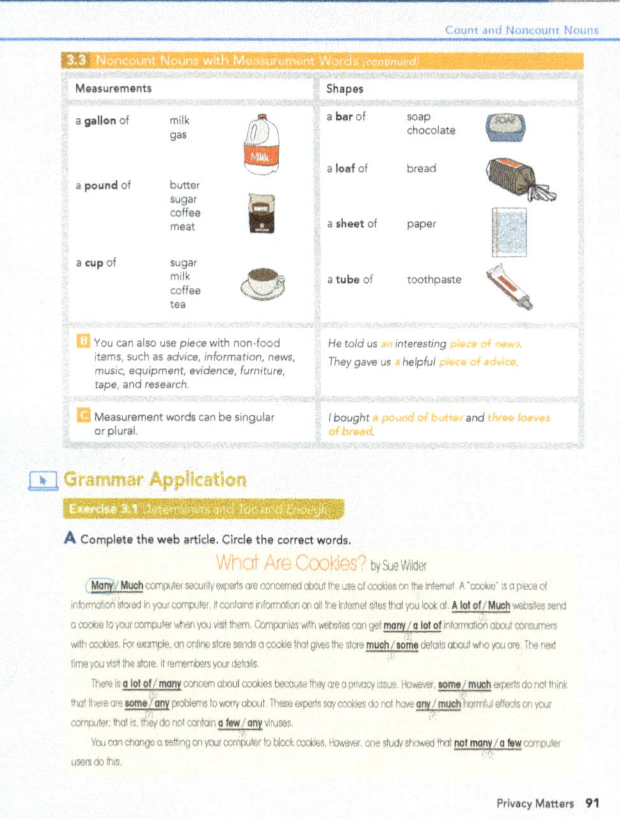

Measurements		Shapes	
a **gallon** of	milk gas	a **bar** of	soap chocolate
a **pound** of	butter sugar coffee meat	a **loaf** of	bread
		a **sheet** of	paper
a **cup** of	sugar milk coffee tea	a **tube** of	toothpaste

| **B** You can also use *piece* with non-food items, such as advice, information, news, music, equipment, evidence, furniture, tape, and research. | He told us *an* interesting *piece of news*.
They gave us *a* helpful *piece of advice*. |
| **C** Measurement words can be singular or plural. | I bought *a pound of butter* and *three loaves of bread*. |

Grammar Application

Exercise 3.1 Determiners and *Too* and *Enough*

A Complete the web article. Circle the correct words.

What Are Cookies? by Sue Wilder

(**Many** / **Much**) computer security experts are concerned about the use of cookies on the Internet. A "cookie" is a piece of information stored in your computer. It contains information on all the Internet sites that you look at. **A lot of** / **Much** websites send a cookie to your computer when you visit them. Companies with websites can get **many** / **a lot of** information about consumers with cookies. For example, an online store sends a cookie that gives the store **much** / **some** details about who you are. The next time you visit the store, it remembers your details.

There is **a lot of** / **many** concern about cookies because they are a privacy issue. However, **some** / **much** experts do not think that there are **some** / **any** problems to worry about. These experts say cookies do not have **any** / **much** harmful effects on your computer; that is, they do not contain **a few** / **any** viruses.

You can change a setting on your computer to block cookies. However, one study showed that **not many** / **a few** computer users do this.

CHARTS

provide clear guidance on the form, meaning, and use of the target grammar for ease of instruction and reference.

GRAMMAR APPLICATION

keeps students engaged with a wide variety of exercises that introduce new and stimulating content.

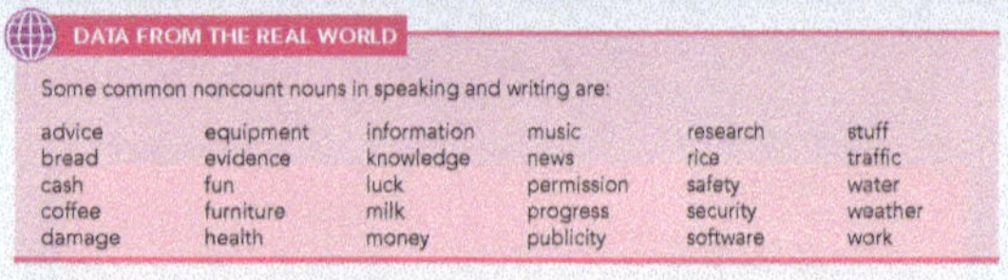

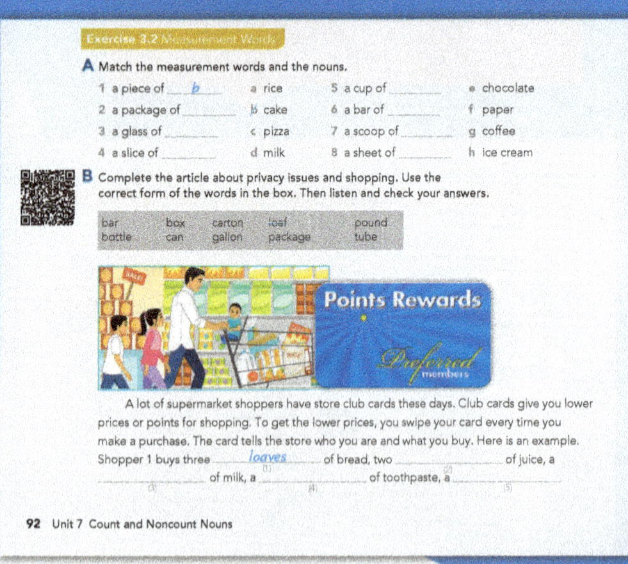

DATA FROM THE REAL WORLD

takes students beyond traditional information and teaches them how the unit's grammar is used in authentic situations, including differences between spoken and written use.

QR CODES

give easy access to audio at point of use.

CONTEXTUALIZED PRACTICE

moves from controlled to open-ended, teaching meaningful language for real communicative purposes.

HOW TO USE A QR CODE

1 Open the camera on your smartphone.

2 Point it at the QR code.

3 The camera will automatically scan the code. If not, press the button to take a picture.

* Not all cameras automatically scan QR codes. You may need to download a QR code reader. Search "QR free" and download an app.

AVOID COMMON MISTAKES

is based on a database of over 135,000 essays. Students learn to avoid the most common mistakes English language learners make and develop self-editing skills to improve their speaking and writing.

EDITING TASK

gives learners an opportunity to identify and correct commonly made errors and develop self-editing skills needed in their university studies.

ACADEMIC WRITING

concentrates on specific stages of the writing process: Brainstorm, Organize, Write, Edit.

REAL WORLD MODEL

incorporates the unit grammar into common types of writing for students to understand and analyze.

LEARNER OUTCOMES

are mapped out at the beginning of each writing cycle and section.

C Group Work What did you buy this week? Write three sentences on a piece of paper. Do not write your name! Read the papers in groups and try to guess who wrote them.

This person bought three loaves of bread, so it might be Nicki.

4 Avoid Common Mistakes ⚠

1 A singular count noun needs a determiner.
I do not have card for this store.

2 Do not use *a/an* with a noncount noun.
You need a permission to use my credit card.

3 Do not use a noncount noun in the plural.
The supermarket has personal informations about shoppers.

4 Do not use *many* or *too many* with a noncount noun.
There was many Internet crime last year.

5 Do not use *much* with a noncount noun in affirmative statements.
She had much cash in her wallet when somebody stole it.

Editing Task

Find eight more mistakes in this article about Internet spyware.

Spyware is type of computer software. Someone sends it to computer without your knowledges or permissions. It takes control of your computer. It can make your computer run slowly or even crash. Spyware often records an information about your computer use. It gives the information to advertisers or
5 other people who want to collect informations on you. Many spyware sneaks into your computer when you are downloading and installing programs from the Internet. One way to prevent a spyware is to put security settings on your Internet browser. Set your browser to a medium or higher setting. There is also much software you can buy that blocks spyware.

Privacy Matters **93**

---

5 Academic Writing

Expository Writing

Brainstorm > Organize > Write > Edit

In this writing cycle (Units 7-9), you are going to write a report that answers the prompt below. In this unit (7), you will analyze an article and brainstorm ideas about the topic.

Choose a new area of technology or invention to analyze. Write a report about its advantages and disadvantages, and include a prediction in the conclusion.

Exercise 5.1 Preparing to Write

Work with a partner. Discuss the questions.

1 What kind of technology is important to you in your life now? Why?
2 Are there disadvantages to this kind of technology? What are they?
3 In the future, what kind of problems could technology solve?

Exercise 5.2 Focusing on Vocabulary

Read the definitions. Complete the sentences with the correct form of the words in the box.

> **artificial** (adj) not natural, made by people
> **benefit** (n) advantage; positive result; (v) to help or give an advantage to
> **convenience** (n) something that makes life or a process easier
> **congestion** (n) a situation when something is blocked or stopped
> **organ** (n) part of a human or animal that has a special purpose
> **power** (n) energy, usually electricity or gas, used to provide heat, light, etc.
> **process** (n) a series of actions to reach a result
> **progress** (n) movement toward an improved situation

1 Designing new technology is often a long ____________. It can take years until it works well.
2 New technology sometimes creates problems, but there are usually ____________ to people, too.
3 Most modern cities have serious traffic ____________ because there are too many cars on the road.

---

7 In medicine, ____________ legs and arms are now so advanced that people use them to run marathons and to climb mountains.

8 With special equipment, doctors can now see a patient's ____________, like the heart, to look for signs of disease.

The World Of Tomorrow

Every generation develops new technology that has both positive and negative effects. In the past 30 years, for example, the Internet has become part of daily life. However, along with more information, faster communication, and greater **convenience**,
5 there are issues with privacy, identity theft, and online harassment. Now, what comes next? What will the world of tomorrow look like? Will it be easier or more difficult? Many people are confident that technology is going to help solve some of today's most challenging problems. Other people worry that new technology may solve
10 old problems but create new ones, like the Internet has. While it is difficult to predict the world of tomorrow, **progress** today in the areas of transportation, production, and safety will probably change the future.

When we dream about the future of transportation, many of us
15 believe that we will be able to exit our garages and take to the skies in our own personal flying cars. In fact, companies like Terrafugia and AeroMobil are already developing them. The advantages of flying cars are obvious. They would allow full freedom of movement. We could fly at 300 miles per hour, avoiding traffic
20 lights, busy roads, and speeding tickets. However, some people point to the disadvantages of flying cars. They claim that there are certain to be problems with controlling traffic. If the cars become popular, there is likely to be more **congestion** in the air. Another big problem is mechanical failure. What will happen if the cars break
25 down? These are problems we must solve when flying cars become a reality.

The way we make, buy, and sell things is also going to change. For example, most people print out electronic documents on sheets of paper at work or school, and many people are probably aware
30 of 3D printing, a **process** by which three-dimensional objects are created. 3D printers build an object using layers of liquid plastic, metal, or other materials. They build up the layers line by line like a normal printer until the object is complete. Car companies like BMW and Volkswagen already use 3D printers to make life-size models
35 of car parts, and medical technology companies have already used 3D printing to make body parts, such as **artificial** ears. Some people print their own small objects at home, such as jewelry and toys, with 3D printers. However, 3D printing has the
40 ability to change the future. It can create something as large as a house in a few days at a low cost. In addition, scientists are conducting experiments to "print" biological tissue. Before long, it might
45 be possible to use 3D printing to create affordable housing, print **organs** for transplants, or even make food.

Finally, the future of personal health and safety is bright. Imagine wearing a real ironman suit. Several companies are trying to build a practical robot "exoskeleton." This is a suit of robot arms
50 and legs that follows the wearer's movements. It allows the wearer to lift heavy objects, walk long distances, and even punch through walls! There are obvious military advantages for this technology, but there are also **benefits** for people with disabilities. The suit could help people walk again after disease or injury. However, the obvious
55 disadvantage at the moment is the cost. Even a simple exoskeleton can cost hundreds of thousands of dollars. Another problem is battery life. This type of suit needs a lot of **power**: at the moment, the batteries last only about 15 minutes. One other problem is that a badly programmed robot suit could injure the wearer if the robot suit
60 bent the leg or arm the wrong way, for instance.

The future is clearly exciting. One day we might be able to fly to work, print out a new pair of shoes, or lift a car above our heads, but there are still a lot of problems to solve before any of these products become part of normal life. However, companies are making
65 progress in all three areas

Privacy Matters **95**

Exercise 5.3 Comprehension Check

Read the text on page 95. Work with a partner. Ask and answer the questions.

1 Will flying cars solve traffic problems? Why or why not?
2 How can 3D printers be used by medical doctors?
3 To which two groups of people could the robot exoskeleton be useful?
4 Does the author believe that technology is always a benefit to people?

Exercise 5.4 Noticing the Grammar and Structure

Complete the tasks. Compare your answers with a partner.

1 Underline the thesis statement. Circle all the non-count nouns in it.
2 Match each invention in the body paragraphs to a non-count noun in the thesis statement.
   a robot suit   b flying car   c 3D printer
3 Circle one advantage and put a box around one disadvantage of each invention.
4 How does the writer organize the information in paragraphs 2-4?
5 Find and highlight two uses of the determiner *a lot of* in paragraphs 4-5. What kind of noun follows it?

Using A T-Chart

A T-chart is a kind of graphic organizer. It is useful for examining two sides or aspects of a topic, such as advantages and disadvantages or pros and cons.

Exercise 5.5 Applying the Skill

Choose one invention in the text, and complete the T-chart. Add at least one advantage and one disadvantage to the T-chart.

Invention: _______________________

Advantages	Disadvantages

My Writing

Exercise 5.6 Brainstorming Ideas

Work with a partner. Write down one modern invention in each area of technology in the chart. Do research online if necessary.

medicine	
home	
space	
transportation	
entertainment	
computers	

Exercise 5.7 Identifying Advantages and Disadvantages

Choose one of the inventions from Exercise 5.6 to write about in your report. Write at least three advantages and three disadvantages of the invention in the T-chart below.

Invention: _______________________

Advantages	Disadvantages

Exercise 5.8 Writing a Paragraph

Write a paragraph about the invention you chose. Include:
* a topic sentence with a description of the invention
* its advantages and disadvantages
* a concluding sentence with a prediction

Exercise 5.9 Editing Your Writing

Use the checklist to edit your paragraph.

Did you use a noncount noun to refer to a general idea and then give details about that idea?	
Did you use the correct determiner with count and noncount nouns?	
Did you avoid the common mistakes in the chart on page 93?	

Kahoot!

for Grammar and Beyond
cambridge.org/kahoot/grammarandbeyond

What is Kahoot!?

Kahoot! is a game-based learning platform that makes it easy to create, share and play fun learning games and trivia quizzes in minutes. You can play Kahoot! on any mobile device or laptop with an internet connection.

What can you use kahoots for?

Kahoots can be used for review, formative assessment or homework.

When should you play Kahoot?

You can play kahoot quizzes before starting the unit as a diagnostic, during the unit as formative assessment, or at the end of a unit to test student knowledge.

To launch a live game in the classroom, find the kahoot for the level and unit and simply click on "play".

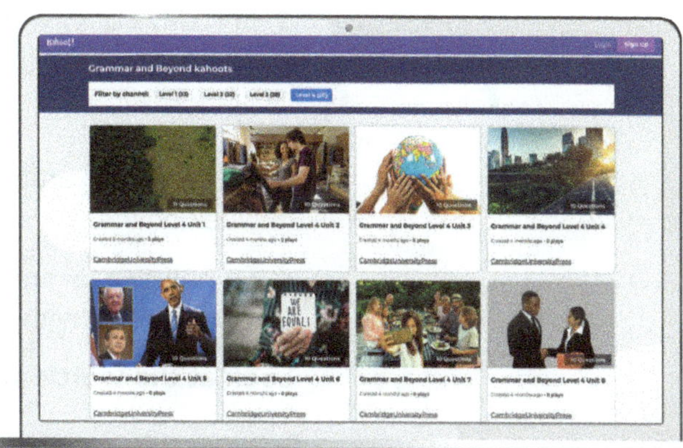

Quiz Your English app

Quiz Your English is a fun new way to practice, improve, and test your English by competing against learners from all around the world. Learn English grammar with friends, discover new English words, and test yourself in a truly global environment.

- Learn to avoid common mistakes with a special section just for *Grammar and Beyond* users
- Challenge your friends and players wherever they are
- Watch where you are on the leaderboards

Are You Often Online?

1 Grammar in the Real World

A What kinds of things do you do on the Internet? Read the magazine article. What is one good thing and one bad thing about spending time online?

B Comprehension Check **Answer the questions.**

1 What do sociologists disagree about?

2 How much time does the average person in the United States spend online per week?

3 What is face-to-face time? What are some examples of face-to-face time?

4 Does the article say not to use computers?

C Notice **Find the sentences in the article and complete them.**

1 In today's busy world, people ________________ a lot of time with computers, and they ________________ less and less time with people.

2 Sociologists ________________ about this.

3 In the United States, the average person ________________ 24 hours a week online.

4 Sometimes technology ________________ people improve their relationships with others.

Look at the words you wrote in the blanks. Which of the verbs end in *-s*?

Balancing
TIME ONLINE and TIME WITH PEOPLE

[1] **sociologist:** someone who studies people and society

[2] **face-to-face:** meeting with someone in the same place directly

In today's busy world, people **spend** a lot of time with computers, and they **spend** less and less time with people. **Does** this **change** how people interact with family and friends? **Does** it **help** or **hurt** people and relationships? Sociologists[1] **disagree** about this. Some **worry** about the Internet's effect on our friends and family. Others **think** this is not a problem.

Studies **show** that people spend less face-to-face[2] time with family and friends than they did a few years ago. Instead, they **play** online games, **shop** online, and also **look** at social networking sites. In the United States, the average person **spends** 24 hours a week online. They **interact** face-to-face less, and this sometimes has bad effects. For example, some people **do not spend time** together as a family very often. They talk less because they spend more time online.

Sometimes technology **helps** people improve their relationships with others. For example, social networking sites **help** people stay in touch with friends and family who live far away. They enable people to reconnect with old friends and classmates.

Are you worried about the time you spend online? If so, try to make a schedule. Schedule time away from the computer to be with family and friends. Try to balance online time with face-to-face time.

Simple Present

Grammar Presentation

The simple present describes habits, general truths, feelings, or thoughts.	Many people **spend** up to 24 hours a week online. I **play** games online every night. My sister **loves** to shop online.

2.1 Affirmative and Negative Statements

AFFIRMATIVE

Subject	Verb	
I You We They	**shop**	online.
He / She / It	**shops**	

NEGATIVE

Subject	Do/Does + Not	Base Form of Verb	
I You We They	**do not** **don't**	**shop**	online.
He / She / It	**does not** **doesn't**		

2.2 Affirmative and Negative Statements with *Be*

AFFIRMATIVE

Subject	*Be*	
I	**am**	
You We They	**are**	online.
He / She / It	**is**	

NEGATIVE

Subject	*Be* + Not	
I	**am not**	
You We They	**are not**	online.
He / She / It	**is not**	

CONTRACTIONS

Affirmative	Negative	
I**'m**	I**'m not**	
You**'re** We**'re** They**'re**	You**'re not** We**'re not** They**'re not**	You **aren't** We **aren't** They **aren't**
He**'s** She**'s** It**'s**	He**'s not** She**'s not** It**'s not**	He **isn't** She **isn't** It **isn't**

 **DATA FROM THE REAL WORLD**

Research shows the contractions *'s not* and *'re not* are more common after pronouns (*he, she, you*, etc.) than *isn't* and *aren't*.

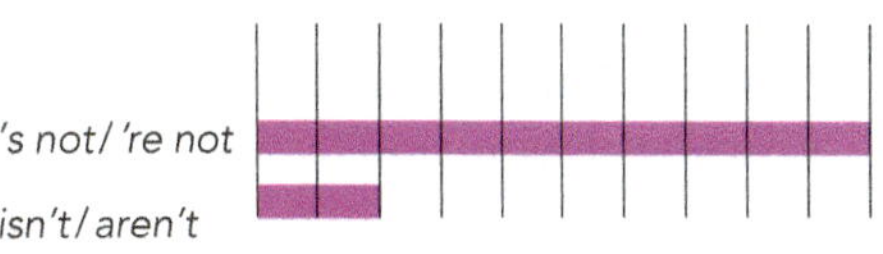

Be careful not to use contractions in formal writing.

Say: *"He's not feeling well today."*
Write: *He is not feeling well today.*

2.3 *Yes/No* Questions and Short Answers

Do/Does	Subject	Base Form of Verb	
Do	I you we they	**shop**	online?
Does	he/she/it		

Short Answers	
Yes, I **do.** Yes, you **do.** Yes, we **do.** Yes, they **do.**	No, I **don't.** No, you **don't.** No, we **don't.** No, they **don't.**
Yes, he/she/it **does.**	No, he/she/it **doesn't.**

2.4 Information Questions and Answers

Wh- Word	*Do/Does*	Subject	Base Form of Verb
Where **When** **How often**	**do**	I you we they	**shop**?
	does	he/she/it	

Answers
I **shop** online. You **shop** at night. We **shop** once a week. They **shop** every day.
He **shops** every night.

Wh- Word	Verb	
Who	**uses**	e-mail?
What	**helps**	people reconnect?

Answers
Everyone **uses** e-mail!
The Internet **helps** people reconnect.

A Use the simple present to describe habits and routines (usual and regular activities).

*I usually **read** the news online.*

*We **eat** together as a family on weekends.*

B Use the simple present to describe facts, general truths, feelings, or thoughts.

*The average person **spends** 24 hours a week online.*

*Some people **worry** about the effects of the Internet.*

C Use the simple present with adverbs of frequency to say how often something happens.

0% → 100%

never	seldom	occasionally	often	usually	always
	hardly ever*	sometimes		almost always	
	rarely			normally	

**ever: at any time*

D Adverbs of frequency come before the main verb in affirmative statements but after the verb *be*.

*I **occasionally** play online games.*

*I am **hardly ever** free.*

E Do not use *sometimes* after *not*.

Note that meaning can change in negative statements with adverbs of frequency.

***Sometimes** people do not check e-mail.*

People ~~do not sometimes~~ check e-mail.

*I don't **always** check e-mail.*

(Does not mean "I never check e-mail.")

F *Sometimes, occasionally, normally, often, usually,* and *almost always* can come before the verb or at the beginning or end of a sentence.

*I **usually** check my e-mail at home.*

***Usually**, I check my e-mail at home.*

*I check my e-mail at home **usually**.*

G Adverbs of frequency come before the main verb in questions.

*Do you **always** <u>study</u> at night? Yes, I do.*

*Do you **ever** <u>watch</u> YouTube? No, I don't.*

H Do not use negative adverbs of frequency in negative sentences.

*I **don't usually** shop online.*

~~I don't never shop online.~~

2.6 Using Simple Present Questions

A Answer *when* or *what time* questions with **time expressions**.	*What time do you shop online? I shop online* **at night**. *When do you check e-mail? I check e-mail* **during the day**. *When do you call your family? I call my family* **on Sunday night**. *When do you shop at the mall? I shop at the mall* **in December**.
B Answer *how often* questions with **frequency expressions**.	*How often do you shop? I shop* **once a week**. *How often do you check e-mail? I check e-mail* **three times a day**.

Grammar Application

Exercise 2.1 Statements

A Complete the sentences. Use the correct form of the verbs in parentheses. Use contractions when possible.

1 My family and friends _______ *use* _______ (use) the computer for all sorts of things.

2 I _______________ (use) an online dictionary for my classes.

3 My friend Mark _______________ (shop) for clothes online.

4 Our classmates Marta and Raul _______________ (check) their e-mail at the library.

5 My best friend Ana _______________ (not be) on any social networking sites.

6 Ana and her sister Claudia _______________ (not buy) groceries online.

7 My family _______________ (spend) a lot of time online.

8 My brother Sam is online a lot, but he also _______________ (interact) with our family.

9 Technology _______________ (not hurt) my relationships.

B Over to You Rewrite three sentences in A so they are true about you. Then compare your sentences with a partner.

A *I don't use an online dictionary. How about you?*
B *No, I don't, but I shop for clothes online.*

Listen to Alex and Karen talk about their online activities. Complete the sentences with the correct adverb of frequency.

1 Karen ___*hardly ever*___ goes to the mall.

2 Karen is _______________ studying.

3 Karen _______________ reserves library books online.

4 Alex _______________ goes to the library on the weekend.

5 Karen _______________ studies in the library.

6 Karen _______________ studies at home.

7 Alex _______________ meets up with friends.

8 Karen needs a break _______________ .

Look at the things Brandon does online. Then complete the sentences. Circle the correct answer.

	Sun.	Mon.	Tue.	Wed.	Thu.	Fri.	Sat.
Watch videos	✓						
Read the news	✓	✓	✓	✓	✓	✓	
Shop for groceries	✓	✓					
Play games						✓	✓
Check e-mail	✓	✓	✓	✓	✓	✓	✓
Shop for clothes							

1 Brandon **occasionally / never** watches videos online.

2 He checks e-mail **sometimes / every day**.

3 He **seldom / often** reads the news online.

4 Brandon always plays games **on Thursday / on Saturday**.

5 He shops for groceries online **twice / once** a week.

6 He **hardly ever / never** plays games.

7 Brandon **always / rarely** checks e-mail.

8 He **never / sometimes** shops for clothes online.

Exercise 2.4 Questions

A Unscramble the words to make questions. Then write two questions of your own.

1 own / Do / a computer? / you   *Do you own a computer?*

2 the news / Do / read / you / online?

3 often / shop online? / do / How / you

4 usually / check / do / you / your / Where / e-mail?

5 website? / your / favorite / is / What

6 music? / you / Do / download / sometimes

7 _______________________________________

8 _______________________________________

B Group Work Ask three classmates the questions in A. Answer your classmates' questions. Give extra information.

A *Do you own a computer?*
B *No, I don't. But I use the computers at the library. They're free!*

C Pair Work Tell a partner some things you learned in B.

I own a computer, but Peter doesn't. He uses the computers at the library.
Peter doesn't shop online, but I do.

3 Time Clauses and Factual Conditionals

Grammar Presentation

Time clauses in the present tense show the sequence of events. Factual conditionals describe things that are generally true in a certain situation.

When I get home, I check my e-mail.
If it's late, I don't stay online for a long time.

3.1 Time Clauses

Time Clause		Main Clause		Main Clause	Time Clause	
Before **After** **As soon as** **When**	I get to work,	I check my e-mail.		I check my e-mail	**before** **after** **as soon as** **when**	I get to work.

Condition		Main Clause
If	**I get an e-mail,**	I feel great!

Main Clause	Condition	
I feel great	**if**	**I get an e-mail.**

3.3 Using Time Clauses

A Use time clauses to say when the main clause happens.

Use *after* to introduce the first event.

SECOND EVENT — FIRST EVENT
*I check my e-mail **after** I get home.*

B Use *as soon as* to introduce the first event when the second event happens immediately after.

FIRST EVENT — SECOND EVENT
***As soon as** I change my password, I forget it.*

C Use *while* when events happen at the same time.

***While** I'm online, I check my e-mail.*

D *When* means "at almost the same time." Use *when* to introduce the first event.

SECOND EVENT — FIRST EVENT
*I visit social networking sites **when** I get home.*

E Use *before* to introduce the second event.

SECOND EVENT — FIRST EVENT
***Before** I go to work, I check my e-mail.*

F Use a comma if the time clause comes first.

***Before I go out,** I check my e-mail.*
***After I check my e-mail,** I read the news.*

G A time clause by itself is not a complete sentence.

Before I go out, I turn off my computer.
~~Before I go out.~~ I turn off my computer.

3.4 Using Factual Conditionals

A Use factual conditionals to describe things that are generally true in certain situations. The condition describes a situation. The main clause describes the result of the situation.

CONDITION — MAIN CLAUSE (RESULT)
***If I need a recipe,** I go to a cooking site.*

B Use *if* when one event depends on another one happening.

If I need directions, I go to a map site.
(I go to a map site only because I need directions.)

C A condition by itself is not a complete sentence.

***If I need directions,** I go to a map site.*
~~If I need directions.~~ I go to a map site.

⬚ Grammar Application

Exercise 3.1 Time Clauses

A Read about Dave. Then complete the sentences. Circle the correct words.

- Dave gets out of bed and immediately turns on his computer.
- Then he checks his e-mail.
- He plays an online game. Then he goes to work.
- At work, Dave checks his e-mail many times a day.
- He gets home and immediately turns on his computer.
- He stays at home all evening and plays online games.
- He sometimes eats dinner and sits in front of his computer.
- He visits a social networking site. Then he goes to bed.

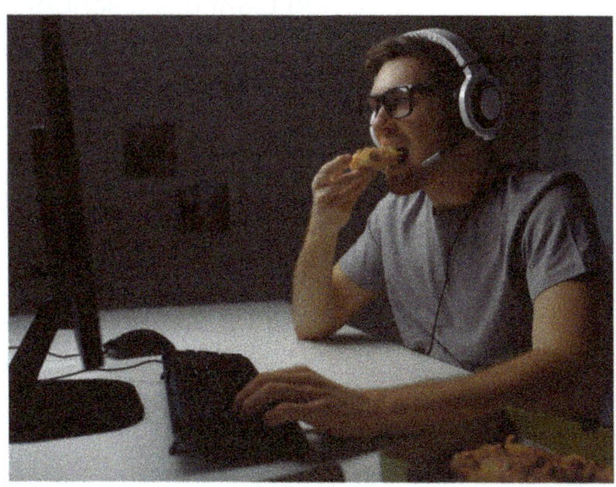

1 **As soon as** / Before he gets out of bed in the morning, Dave turns on his computer.

2 **After** / **Before** he turns on his computer, he checks his e-mail.

3 He plays an online game **when** / **before** he goes to work.

4 **As soon as** / **While** he is at work, Dave checks his e-mail many times a day.

5 **Before** / **As soon as** Dave gets home, he turns on his computer again.

6 Dave usually plays online games **after** / **while** he is at home in the evening.

7 Dave sometimes eats dinner **while** / **after** he sits in front of his computer.

8 Dave visits a social networking site **before** / **as soon as** he goes to bed.

B Pair Work Compare your behavior with Dave's. Discuss it with a partner.

A *As soon as I get out of bed in the morning, I turn on my computer. How about you?*

B *I turn my computer on after I make coffee.*

Read the sentences about Internet research. Underline the time clause or condition.
Circle the main clause.

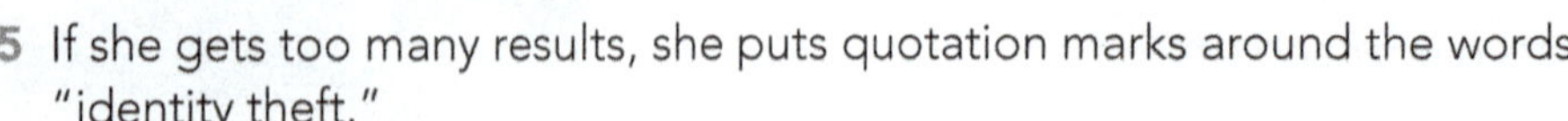

1 When Dani has a school assignment, she often does research on the Internet.

2 She usually starts with a search engine when she does research.

3 If the topic is general, Dani thinks about the best words to put into the search engine.

4 For example, if the topic is "How to avoid identity theft," Dani uses *avoid identity theft*.

5 If she gets too many results, she puts quotation marks around the words "identity theft."

6 She clicks on a result if it comes from a useful site.

7 When she gets to the page, she usually skims the information first.

8 She reads the entire page if the information seems useful.

A Match the task with the website you go to.

If you . . .
1 forget the actors in an old movie, __*e*__
2 need the definitions of some words, _____
3 want to know the score of a soccer game, _____
4 need to know the temperature in Chicago today, _____
5 need a book at the library, _____
6 drive to a new friend's house, _____
7 want to cook something new for dinner, _____
8 forget the birth date of a famous person, _____

you go to . . .
a a sports site.
b an online encyclopedia.
c a recipe site.
d your library's website.
e a movie site.
f an online dictionary.
g a weather site.
h a map site.

B Over to You Write conditional sentences about your own Internet research.
Use the ideas in A or your own ideas. Then compare your sentences with a partner.

1 If I __*forget the title of a book,*__ I __*go to an online bookstore*__ .

2 If I ____

   I ____ .

3 If I ____

   I ____ .

4 I ____

   If I ____ .

5 I ____

   if I ____ .

 **4** Avoid Common Mistakes  

1 Do not contract *not* with *am*.

I'm not
~~I amn't~~ online every day.

2 Use the correct form of *do* with singular and plural subjects.

doesn't
He ~~don't~~ own a computer.

3 Remember to form information questions correctly.

does the professor
Where ~~the professor does~~ post his comments?

4 Do not use *sometimes* after *not*.

Sometimes I do not check
~~I do not sometimes check~~ e-mail on the weekends.

5 Always use a comma if a time clause or a condition clause begins a sentence.

When I change my password, I write it down.
~~When I change my password I write it down.~~

Editing Task

Find and correct 10 more mistakes in this blog entry.

doesn't

My roommate Mark plays online games. He ~~don't~~ own a computer, so he goes to a computer lab. How often he does play? He plays every night! As soon as he finishes his homework he goes to the lab. He does not sometimes come home until midnight. He usually plays with people from around the world. He don't know the

5 other players, but it doesn't matter. When Mark gets home he always has stories about the games he plays. Why people play these games? I do not understand. I amn't like Mark. I always play with people face-to-face when I play a game. When I play a game I know the people. Does many people play online games? How often you do play online games?

5 Academic Writing

Doing Research Online

In this unit (1), you will learn how to find and evaluate online sources and information to support your academic writing.

Exercise 5.1 Preparing to Write

Work with a partner. Ask and answer the questions.

1 Have you ever done research online? Give an example.
2 What types of websites can you use in academic writing? What types of websites should you avoid in academic writing? Explain your answers.
3 What should you look for when you evaluate an Internet source for academic writing?

Finding a Reliable Source

When you write in an academic setting, you must include reasons, facts, and examples to support your opinions and statements. In order to find this kind of support, you will often do research online. There are some excellent online resources for your academic writing, but there are also many sites that are not reliable. It is important to use reliable sources for your research.

Reliable Sources

- **Educational sites:** Look for websites that end in **.edu**. The writers are often professors or researchers. These articles are usually based on academic or scientific studies and research.
- **Government sites:** Look for websites that end in **.gov**. They often present data or statistics from government agencies. Experts usually write the reports.
- **Professional or academic journals:** These sources, which often end in **.edu** or **.org**, are based on research, and they present balanced information. Professionals and experts in that field write the articles.

Unreliable Sources

- **Blogs:** Anyone can write a blog. The writer may not be an expert or even have any real knowledge of the subject. Blogs often include biased information and personal opinions, not facts, data, or research.
- **Company sites:** Many websites that end in **.com** are commercial sites. They provide information for customers, but their main purpose is usually to sell products or services. As a result, they may have a biased point of view.

Sources That Need More Research

- **Major newspapers:** Look for sources that are known for accuracy and balanced reporting. You can usually use them even though their web addresses end in **.com.** However, these sites often include both news reports and opinion writing. It is important to pay attention to the kind of article you find.
- **Nonprofit sites:** These sites end in **.org**. The Red Cross is an international relief organization and a reliable source. However, many nonprofit organizations have a religious or political bias, so they are not always objective.
- **Wikipedia:** This website is useful because it can give you background information on a topic, key words for more research, and a list of reliable sources. However, it is not a reliable primary (main) source because its writers are not necessarily experts in the field.

Exercise 5.2 Applying the Skill

Work with a partner. Match the website with the type of source. Then discuss two topics for which you could use each website in academic writing. If necessary, go to the websites for information.

1 Educational
2 Government
3 Professional
4 Major newspaper
5 Company
6 Nonprofit organization

a World Wildlife Fund (worldwildlife.org)
b Microsoft (microsoft.com)
c Princeton University Library (library.princeton.edu)
d *New England Journal of Medicine* (nejm.org)
e *New York Times* (nytimes.com)
f Centers for Disease Control and Prevention (cdc.gov)

Evaluating an Internet Source

You should evaluate any article or report that you find online before you use it as a resource in your academic writing. To evaluate a resource, ask the following important questions.

Who wrote it? Reliable sources usually include some information about the author of an article. You can use a source if the author is an expert or respected person in the area. In addition, look for any connections the author has with larger institutions, like universities or research organizations, in order to evaluate the source.

When was it published? In many academic areas, like technology, politics, and fashion, things change quickly, so look for recent information. If you cannot find a date, then you may not want to use it as a resource.

Who is it for? Resources that are written for college students, professors, or other professionals are better than those for younger students or for political or religious audiences.

This information is also important if your instructor or professor asks you to cite your source.

Exercise 5.3 Applying the Skill

Work with a partner. Imagine that your writing assignment is about the benefits and dangers of spending time online. Complete the tasks.

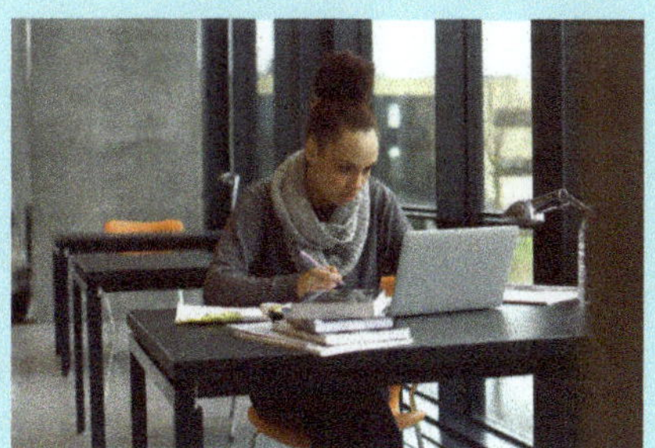

1 Find three reliable online sources for the topic.
2 Answer the three important questions in "Evaluating an Internet Source" for each source.
3 Compare your results with another student pair.

1 Grammar in the Real World

A What do you do to improve your brain? Read the article from a health magazine. How are the people in the article improving their brains?

B Comprehension Check Match each item with its benefit.

1 Chemicals in blueberries _**b**_   a helps the brain, not just the body.

2 Calm thoughts _____   b improve your memory and ability to learn.

3 Word puzzles _____   c are good for your memory.

4 Exercise _____   d make your brain younger.

C Notice Find the sentences in the article. Circle the answer you find in the article.

1 It is 9:00 a.m. in Portland, Oregon. Hannah Lewis **sits / is sitting** at her computer.

2 They all **live / are living** in Portland, of course.

3 Exercise **helps / is helping** the brain, not just the body.

Which sentences describe things that are true in general? Which describe things in progress now or around the present time?

A HEALTHY BRAIN

It is 9:00 a.m. in Portland, Oregon. Hannah Lewis is **sitting** at her computer. She **is looking** at websites that interest her. Bill Green **is doing** a word puzzle at his kitchen table. Kelly South **is eating** a bowl of cereal with blueberries. Nina Ritch **is brushing** her teeth after breakfast.
5 Anthony Owens **is jogging** in the park. Olga Prince **is sitting** on the floor of her apartment with her eyes closed. She **is thinking** beautiful, calm thoughts.

What do these people have in common? They all **live** in Portland, of course. In addition, they **are** all **improving** their brains. We **are**
10 **learning** more about the brain every day. Do things like word puzzles and blueberries help your brain? Many scientists **think** so. They **believe** that exercise, food, and other activities give people sharper memory and stronger, healthier brains.

These things **help** the brain in different ways. For example, the
15 **chemicals** in blueberries **improve** your memory and your ability to learn. Calm thoughts **are** also good for your memory. Using interesting websites **makes** your brain stronger, and word puzzles **make** it younger. Take Bill Green, the word-puzzle lover. He **is** 60, but his brain is like
20 the brain of a 40-year-old. Exercise **helps** the brain, not just the body. Even oral health is connected to the health of the brain, so don't forget
25 to brush your teeth!

Improving your brain **does not stop** at any particular time. It can continue for life.

2 Present Progressive

Grammar Presentation

The present progressive describes things that are in progress now or around the present time.	Hannah *is sitting* at her computer. She *is exercising* a lot these days.

2.1 Affirmative and Negative Statements

AFFIRMATIVE

Subject	*Be*	Verb + *-ing*
I	am	
You / We / They	are	**thinking.**
He / She / It	is	

NEGATIVE

Subject	*Be + Not*	Verb + *-ing*
I	am not	
You / We / They	are not	**working.**
He / She / It	is not	

CONTRACTIONS

Affirmative	Negative	
I**'m**	I**'m not**	
You**'re** / We**'re** / They**'re**	You**'re not** / We**'re not** / They**'re not**	You **aren't** / We **aren't** / They **aren't**
He**'s** / She**'s** / It**'s**	He**'s not** / She**'s not** / It**'s not**	He **isn't** / She **isn't** / It **isn't**

▶▶ Spelling Rules for Verbs Ending in *-ing*: See page A4.

DATA FROM THE REAL WORLD

Isn't and *aren't* are more common after nouns than *'s not* and *'re not*.	*Bill and Olga* **aren't** *exercising.*

2.2 Yes / No Questions and Short Answers

Be	Subject	Verb + *-ing*
Am	I	
Are	you / we / they	**thinking?**
Is	he / she / it	

Short Answers

Yes, I **am.**	No, I**'m not.**	
Yes, you **are.**	No, you**'re not.**	No, you **aren't.**
Yes, we **are.**	No, we**'re not.**	No, we **aren't.**
Yes, they **are.**	No, they**'re not.**	No, they **aren't.**
Yes, he **is.**	No, he**'s not.**	No, he **isn't.**
Yes, she **is.**	No, she**'s not.**	No, she **isn't.**
Yes, it **is.**	No, it**'s not.**	No, it **isn't.**

 **DATA FROM THE REAL WORLD**

The 's not and 're not contractions are more common in short answers than the isn't and aren't contractions.

Are they exercising?
No, they're not.

2.3 Information Questions and Answers

Wh- Word	Be	Subject	Verb + -ing	Answers
Who	are	you	**helping**?	I**'m helping** my brother.
What	is	your brother	**reading**?	He**'s reading** a news article.
Why	are	you	**jogging**?	Because I**'m trying** to improve my brainpower.

Wh- Word	Be	Verb + -ing	Answers
Who	is	**doing** a word puzzle?	Bill **is doing** a word puzzle.
What		**happening** at Kelly's house?	She**'s eating** blueberries.

2.4 Using Present Progressive

A Use the present progressive for things in progress now or around the present time.

Lorna's doing a puzzle right now.
I'm reading a great book about brain training exercises.

B You can use the present progressive with time expressions that mean "right now" and "around now": *now, right now, at the moment, this week, these days, this month.*

She's working on her essay right now.
He's exercising at the gym now.
What's Felipe reading these days?
I'm not doing anything interesting this week.

C Use the full forms when writing in class. Use contractions in everyday speaking.

Anthony is not running today.
I'm improving my brainpower.

D You can contract *Wh-* words + *is* in informal speaking and writing.

Who's she working for?
Why's the printer not working?

You can contract *Wh-* words + *are* in speaking but **not** in formal writing.

Say: "*What're you doing?*"
Write: *What are you doing?*

Grammar Application

A Complete the article about improving brainpower. Use the correct form of the verb in parentheses. Use full forms.

There are a lot of ways to improve brainpower, such as doing word puzzles and exercising. Here are a few more things our readers are doing.

Jane R., from Chicago, usually wears her watch on her right arm. This week she _is wearing_ (wear) it on her (1) left arm. Jane uses her right hand a lot, but now she ________________ (use) her left hand more. (2)

Joe M., from Dallas, usually drives to work. This month he ________________ (not drive). Instead, he (3) ________________ (walk) to work every day. Also, he (4) ________________ (run) three times a week this month. (5)

Isabel and Max V., from Los Angeles, ________________ (go) to the gym together every day this week. (6) They ________________ (try) to improve their mental and physical health, too. (7)

Mario S., from Boston, always goes to bed after midnight, but this week he ________________ (not go) to bed so late. Also, he ________________ (8)   (9) (not eat) junk food this week.

B Over to You Here are more things people do to improve their brainpower. Are you or people you know doing any of these things? Use the words to write sentences about you and people you know.

1 I / learn / a musical instrument   _I'm not learning a musical instrument._

2 My best friend / learn / a musical instrument   ________________

3 I / improve / my vocabulary   ________________

4 My friends / improve / their vocabulary   ________________

5 I / eat / less junk food   ________________

6 My family / eat / less junk food   ________________

7 I / study / math   ________________

8 My co-workers / study / math   ________________

Exercise 2.2 Questions and Answers

A Complete the questionnaire with the present progressive. Then write true answers.

1 a _Are_ you _doing_ (do) anything to improve your brainpower right now?
   Yes, I am.
   b If yes, what _________ you _________ (do)? _________________________________
2 a _________ you _________ (try) to improve your health? _________________________
   b If yes, what _________ you _________ (do)? _________________________________
3 a _________ you _________ (read) an interesting book? _________________________
   b If yes, what _________ you _________ (read)? _________________________________
   c If no, _________ you _________ (read) anything else? _________________________
4 a _________ you _________ (get) enough exercise right now? _________________________
   b _________ you _________ (eat) the right kinds of food? _________________________
5 a _________ your friends also _________ (take) classes? _________________________
   b If yes, what _________ they _________ (study)? _________________________________
6 a _________ you and your classmates _________ (work) hard this semester?
   ____
   b _________ you all _________ (get) good grades?

B Pair Work Ask and answer the questions with a partner. How many of your answers are the same?

C Pair Work Change partners. Ask and answer questions about your first partner.

   A *Is Andrea doing anything to improve her brainpower right now?*
   B *Yes, she is. She's doing a lot! She's . . .*

3 Simple Present and Present Progressive Compared

Grammar Presentation

The simple present describes actions that are true in general or that happen regularly. The present progressive describes things that are happening now or around the present time.	He **runs** every evening. He**'s running** right now.

A Use the simple present to describe habits, routines, facts, or general truths.

He **runs** in the park every day.
Physical exercise **improves** the brain.

Use the present progressive when an action is happening right now or around the present time.

Mark **is doing** brain exercises these days.
Right now, he**'s improving** his memory.
He**'s** not **running** today.

B Use the simple present for situations that are true in general. The situations are settled, and we do not expect them to change.

Exercise **helps** the brain, not just the body.
Many people **don't get** enough exercise.

The present progressive often describes temporary or changing actions.

Lara **is eating** fish this week. (She's trying fish just for this week.)

I**'m reading** a lot these days because I have an exam next week. (I'm reading a lot, but it's just for the exam.)

C Use the simple present with stative verbs, such as *like*, *know*, and *want*. Stative verbs do not describe actions. They describe states or situations.

I **like** your new laptop.
I don't **know** her e-mail address.
I **want** a new cell phone.

D We do not usually use stative verbs in the present progressive, even if we are talking about right now.

~~I'm liking~~ your new laptop.
~~I'm not knowing~~ her e-mail address.
~~I'm wanting~~ a new cell phone.

Exception Some stative verbs can be used in the present progressive. These verbs have an action meaning as well as a stative meaning.

I **have** a new puzzle book. (have = own)
He's **having** fish for lunch these days. (have = eat)
I **think** blueberries are good for brain health. (think = believe)
I'm **thinking** about a word problem. (think = using my mind)

DATA FROM THE REAL WORLD

Research shows that these are the 25 most common stative verbs in spoken and written English:

agree	dislike	hope	love	see
believe	expect	hurt	need	seem
care (about)	hate	know	notice	think
cost	have	like	own	understand
disagree	hear	look like	prefer	want

▸▸ Stative (Non-Action) Verbs: See page A2.

Grammar Application

Complete the article. Use the correct form of the verbs in parentheses. Use the simple present or the present progressive.

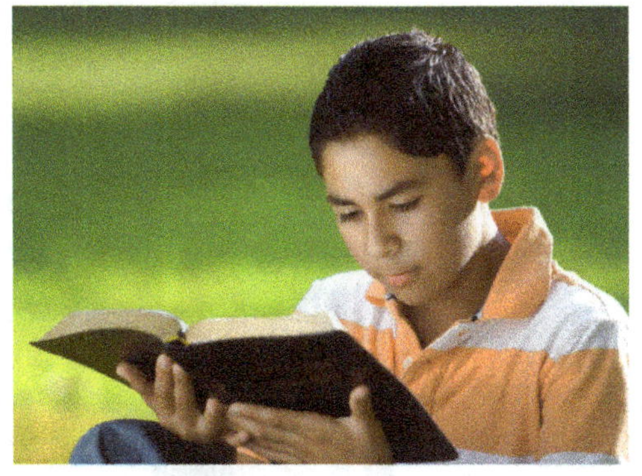

Rafael Sosa is only 12 years old, but he _is getting ready_ (get ready) to go to college this
(1)
week. At 12 years old, Rafael ___________________
(2)
(seem) young for college, but Rafael is not a
typical child. He ___________________ (have)
(3)
high intelligence-test scores, and he easily
___________________ (understand) difficult ideas.
(4)
He ___________________ (love) both science and
(5)
music. Rafael ___________________ (write) music and ___________________ (design) electronic
(6) (7)
devices. He ___________________ (own) a lot of college textbooks, and he ___________________
(8) (9)
(read) engineering textbooks every day. These days, he ___________________ (study) Japanese
(10)
and Chinese. Rafael ___________________ (look) like a normal child, and he ___________________
(11) (12)
(like) normal activities, too. He ___________________ (not spend) all his time reading and studying.
(13)
Right now, he ___________________ (play) soccer with a group of friends and ___________________
(14) (15)
(have) a great time.

Complete the conversation with the correct form of *have, look,* or *think.* Use the simple present or the present progressive.

Clerk	Can I help you?
Sally	Yes. I _'m looking_ for some brain-training software. What do you have? (1)
Clerk	We ___________ several good products for brain training. Here's one: *Memory Plus.* (2)
Sally	That ___________ good. Does it work? (3)
Clerk	I ___________ all these products work well. (4)
Sally	We're also ___________ about our eight-year-old son. What do you (5) ___________ for children? (6)
Clerk	Here's *Memory Plus Kids.*
Sally	OK . . . I'm ___________ for the price . . . (7)
Clerk	Here it is: $25.
Sally	That's not bad.
Clerk	And we're ___________ a sale this week, too. Twenty percent off all week. (8)
Sally	OK. These ___________ perfect. I'll take them. (9)

A Complete the text about a company's idea for market research with the correct form of the verbs in parentheses. Use the simple present or the present progressive. Then listen and check your answers.

Large corporations often __*need*__ (need) to make
(1)
decisions about new products. __*Do*__ people __*want*__
(2)   (2)
(want) this product? At the present moment, ______________
(3)
people __________ (look) for a product like this in the
(3)
stores? New products __________________ (cost) a lot of
(4)
money and __________________ (need) a lot of research.
(5)
Corporations usually __________________ (pay) experts
(6)
to do market research. But there is another way. One
large corporation __________________ (try) a new idea
(7)
this year. Every time the company __________________
(8)
(need) market information for a new product, managers __________________ (ask) the
(9)
employees for their opinions. The employees __________________ (vote) yes or no on
(10)
the new idea. They __________________ (tell) the managers, "I __________________
(11)   (12)
(like) the idea" or "I __________________ (not like) the idea."
(13)

Manager Rick Jons said, "Right now we __________________ (use) the collective
(14)
brain of our employees, and it __________________ (seem) to work. The results are
(15)
more reliable than expensive market research."

B Imagine you are doing market research for a new dictionary. Write market research questions about dictionary use. Use the simple present or the present progressive.

1 how often / use a dictionary? _____*How often do you use a dictionary?*_____

2 look for / a better dictionary right now? ___________________________________

3 use a dictionary / in this class today? ___________________________________

4 prefer / an online dictionary or a paper one? ___________________________________

5 use a dictionary / when you prepare for tests? ___________________________________

6 prepare / for a test at the moment? ___________________________________

C Group Work Ask and answer the questions in B. Based on the results, what is the best dictionary for your group?

The best dictionary is an electronic one, like the one Sam is using in this class.

 4 Avoid Common Mistakes  

1   Use a form of *be* with the present progressive.

am listening
I ~~listening~~ to the radio.

2   Use the *-ing* form of the verb with the present progressive.

is studying.
Fred ~~is study.~~

3   Spell the *-ing* form of the verb correctly. (See page A4 for more information.)

planning   *writing*   *enjoying*
plan ➞ ~~planing~~   write ➞ ~~writting~~   enjoy ➞ ~~enjoing~~

4   Do not use the present progressive with verbs of stative meaning.

I have
~~I'm having~~ a very smart brother.

5   Use the simple present for habits, routines, and general truths. Use the present progressive for actions in progress now or around the present time.

I'm watching
Can you call me back later? ~~I watch~~ the news right now.

improves
Exercise ~~is improving~~ physical and mental health.

Editing Task

Find and correct nine more mistakes in this article about the brain.

resembles
   The human brain ~~is resembling~~ a computer. It stores a lot of information.
But humans are smarter than computers because we store things outside of our brains
that we do not need to store *in* our brains. For example, we are storing information
in books, newspapers, images, and of course, computers. Another example is this
5   text. At this moment, you are read this text. You are not needing to remember all
the information in it. The book is having the information, and you read it when you
need it. If you are planing an essay, you can make notes on paper or on a computer.
When you are writting the essay, you can read those notes again. If you are studing
a subject, you can go online and find information about it. The information is on the
10   Internet. We do not look into people's brains to see it. When we are enjoing an online
video, we watching something that is outside of the human brain. So computers are
like extensions[1] of our brains.

[1] **extension:** something added or extra

Opinion Writing

Brainstorm > Organize > Write > Edit

In this writing cycle (Units 2-6), you are going to complete an opinion essay for the prompt below. In this unit (2), you will look at an opinion essay and start brainstorming ideas.

Should governments spend more money on space exploration?

Exercise 5.1 Preparing to Write

Work with a partner. Ask and answer the questions.

1 What do you think are the best ways to improve brainpower?
2 What are you studying in school? Does it take a lot of brainpower to learn?
3 Is learning about space important? Why or why not?
4 In your opinion, does life exist on other planets?

Exercise 5.2 Focusing on Vocabulary

Read the sentences. Circle the definition for each word in bold. Pay special attention to the verbs. Are they stative or active?

1 People **assumed** that the sun traveled around the Earth until scientists and mathematicians showed the opposite was true.

  a to think that something is true without question or evidence

  b to think about something and try to understand it

2 Research does not **support** the claim that bats are blind.

  a to do something physical, like running or swimming

  b to help show that something is true

3 Scientific **evidence** shows that Mars once had flowing water.

  a opinions that people have about a topic

  b information or research that shows that something is or is not true

4 Many people think that there is life on other planets, but no one can **prove** it.

  a show that something is true

  b ask questions about something

5 Science tells us that life cannot **exist** without air or water.

  a be real, alive, or present

  b have ideas

6 The astronauts are training every day to prepare for the difficult **conditions** they will face next month in space, such as very cold temperatures and zero gravity.

   a the location of something

   b the physical state that someone or something is in

We stand in line to watch movies about them. We buy science fiction books about them. In fact, right now we are sending radio signals into space to them. But do aliens really **exist**? Is there life
5 on other planets? Some scientists believe that there must be because the universe is so big and because at least one planet in another solar system has similar **conditions** to those on Earth. However, until scientists can **prove** that there is life outside
10 of Earth, we must **assume** that we are alone in the universe.

First of all, it is true that the universe is huge. It has billions of stars and thousands of solar systems. As of 2016, experts using the very powerful Kepler
15 telescope have found more than 2,300 planets in orbit around stars. Many of these planets are similar to Earth. In fact, a number of scientists think that one of these planets, named Kepler 22b, has the right conditions—the right atmosphere and
20 temperature—to **support** life. However, there is no **evidence** that there is life on Kepler 22b. Experts with the best technology can see no signs of life there. Until there is hard evidence, we cannot use Kepler 22b to support the idea of life
25 on other planets.

Secondly, a planet needs very particular conditions to support life. A planet with life would need to have water, the right temperature, and the right mix of chemicals in the atmosphere.
30 Earth has the perfect conditions for life, and it is highly unlikely that another planet has exactly the same environment as Earth. In addition, although scientists believe that life might exist on other planets, they have never found evidence to
35 prove it. A recent report from Princeton University suggests that there probably is no life on other planets. The researchers agree that we do not have enough scientific evidence to decide if there is life on other planets. They say that just because
40 conditions similar to Earth exist on other planets, it does not mean that life exists there.

For these and other reasons, I do not believe that there is life on other planets. Although the universe is very big, a planet needs very special
45 conditions to support life, and Earth has them. It is not too hot or too cold. It has water, air, and the right chemicals. In my opinion, we are living on the only planet that can support life because no other planets have these conditions.

Read the text on page 27. Answer the questions.

1 Are scientists trying to find life on other planets? If so, what are they doing?
2 What is the name of the planet with similar conditions to Earth's?
3 Does the writer think there is life on other planets?

Complete the tasks. Then compare your answers with a partner's.

1 Underline the main verbs in the first three sentences of paragraph 1. Are they in the simple present or present progressive? Why does the writer use these verb forms?
2 Circle at least five stative verbs (see the list on page 22). How does the writer use these verbs?
3 Highlight one more example of the present progressive. How does the writer use this form?
4 Why doesn't the writer use the present progressive in paragraphs 2 and 3?

Identifying Purpose

There are many reasons to write, for example, to inform, explain, entertain, or persuade. Writers may state their purpose clearly in the text, or they may imply it. Writers use key words, tone, and language to help show the purpose of their writing.

Work with a partner. Ask and answer the questions.

1 What is the main idea of the text?
   a Earth is the only planet with life.
   b Kepler 22b may be able to support life, but scientists cannot prove it.

2 What is the writer's purpose?
   a to entertain   b to inform   c to persuade

3 Why does the writer include information from a recent report from Princeton University?
   a to show that experts agree with his opinion
   b to show that there are two sides to the argument

4 How can stative verb forms like *believe* and *think* help identify the writer's purpose?
5 What is the purpose of most academic writing?

Supporting Details

In academic writing, writers give details - facts, examples, or reasons - to support their statements or opinions and show that they are true.

Exercise 5.6 Applying the Skill

Work with a partner. Complete the tasks.

1 Underline the writer's main argument (thesis) in paragraph 1 on page 27.
2 What details does the writer give to support the argument in paragraph 2?
3 What details does the writer give to support the argument in paragraph 3?

My Writing

Exercise 5.7 Brainstorming

Answer the questions. Write your opinion and one detail to support it.

1 Which of the following scientific areas is the most important for governments to spend money on: health, environment, or space?

2 Who should explore space, governments or private companies?

3 What is the best reason to explore space?

Exercise 5.8 Writing a Paragraph

Choose one of your answers in Exercise 5.7. Write a paragraph with a topic sentence, more supporting details and information, and a concluding sentence. Include at least two stative verbs and one example that uses the present progressive form.

Exercise 5.9 Editing Your Writing

Use the checklist to edit your paragraph.

Did you use the simple present for things that often happen or are general truths?	
Did you use the present progressive for things that are happening now?	
Did you use the simple present for stative verbs or verbs with stative meaning?	
Did you avoid the common mistakes in the chart on page 25?	

Imperatives

What's Appropriate?

1 Grammar in the Real World

A Who do you usually send e-mails to – friends, family, your professors? Do you write the same way to all of them? Read the web article about e-mailing. What are some good rules to follow in an e-mail to a professor?

B Comprehension Check Read the e-mail. Label the parts *A* for appropriate or *NA* for not appropriate.

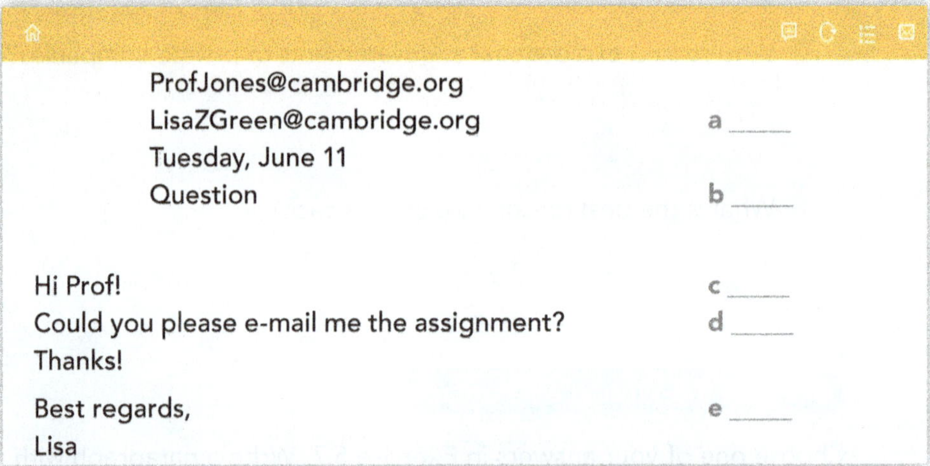

C Notice Find and write the sentences from the article with these meanings.

1 You need an e-mail address that shows your name.

____

2 You need to write a greeting.

____

3 It is not good to write pages and pages of text.

____

4 Text messaging abbreviations are not appropriate.

____

How to Write an **E-Mail** to a Professor

At some point in the school year, you may need to e-mail a professor. **Make sure** that you create a positive impression[1] by following these simple rules.

1   **Use** an e-mail address that shows your name. A fun e-mail address like soccerfan@cambridge.org does not look professional. Your e-mail may go to the professor's spam folder if there is no name in the e-mail address. **Use** your name or your school e-mail address instead.

2   **Write** the purpose of your e-mail in the subject line. Do not write "Hi" or "Question." **Include** your class name and time so your professor can immediately see this information.

3   **Always start** with a greeting, for example, "Dear Prof. Smith." **Never send** an e-mail, especially a request, without one. Your professor might be friendly and informal in class. However, it is not appropriate[2] to be informal in an e-mail to him or her, so **don't start** an e-mail with "Hi there!" or "What's up?"

4   **Be** brief,[3] clear, and specific. **Do not write** pages and pages of text. Remember, your professor is very busy. **Do not write** more than one screen.

5   **Always be** polite. **Say** "please" and "thank you." **Don't tell** your professor what to do. For example, **don't say** "Reply ASAP,[4]" "Please respond immediately," or "Urgent!!!" **Do not write** "I need the assignment. Please send it." Instead, **write** "Could you please e-mail me the assignment?"

6   **Don't use** text messaging abbreviations. This is an e-mail to a professor, not a friend, so **avoid** "LOL" (laughing out loud), "TTYL" (talk to you later), or emojis ().

7   **Thank** your professor at the end of the e-mail. **Write** something like "Thanks" or "Thanks for your time" and a polite ending like "See you in class on Tuesday" or "Best regards." **Remember** to type your name.

8   Finally, **don't forge**t to check your grammar and spelling. If you follow these rules, you will always communicate appropriately with your professors.

[1] **a positive impression:** a good opinion

[2] **appropriate:** right for a particular situation

[3] **be brief:** do not write a lot

[4] **ASAP:** an abbreviation for "as soon as possible"

2 Imperatives

Grammar Presentation

Imperatives tell people to do things. For example, they can give instructions, directions to a place, or advice.

Write the purpose of your e-mail in the subject line.
Don't use text messaging abbreviations.

2.1 Affirmative and Negative Statements

AFFIRMATIVE			NEGATIVE		
Base Form of Verb			Do + Not	Base Form of Verb	
Avoid	abbreviations.		**Don't**	**make**	demands.
Be	clear.		**Do not**	**write**	pages and pages of text.

DATA FROM THE REAL WORLD

Don't is much more common than *do not* in conversation. *Do not* is also very strong.

2.2 Using Imperatives in Writing

A	Imperatives are common in rules, road signs, orders, warnings, forms, and directions.	*Stop.* *Do not enter.* *Write clearly.* *Turn left at the next intersection.*
B	They are common in texts with instructions and advice, such as manuals, recipes, and magazine articles.	*Set the date and time.* *Chop the onions.* *Finish your e-mail with something polite.*
C	You can use *always* and *never* to give emphasis in writing.	*Always start with a greeting.* *Never send an e-mail without one.* (= Don't send.)
D	You can use imperatives with time clauses and with *if* clauses.	*Check the e-mail for spelling errors before you send it.*
E	Use a comma when the main clause is second.	*If you e-mail a professor, do not use texting language.*

2.3 Using Imperatives in Speaking and Informal Writing

A	Don't use imperatives to tell people you don't know well what to do. It can sound rude. Saying *please* doesn't make it polite.	~~*Send me* the assignment, *please.*~~ *Could you please send me the assignment?*
B	When you know people very well, you can use imperatives in everyday situations to ask for things, give instructions or advice, and to make offers or invitations.	*Give me that pen.* *Call the doctor.* *Don't forget.* *Have a cookie.* *Come over Saturday.*

Grammar Application

Exercise 2.1 Forming Imperatives

A Complete the sentences in this advice column about using cell phones. Use the affirmative or negative imperative form of the verbs in the box.

answer	find	keep	leave	let	send	take	~~turn~~	~~use~~

Rules for Using Cell Phones

What is appropriate use of a cell phone at the office? Here are some simple rules to follow so that you do not upset your friends, co-workers, business clients, and most of all, your boss!

1 __Turn__ your cell phone ringer off in the office, or put it on vibrate.

2 __Don't use__ a pop song for a ring tone. It is not professional.

3 ________________ unimportant calls go to voice mail. Your co-workers do not want to know what you are having for dinner tonight.

4 If your cell phone rings in a restroom, ________________ it! People can hear you.

5 ________________ your voice down. On a modern cell phone, there is no need to shout.

6 ________________ text messages instead of making phone calls in the office. They are less annoying to other people.

7 ________________ a quiet, private place to take calls, and be brief.

8 ________________ a call in a meeting. Just ________________ the room and take the call outside.

B Over to You Rewrite two of the imperatives above using *Always* and two with *Never*. Compare with a partner.

I wrote, "Always turn your cell phone ringer off." How about you?

Use the words to write sentences about appropriate cell phone use.
Use affirmative or negative imperatives. Write each sentence two different ways.

1 go into a meeting / turn your cell phone off

Before __*you go into a meeting, turn your cell phone off*__ .
__*Turn your cell phone off*__ before __*you go into a meeting*__ .

2 be in a face-to-face meeting / check your messages

When ____ .

_______________________ . when _______________________ .

3 be in a meeting / keep checking your messages

If ____ .

_______________________ if _______________________ .

4 be in a presentation / reply to a call or an e-mail

When ____ .

_______________________ . when _______________________ .

5 be expecting a call / tell the other people in a meeting

If ____ .

_______________________ if _______________________ .

6 take a phone call in a meeting / leave the room to talk

If ____ .

_______________________ if _______________________ .

7 leave the room to take a call / be brief

If ____ .

_______________________ if _______________________ .

8 finish your call and come back to the room / apologize

After ____ .

_______________________ after _______________________ .

Exercise 2.3 Making Rules with Imperatives

A Group Work **Discuss the questions about cell phone use. Do you all do the same things?**

- When do you turn off your phone?
- When do you set it to vibrate?
- Do you take calls during dinner? At a restaurant?
- Do you talk on the phone when you're out with friends?
- Do you sometimes go someplace quiet to talk?
- Do you always answer your phone when someone calls you?

B Group Work **Agree on four rules for using a cell phone appropriately. Write four rules with imperatives. Use time clauses and *if* clauses. Share your ideas with the class.**

When you're in class, turn off your cell phone.

Exercise 2.4 Imperatives with Subject Pronouns

DATA FROM THE REAL WORLD

You can use *You* with imperatives in informal situations, for example, to decide who does what or to add emphasis and make the imperative stronger.

You write the e-mail, and I'll check it.
You take care now.
Don't you scare me like that again!

You can use *somebody, someone, everybody,* and *everyone* with imperatives when there are a lot of people, for example, in class or at a party.

Use *someone / somebody* to refer to one person.
Use *everyone / everybody* to refer to a group.

Someone turn off the lights.
Everybody please sit down.
Everyone please take your seats.

A Complete these sentences people might say while doing group activities in class. Use *you* and the imperative form of the verbs in parentheses.

1 _____*You write*_____ (write) the questionnaire, and I'll write the answers. Does that sound fair?

2 Kate, _____________ (do) some research on the Internet.

3 Dale, _____________ (be) the salesperson, and Josh, _____________ (play) the role of the customer.

4 We'll get a good grade, _____________ (not worry).

5 Who's going to be A and B? I'll be A, and _____________ (be) B.

6 Binh, _____________ (be) the group leader, and Ana, _____________ (take) notes.

7 Claudia, _____________ (think) of a clever title for our report.

8 Asha, _____________ (find) the pictures, and I'll print them.

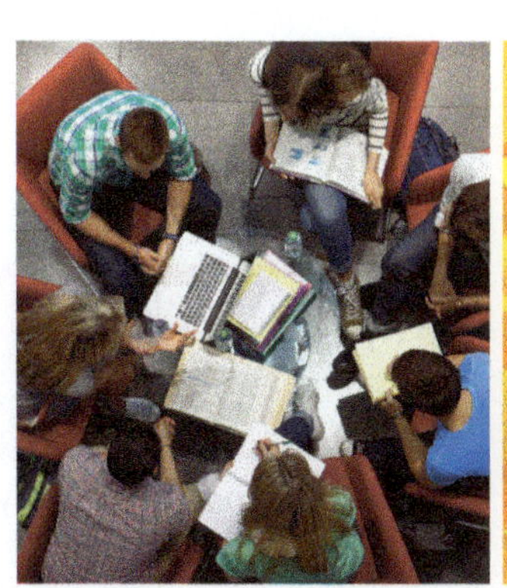

B Complete the sentences from a student's presentation with *somebody / someone* or *everybody / everyone*.

1 _Everybody / Everyone_ take a seat, please.

2 _________________ pass out the worksheet, OK?

3 Now, before I start, _________________ choose a partner. We're going to do some pair work.

4 Do you need a pencil, Raffi? _________________ hand this pencil to Raffi, please.

5 I want to use the projector now, so _________________ turn off the lights, please.

6 _________________ please write the answer on the board.

7 Now, _________________ go back to your first partner and discuss the questions.

8 Before you leave the room, _________________ take a handout.

3 Let's . . .

Grammar Presentation

Let's is a kind of imperative that makes suggestions or gives instructions to other people in a group you are in.	***Let's stop*** *there and talk about this in the next class.*

3.1 Affirmative and Negative Statements

AFFIRMATIVE	NEGATIVE
Let's + Base Form of Verb	*Let's not* + Base Form of Verb
Let's stop there. **Let's be** clear.	**Let's not talk** about that now. **Let's not confuse** writing to friends and writing to professors.

DATA FROM THE REAL WORLD

In very formal academic writing, people use *Let us*. Research shows that the negative form, *Let's not*, is not very common in academic writing or conversation.

Let us now look at the use of smartphones.

3.2 Using Imperatives with *Let's*

A You can use *Let's* to make suggestions to do things with other people.	***Let's meet*** *after class today.*
B You can also use *Let's* to give instructions, for example, in class.	***Let's get started.*** ***Let's stop*** *there.* ***Let's discuss*** *this in the next class.*
C You can soften (say in a nice way) *Let's* imperatives with *just* in speaking.	***Let's just*** *do this exercise, and then we can stop for today.*

DATA FROM THE REAL WORLD

Research shows that the most common expressions with *Let's* in formal academic speaking are *Let's say*, *Let's see*, and *Let's look at*.
Let's say often means "imagine."
Let's see gives you time to think.

Let's say *you're writing to a professor. How do you start your e-mail?*
You can say this in several ways. ***Let's see***, *you can say . . .*
Are you still confused? ***Let's look at*** *page 12.*

Grammar Application

Exercise 3.1 Imperatives with *Let's* and *Let's Not*

A Some students are creating a questionnaire on text messaging. Complete the conversation with *Let's or Let's not* and the words in the box.

ask	choose a topic	put it first	see	start	write down

A OK. _____*Let's start*_____.
(1)

B Right. _________________. How about text messaging?
(2)

A Yeah. That's a good topic for a questionnaire.

B All right. First, _________________ some questions. What
(3)
can we ask?

A _________________. Oh, here's one: "Do you ever text
(4)
friends when you're in class?"

B Yes, that sounds good, but _________________. It can
(5)
be second. The first question can be: "Do you turn off your
cell phone in class?" What do you think?

A OK. So that's two questions. For question three,
_________________ : "Do you ever text your instructors?"
(6)

B Sounds good!

B Listen to the rest of the conversation and write the missing words with *Let's / Let's not*.

A OK, group, ___*let's think*___ of two more questions.
(1)

B Wait a minute. How will we distribute the questionnaire to everyone?

A _______________ about that now. We can ask the teacher for help when we're ready.
(2)

B I have some ideas for the presentation. _______________ about that.
(3)

A _______________ the questionnaire first. We still need two more questions.
(4)

C _______________ . How about: "How many text messages do you send in a day?"
(5)

A Great question. One more.

B What about: "Do you sleep with your cell phone near you?"

A I love it! That's six questions. _______________ there for today, OK? Can we meet again
(6)
on Thursday or Friday?

C _______________ on Friday. I have to work all day. Thursday's good. Same time?
(7)

A OK, _______________ on Thursday.
(8)

Read the situations for preparing a group presentation on appropriate work behavior. Write suggestions using *Let's / Let's not*.

1 You arrive at school to meet with your group. You are the group leader. Everyone is talking.

You want to start the meeting. You say: OK, everybody, ___*let's start the meeting.*___

2 One member wants to talk about handouts. You don't want to think about that until later.

You say: ___*Let's not think about that until later.*___

3 The group isn't sure what to do. You want to try brainstorming ideas. You say:

Well, ____

4 The group thinks of many ideas. You want to divide the ideas up so that everyone presents

something. You say: ____

5 A member thinks that the presentation might be too long. You don't want to worry about

that now. You say: ____

6 Your group is deciding who will introduce the presentation. You want to vote on it.

You say: I have an idea. ____

7 It's getting late and everyone seems tired. You want to stop for now and meet tomorrow.

You say: It's getting late. ____

4 Avoid Common Mistakes 

1 **Negative imperatives are _Don't_ / _Do not_ + base form. _No_ is not used in imperatives.**

Don't use
~~No use~~ text messaging abbreviations.

2 **_Do not_ is two words, not one.**

Do not
~~Donot~~ write pages and pages of text.

3 **There are apostrophes in _Don't_ and _Let's_.**

Don't
~~Dont~~ send text messages during class.

Editing Task

Find and correct four more mistakes in this article about how to set up a professional social networking profile.

5 Academic Writing

Opinion Writing

Brainstorm 〉 Organize 〉 Write 〉 Edit

In Unit 2, you looked at an essay and brainstormed ideas for the prompt below. In this unit (3), you are going to identify and evaluate evidence to support your opinion.

Should governments spend more money on space exploration?

Evaluating Evidence

In an opinion essay, you must support your opinions with evidence (reasons, facts, and examples) to produce valid arguments. Some evidence is stronger than other evidence. It is important to evaluate its strength for and against your opinion. This can help you decide your opinion and the evidence to include.

Exercise 5.1 Applying the Skill

Read the emails about spending money on space exploration. Then work with a partner and complete the tasks.

Dear Senator Darcy,

I'm a big supporter of the International Space Agency, and I think we should spend more money on space programs. The International Space Station (ISS) is a good example why. It has existed since 1998 and brings together many countries. Astronauts live in space and take part in important experiments. In 2015, Russia and the United States sent astronauts to live on the ISS for one year to observe the effects of space on the human body. Long-term journeys, such as traveling to Mars, will never happen without this research. The ISS cost about $100 billion, and one country could not pay for that on its own. International space exploration proves that countries can work together. It represents the spirit of partnership. With so much war in the world, governments should spend more money on things they can achieve together. Maybe that will help bring peace. So please vote to continue funding the ISS. Let's work together for a better planet.

Sincerely,

Jessica Park

Dear Senator Darcy,

We have spent more than $16 billion per year on our space program since 1958. For a long time, the cost was worth it because of the advances made in science and technology. However, space travel is not only expensive but dangerous. Astronauts have been killed as recently as 2014. Also, we shouldn't waste natural resources on building new spacecraft. Nowadays, more money should be spent on people who need clean water and food, access to education, and medical research. For example, a Japanese study found that a drug made from sea sponges helps treat several types of cancer, and yet 90% of the oceans are still unexplored. Please vote against funding future space exploration. Instead, let's spend our money on ocean exploration and finding cures for diseases instead of wasting it on trips to Mars.

Best,

Ricardo Luna

1 Underline the sentence or sentences that show each writer's opinion about the topic.

2 Highlight the reasons and evidence the writers give for and against funding space exploration.

3 Complete the T-chart with the information you highlighted.

for	against

4 Think of at least three more reasons or examples for each side. Write them in the T-chart.

5 Evaluate the evidence in the T-chart. Which makes the strongest argument?

6 After evaluating the information, which opinion do you agree with the most? Why?

   a Governments should spend more money on space exploration.

   b Governments should not spend more money on space exploration.

7 Underline four examples of imperatives in the emails. Why do the writers use the imperative?

My Writing

Using the Imperative in Academic Writing

It is not common to use the imperative form in academic writing except in the following situations: a process paragraph or essay; instructions; or an email. When you write an opinion essay, use phrases like *It is important*, *We should*, *In my opinion*, and *I believe* to introduce your opinion.

Exercise 5.2 Writing an Opinion Email

Look at the evidence you added to the T-chart. Write an email to Senator Darcy. Include your opinion and evidence to make a strong argument for or against the funding of space exploration. Use the emails on page 40 as models.

Exercise 5.3 Editing Your Writing

Use the checklist to edit your email.

Did you use imperatives to signal what to do and what to avoid?	
Did you use time clauses and *if* to explain when to do something?	
Did you avoid the common mistakes in the chart on page 39?	

Simple Past

Entrepreneurs

ACADEMIC WRITING

Opinion writing

1 Grammar in the Real World

A What is the best way to find information today? Read the article from a technology magazine. How did Google start?

B Comprehension Check Answer the questions.

1 Where did Larry Page and Sergey Brin meet?

2 Why did they work in a garage?

3 What other products did Google start?

4 How many people worked at Google after 20 years?

C Notice Look at the article. Find the simple past forms of these verbs.

Group A

1 start ___________________

2 move ___________________

3 study ___________________

4 happen ___________________

Group B

5 come ___________________

6 be ___________________,
___________________ (two forms)

7 become ___________________

8 meet ___________________

How are the two groups of verbs different?

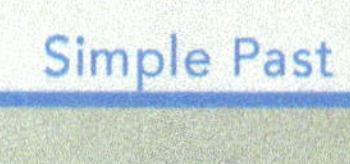

The STORY OF Google

Who started Google?

Sergey Brin and Larry Page **started** the company. Sergey **came** from Moscow, Russia. He **moved** to the United States as a young child and later **studied** mathematics and computer science. Larry **was** born in
5 Michigan and **became** interested in computers as a child.

How did they meet?

They **met** in 1995 at Stanford University, in California, where they **were** both computer science students. They **did not get along** at first, but they soon **became** friends.

10 What happened next?

They **designed** a new Internet search engine. At first, they **worked** in their rooms in college. Then they **rented** a friend's garage because Sergey's roommate **complained** about the noise from his computers. Three years later, they **started** Google.

15 Was it an immediate success?

The company **was** an immediate success. Before Google, **there were** other search engines, but Google soon **became** the most popular one. The company **grew** quickly. They **did not stop** at just one product. Very soon, **there were many** other Google products, including Google
20 Maps, Android phones, and YouTube, of course. Twenty years later, Google **was** one of the top ten most valuable companies in the world and **had** about 60,000 employees.

So what did people do before Google?

Before Google, people **went** to libraries. They **got** information from
25 books. These days, they just "google" for information.

Simple Past

Grammar Presentation

You can use the simple past to talk about completed events in the past.	*Brin and Page* **started** *Google in 1998.* *They* **did not get along** *at first.*

2.1 Affirmative Statements

Subject	Verb + -ed (Regular Verbs)
I You He / She / It We They	**started** in 1998. **employed** 80,000 people.

Subject	Irregular Verb
I You He / She / It We They	**grew** quickly. **became** successful.

▸▸ Spelling Rules for Regular Verbs in Simple Past: See page A4.   ▸▸ Irregular Verbs: See page A3.

🌐 DATA FROM THE REAL WORLD

Research shows that these are six of the most common **regular** simple past verbs.	work start call	work**ed** start**ed** call**ed**	live try plan	lived tried plan**ned**
Research shows that these are eight of the most common **irregular** simple past verbs.	have get do say	**had** **got** **did** **said**	go come take make	**went** **came** **took** **made**

2.2 Negative Statements

Subject	Did + Not	Base Form of Verb	
I You He / She / It We They	**did not** **didn't**	**start**	slowly.

2.3 Yes/No Questions and Short Answers

Did	Subject	Base Form of Verb	
Did	I you he / she / it we they	**work** **start**	every day? quickly?

Short Answers

Yes, I **did**.	No, I **didn't**.
Yes, you **did**.	No, you **didn't**.
Yes, he / she / it **did**.	No, he / she / it **didn't**.
Yes, we **did**.	No, we **didn't**.
Yes, they **did**.	No, they **didn't**.

2.4 Information Questions

Wh- Word	Did	Subject	Base Form of Verb
What **Where** **When** **Who** **Why**	**did**	I you he / she / it we they	**study**?

Wh- Word	Simple Past Verb	
What **Who**	**happened** **started**	next? the company?

2.5 Using Simple Past

A Use the simple past to talk or write about:
- a single action that started and ended in the past.

*They **started** Google in 1998.*

x

——————————————————→

past ———————————————— now

- a repeated action or habit in the past.

*They **worked** in their rooms every day.*

xxx

——————————————————→

past ———————————————— now

- a state, situation, or feeling in the past.

*They **didn't get along**.*

▬▬▬▬▬——————————————→

past ———————————————— now

B Time expressions can come at the start or end of a statement. Examples: *last week / month / year, 10 years ago, in 1998, yesterday.*

Last year, I joined a new company.
I joined a new company last year.

Two years ago, I graduated.
I graduated two years ago.

C Remember to use a comma when the time expression comes at the beginning of the sentence.

In 1998, they started Google.

They started Google in 1998.

D Adverbs of frequency often come before the main verb in simple past statements. Some examples of adverbs of frequency are *never, rarely, sometimes, often, usually,* and *always.*

*They **often had** meetings at a pizza parlor.*

*They **sometimes worked** in their room.*

DATA FROM THE REAL WORLD

Research shows that *didn't* is not common in formal writing. Use *did not* instead. Writers sometimes use *didn't* in quotes of people speaking.

Use *didn't* in conversation and informal writing. In conversation, *did not* can sound formal, emphatic, or argumentative.

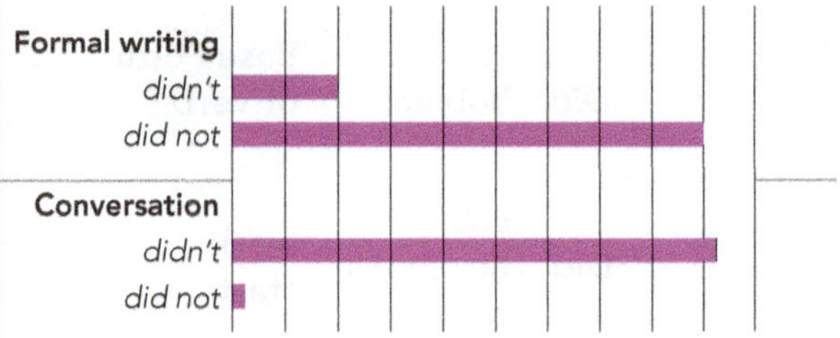

Grammar Application

Exercise 2.1 Statements and Questions

A **Complete the article with the simple past form of the verbs in parentheses.**

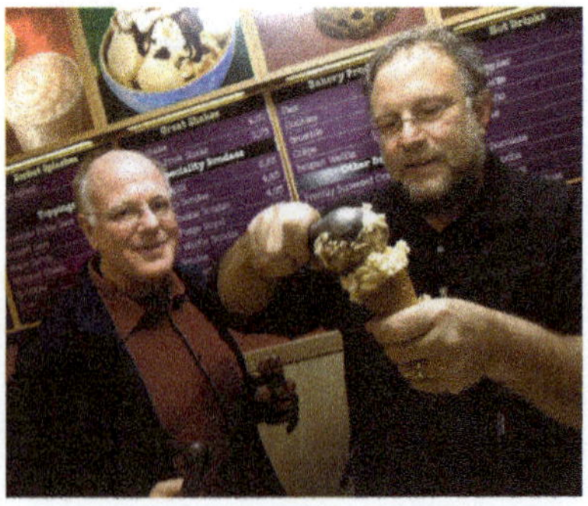

Ben Cohen and Jerry Greenfield grew up (1) (grow up) in Merrick, Long Island. They ________ (2) (meet) in middle school, and they ________ (3) (graduate) from high school together. Their connections to ice cream ________ (4) (begin) at an early age. Ben ________ (5) (drive) an ice cream truck in high school. Jerry ________ (6) (work) in his college cafeteria as an ice cream scooper.

Ben ________ (7) (try) different colleges, but he ________ (8) (not graduate). At one time, he ________ (9) (teach) crafts in a school. At the school, he sometimes ________ (10) (make) ice cream with his students. Jerry ________ (11) (want) to be a doctor. After he ________ (12) (graduate) from college, he ________ (13) (apply) to medical school, but he was not successful. During those years, Ben and Jerry ________ (14) (stay) friends.

After a few years, Ben and Jerry ________ (15) (go) into the food business together. At first, they ________ (16) (think) about making bagels, but the equipment was expensive. So they ________ (17) (choose) ice cream and ________ (18) (take) a $5 class on ice cream making.

Ben and Jerry ________ (19) (see) an opportunity in Burlington, Vermont. This college town ________ (20) (not have) an ice cream shop. They ________ (21) (find) an old gas station, and in 1978 they ________ (22) (open) the first Ben & Jerry's store.

Ben & Jerry's quickly ________ (23) (become) popular because it ________ (24) (have) great ice cream and a caring approach to the community. On their first anniversary, they ________ (25) (give) everyone free ice cream as a "thank you." They still give away free ice cream every year on their anniversary.

B Pair Work Complete the *Yes/No* questions and answers about Ben and Jerry. Then ask and answer the questions with a partner. Give more information.

1 _______*Did*_______ Ben and Jerry _____*grow up*_____ (grow up) on Long Island?
   ___*Yes, they did.*___

2 _________________ they _________________ (meet) in college?

3 _________________ Ben _________________ (graduate) from college?

4 _________________ Ben _________________ (teach) in a school?

5 _________________ Jerry _________________ (go) to college?

6 _________________ Jerry _________________ (apply) to law school?

7 _________________ they _________________ (think) about making ice cream at first?

8 _________________ they _________________ (open) their first store in 1978?

A *Did Ben and Jerry grow up on Long Island?*
B *Yes, they did. They grew up in Merrick, Long Island.*

C Complete the information questions about Ben and Jerry. Use the answers to help you.

1 **A** Where _____*did Ben and Jerry grow up*_____ ? **B** On Long Island.
2 **A** Where _________________________________ ? **B** In middle school.
3 **A** What _________________________________ ? **B** Crafts.
4 **A** What kind of course _____________________ ? **B** An ice cream-making course.
5 **A** How much _____________________________ ? **B** $5.
6 **A** When _________________________________ ? **B** In 1978.
7 **A** Why __________________________________ ? **B** The ice cream was good.
8 **A** What _________________________________ ? **B** Free ice cream.

D Pair Work Complete the information questions about Ben and Jerry. Write *did* in the blank, if necessary. If *did* is not necessary, write an **X**. Then take turns asking and answering the questions with a partner.

1 Who _____*X*_____ drove an ice cream truck in high school?
2 Who ___________ worked in the college cafeteria?
3 What ___________ he do in the cafeteria?
4 Who ___________ graduated from college?
5 What ___________ he want to study after college?
6 Who ___________ taught in a school?
7 What ___________ happened on their first anniversary?
8 Why ___________ they open a store in Burlington?

Verbs ending in /t/ or /d/	/ɪd/ or /əd/	
If the base form of the verb ends with the sound /t/ or /d/, say -ed as an extra syllable /ɪd/ or /əd/.	/t/ rent – rented	/d/ decide – decided

Verbs ending in voiceless consonants	/t/	
If the base form of the verb ends in /f/, /k/, /p/, /s/, /ʃ/, and /tʃ/, say the -ed as /t/.	/f/ laugh – laughed /s/ miss – missed /k/ look – looked /ʃ/ finish – finished /p/ stop – stopped /tʃ/ watch – watched	

Verbs ending in voiced consonants or vowels	/d/	
If the base form of the verb ends in a voiced consonant or vowel, say the -ed endings as /d/.	live – lived learn – learned change – changed play – played	

A Listen and repeat the verbs with -ed endings in the chart above.

B Circle the -ed endings that have an extra syllable (/ɪd/ or /əd/) in these sentences. Then listen, check, and repeat.

1 My family moved here six years ago.

2 I needed to earn some money, so I decided to get a job in a factory.

3 I earned a lot of money, but I wanted to be my own boss.

4 I studied business and learned how to start a company.

5 I finished the program and graduated two years ago.

6 Finally, I started my own business.

C Over to You Write six sentences about your own life. Use the ideas in B or your own ideas. Compare sentences with a partner. Ask your partner for more information.

A *My family moved here in 1998.*
B *Really? Where did you live before that?*

A Complete the article with the simple past form of the verbs in parentheses.

Today, Oprah Winfrey is one of the most successful broadcasters, publishers, and entrepreneurs in the world. However, she did not have an easy start in life. Oprah _had_ (1) (have) a difficult childhood. She _______________ (2) (not have) a lot of opportunities as a child, but she was very intelligent. She _______________ (3) (learn) to read before the age of three. Her broadcasting career _______________ (4) (begin) in high school. In 1971, she

_____________________ (go) to Tennessee State University.
(5)

During high school and college, she _____________________
(6)

(work) on a radio show. She also _____________________ (work)
(7)

at a TV station in Nashville as a student. At the age of 19,

she _____________________ (become) the first African-American
(8)

woman news anchor[1] at the station.

In 1976, she _____________________ (graduate) from
(9)

college. That year, she _____________________ (move) to
(10)

Baltimore. There she _____________________ (host) a
(11)

TV talk show called *People Are Talking*. Eight years

later, she _____________________ (start) working on a morning show in Chicago.
(12)

It _____________________ (become) *The Oprah Winfrey Show*. Oprah's popularity
(13)

_____________________ (grow) quickly, and in 1986, it _____________________ (become) a
(14)   (15)

national show.

[1]**anchor:** a person who reports the news

B Pair Work **Complete the questions about Oprah Winfrey. Use the information in the article. Then ask and answer the questions with a partner.**

1 What kind of childhood _____________________________________ ?

2 What _____________________________________ before the age of three?

3 Which university _____________________________________ ?

4 What _____________________________________ during high school and college?

5 What else _____________________________________ as a student?

6 Where _____________________________________ after college?

7 What _____________________________________ working on in Chicago?

8 When _____________________________________ a national show?

A *What kind of childhood did Oprah Winfrey have?*
B *She had a difficult childhood.*

3 Simple Past of *Be* and *There Was / There Were*

Grammar Presentation

The simple past of *be* and *There was / There were* describe people, places, and things in the past.	*Oprah Winfrey* **was** *an intelligent child.* ***There were*** *millions of visitors to Oprah's website last month.*

3.1 Simple Past of *Be*: Affirmative and Negative Statements

AFFIRMATIVE

Subject	Was / Were	
I He / She / It	**was**	at Stanford University.
You We They	**were**	

NEGATIVE

Subject	Was / Were + Not	
I He / She / It	**was not** **wasn't**	in Chicago.
You We They	**were not** **weren't**	

DATA FROM THE REAL WORLD

Research shows that *wasn't* and *weren't* are not common in academic writing. Use *was not* and *were not* instead.

Use *wasn't* and *weren't* in conversation, where they are very common.

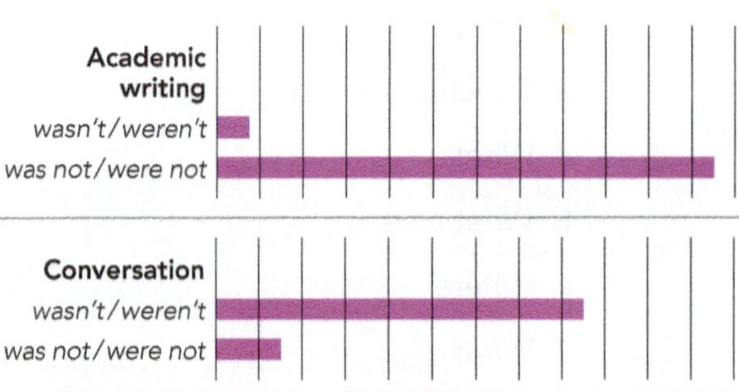

3.2 Simple Past of *Be*: Yes / No Questions and Short Answers

Was / Were	Subject	
Was	I he / she / it	popular?
Were	you we they	

Short Answers	
Yes, I **was**. Yes, he / she / it **was**.	No, I **wasn't**. No, he / she / it **wasn't**.
Yes, you **were**. Yes, we **were**. Yes, they **were**.	No, you **weren't**. No, we **weren't**. No, they **weren't**.

3.3 Information Questions with Simple Past of *Be*

Wh- Word	Was / Were	Subject
Who **Where** **What** **How**	**was**	I? he / she / it?
	were	you? we? they?

Wh- Word	Was	
Who **What**	**was**	there at the beginning? next for the company?

3.4 *There Was / There Were*

There Was / Wasn't + Singular or Noncount Noun	There Were / Weren't + Plural Noun
There was a problem. **There wasn't any** software. **There was no** software.	**There were** some problems. **There weren't any** programs. **There were no** programs.

3.5 Using *There Was / There Were*

A Use *There was (not) / There were (not)* to talk about things that did or did not exist in the past.	*Before Google,* **there were** *other search engines.* **There was** *no software.*
⊕ Research shows that *There was/were no* is more common than *There wasn't/weren't any*.	
B The form of *be* always agrees with the noun that follows it.	**There were** *other search engines.* *There was other search engines.*

A Complete the lecture about Sarah Breedlove McWilliams Walker (1867–1919). Use the affirmative or negative form of *was*, *were*, *there was*, and *there were*.

Sarah Breedlove McWilliams Walker **was** the (1) first American female self-made millionaire. However, before she became a millionaire, life _________________ (2) easy for young Sarah. Her parents died, and Sarah _________________ (3) an orphan at the age of seven. For a time, Sarah and her sister _________________ (4) cotton pickers. By the age of 14, Sarah _________________ (5) already married. Her husband died two years later, and she went to live with her brothers. They _________________ (6) barbers.

In the 1890s, Sarah lost some of her hair. At that time, _________________ (7) no good products in the stores for this problem. In fact, _________________ (8) a lot of hair care products for African Americans in those days. Sarah saw that _________________ (9) an opportunity for a new business, so she invented "Madam Walker's Wonderful Hair Grower." The business grew. Soon _________________ (10) other "Madam Walker" products, such as shampoos and cosmetics. She _________________ (11) very successful and eventually became a millionaire.

B Pair Work Now listen to the lecture. It has some extra information about Madam Walker. Write down three new things you hear. Then tell your partner.

1 ____

2 ____

3 ____

A *Her brothers were barbers in St. Louis.*

B *Right. And she worked for . . .*

Exercise 3.2 Questions with *Be* and Other Verbs

Pair Work **Write the simple past questions. Then interview a classmate. Ask for more information as you talk.**

1 What / be / your first job   *What was your first job?* _______________

2 be / it / a good job   _______________________________

3 What / be / your co-workers like   _______________________________

4 What / you / do there   _______________________________

5 Why / you / leave   _______________________________

6 What / be / your best job   _______________________________

7 Why / you / like it   _______________________________

8 Where / be / your worst job   _______________________________

4 Avoid Common Mistakes ⚠

1 Use the simple past, not the simple present, when you write about the past.

started
I ~~start~~ my first job in 2008.

2 After *did not* or *didn't*, use the base form of the verb, not the past form.

They didn't earned a lot of money.

3 Put time expressions at the beginning or end of a statement, not between the subject and the verb, and not between the verb and the object.

yesterday
I bought ~~yesterday~~ a computer ⌃.   OR   *Yesterday,* ⌃ I bought ~~yesterday~~ a computer.

4 Use *there were* with plural nouns. Use *there was* with singular or noncount nouns.

were   *was*
There ~~was~~ a lot of people. There ~~were~~ no information.

Editing Task

Find and correct nine more mistakes in the blog.

moved
My family ~~move~~ from Mexico City to the United States in 2018. I went to Hamilton High School in Los Angeles. I did not knew anybody, and I did not had any friends here. I in 2009 met Jun. He became my first friend.

We in 2012 graduated. I got a job at a nice restaurant, but I did not enjoyed my job. Jun drove
5 a taco truck, but he did not liked the food. I wanted to be my own boss, and I always liked food and cooking. Jun wanted his own business, too. Jun saw an opportunity. There was hungry office workers downtown at noon, but there weren't a nice place to eat. We bought a food truck and we start Food on the Move in 2014.

5 Academic Writing

Opinion Writing

Brainstorm > **Organize** > Write > Edit

In Unit 3, you identified and evaluated evidence to support an opinion. In this unit (4), you are going to study the organization of an essay and write thesis statements for the prompt below.

Should governments spend more money on space exploration?

Organizing an Essay

An essay is a group of paragraphs about the same topic. Essays are common in academic writing. They respond to questions, or writing prompts. An essay has three main parts:

Introductory Paragraph: The introductory paragraph gives background information about a topic. This can be general information about the topic, historical information, or a brief story or example that helps readers understand why the topic is important. The last sentence of the introductory paragraph is usually the **thesis statement**, which tells the reader what the essay is about. It is similar to a topic sentence for a paragraph, and it includes the writer's point of view, or opinion, on the topic.

Body Paragraphs: Each body paragraph relates to the thesis of the essay and has a topic sentence and supporting sentences. Supporting sentences include facts, reasons, and examples that support the main ideas. There can be one or more body paragraphs in an essay, but usually there are at least two.

Concluding Paragraph: The concluding paragraph retells or summarizes the main points in the essay and restates the writer's opinion or point of view. It can also present a conclusion, recommendation, or prediction.

Exercise 5.1 Understanding the Skill

Use the words in the box to complete the summary about essay organization.

middle   last   first   one

The introductory paragraph is the (1) __________ paragraph in an essay. The body is the (2) __________ paragraph or set of paragraphs of the essay. The body can be (3) __________ paragraph or many paragraphs. The concluding paragraph is the (4) __________ paragraph in an essay.

My Writing

Thesis Statements

Thesis statements can be either general or specific. A **general thesis statement** includes the topic and the writer's point of view on the topic, but it does not include any specific information about what aspects of the topic the writer will discuss.

The United States helps entrepreneurs succeed in business in two main ways.

A **specific thesis statement** includes the main areas or reasons that the writer will discuss in the essay.

The United States helps entrepreneurs succeed in business through its educational and economic systems.

Exercise 5.2 Applying the Skill

Read the prompt on page 54, and review your My Writing work in Units 2 and 3.

1 Write a general thesis statement that answers the prompt.

2 Write a specific thesis statement that answers the prompt.

Using the Simple Past in Academic Writing

The simple past is often used in narrative writing or reports. In opinion writing, it can be used to describe a past event that is an example to support one of the writer's main points.

Exercise 5.3 Applying the Skill

Think of a past event that supports one of the main points in the specific thesis you wrote in Exercise 5.2. Write a body paragraph. Include the past event as one of your supporting details.

Exercise 5.4 Editing Your Writing

Use the checklist to edit your paragraph.

Did you use the simple past for all past single actions, repeated actions, and states?	
Did you use the correct forms for irregular verbs?	
Did you avoid the common mistakes in the chart on page 53?	

Simple Past, Time Clauses, *Used To*, and *Would*

Science and Society

1 Grammar in the Real World

A What is your favorite ice cream flavor? Read the article from a textbook. How is ice cream today different from ice cream in the past?

B Comprehension Check **Circle the correct answer.**

1 Persians made a frozen dessert with **noodles / buffalo milk**.

2 In ancient Rome, people mixed snow with **fruit / cream**.

3 A duchess brought sorbet to **Italy / France**.

4 British chemists invented ice cream that **lasted longer / had no air in it**.

C Notice **Find the sentences in the article. Complete them with** *after*, *before*, **or** *as soon as.*

1 ___________________ refrigeration existed, people needed ice to make frozen desserts.

2 ___________________ scientists found better processes for freezing things, ice cream became popular with all classes, rich and poor.

3 ___________________ ice cream became more available, people began to buy it more often.

In each sentence, two events happen. Circle the event that happened first.

Ice Cream:
A Food Revolution

Science can have a great effect on society. Take ice cream, for example. Today, people all over the world, rich or poor, eat ice cream. **Before there were modern refrigerators**, however, ice cream was a luxury food.

The history of ice cream goes back to ancient times. In 400 BCE,[1]
5   Persians made a frozen dessert with noodles and fruit. There are early records of frozen milk and rice in China from around 200 BCE. In 618 CE, King Tang of Shang (China) ate frozen buffalo milk.

Before refrigeration existed, people needed ice to make frozen desserts. For example, in ancient Rome, people would go into the
10 mountains and collect snow. They would bring it to the city and mix the snow with fruit. This was later called "sorbet."

When an Italian duchess[2] moved to France, she brought sorbet and other frozen desserts with her. **After sorbet and ice cream became popular in France**, they spread to the rest of Europe. However, only the rich
15 ate them.

In the twentieth century, ice cream became easier to make and keep. **After scientists found better processes for freezing things**, ice cream became popular with all classes, rich and poor. Then, in the 1940s and
20 1950s, British chemists discovered a new way to make ice cream. They put air into it. This made the ice cream bigger and softer. Now, ice cream was less expensive. It lasted longer, too. **As soon as ice cream became more available**, people
25 began to buy it more often.

Today, almost anyone, rich or poor, can buy ice cream and keep it at home. Ice cream is a universal dessert, popular all over the world. Together, traditional ice cream makers and
30 scientists created a food revolution.

[1]**BCE:** before common era

[2]**duchess:** a woman of very high social rank in some European countries

Time Clauses and the Order of Past Events

Grammar Presentation

Time clauses can show the order of events in the past.	**After** scientists developed better processes for freezing things, ice cream became popular with everyone.

2.1 Time Clauses

A A time clause can come first in a sentence. When it comes first, use a comma after it.

A time clause can also come second in a sentence. No comma is needed.

┌──────TIME CLAUSE──────┐ ┌──MAIN CLAUSE──┐
After sorbet became popular in France, it spread to the rest of Europe.

┌────────MAIN CLAUSE────────┐ ┌──────TIME CLAUSE──────┐
Sorbet spread to the rest of Europe after it became popular in France.

B Use *after* to introduce the first event.

FIRST EVENT · SECOND EVENT
***After** an Italian duchess brought ice cream to France, it became popular.*

SECOND EVENT · FIRST EVENT
*Ice cream became popular **after** an Italian duchess brought it to France.*

C Use *before* to introduce the second event.

SECOND EVENT · FIRST EVENT
***Before** there were freezers, people needed ice to make frozen desserts.*

FIRST EVENT · SECOND EVENT
*People needed ice to make frozen desserts **before** there were freezers.*

D Use *when* to refer to the time that something started.

***When** scientists found new ways to make ice cream, it became cheaper.*

*Ice cream became cheaper **when** scientists found new ways to make it.*

E Use *as soon as* to refer to something that happened right after or immediately after.

FIRST EVENT · SECOND EVENT
***As soon as** scientists found ways to freeze things, people began buying more ice cream.*

(Scientists invented ways to freeze things. Soon after, people started buying ice cream more often.)

2.1 Time Clauses *(continued)*

F Use *until* to refer to things that continued up to a certain time.	*Until* people had refrigerators, it was difficult to keep food for a long time. (Up to the time when people got refrigerators, it was difficult to keep food for a long time.)

Grammar Application

Exercise 2.1 Time Clauses

Read the sentences about Ernest Hamwi, the possible inventor of the ice cream cone. Label the first event *1* and the second event *2*.

1 Until Ernest Hamwi invented the ice cream cone, most people ate ice cream in a dish.

2 Hamwi was a waffle seller at the 1904 World's Fair when he invented the ice cream cone.

3 When an ice cream seller at the fair ran out of dishes, Hamwi rolled up a waffle.

4 The warm waffle turned hard when Hamwi filled it with ice cream.

5 As soon as they saw Hamwi's cones, all the other ice cream sellers started using them.

6 Before Hamwi started an ice cream cone business, he returned from the fair.

7 After Hamwi's story became popular, many people said that *they* invented the ice cream cone.

8 Another man, Italo Marchiony, invented an edible ice cream *cup* before Hamwi invented his cone.

Exercise 2.2 Time Words

Complete the sentences. Circle the correct answer.

1 **Before** / **After** people drove cars, they rode horses.

2 **When** / **Until** the Internet became popular, people wrote letters and sent faxes.

3 **Before** / **After** the first men landed on the moon in 1969, U.S. astronauts made five more trips to the moon between 1969 and 1972.

4 **As soon as** / **Before** people used digital cameras, they took photographs using film.

5 Public transportation changed completely **until** / **when** the first airlines began to operate.

6 People did not understand the solar system **when** / **until** scientists invented telescopes.[1]

7 **Before** / **As soon as** telephones existed, communication was very slow.

8 **As soon as** / **Until** scientists developed medicines such as vaccines,[2] public health improved rapidly.

[1]**telescope:** a device you look through to make objects that are far away look bigger | [2]**vaccine:** a special substance that you take into your body to prevent disease and that has a weak or dead form of the disease-causing organism

DATA FROM THE REAL WORLD

We often answer information questions about time (e.g., *When . . . ?*, *What time . . . ?*, and *How long . . . ?*) with time clauses. In conversation, these answers do not usually contain a main clause.

A *When did you start studying English?*

B *After I got my job at the museum.*

A *How long did you study at a community college?*

B *Until I got my degree.*

A Listen to a radio interview with an inventor of a new printer. Match the interview questions with the answers.

1 When did you come to the United States? ___*d*___

2 So, when did you get the idea for your invention? ______

3 And how long did you study at college? ______

4 When did you build your first printer? ______

5 And when did you start your printer company? ______

6 So, when did you get the money for your company? ______

7 And when did the company start making a profit? ______

a As soon as my first printer reached the stores.

b After I graduated from college.

c As soon as we got the money to start.

d After I graduated from high school.

e Until I got my degree.

f When I was a student in college.

g After I presented my idea to some banks and investors.

B Listen again and check your answers.

A Write sentences in the simple past about inventions and discoveries. Use an event in Column A, an event in Column B, and *after*, *before*, *when*, *until*, or *as soon as*.

A	B
1 TV / exist	a people / start to fly more
2 cheap air travel / become possible	b credit cards / become popular
3 everyone / have a cell phone	c families / listen to the radio together
4 people / pay for things with cash or checks	d millions of people / learn to drive
5 free education / be available	e roads / become safer
6 traffic lights / come into our cities	f people / buy food from small local stores
7 Ford / make the first mass-produced car	g people / make calls from pay phones
8 the first supermarket / open	h most people / not read or write

1 *Before TV existed, families listened to the radio together.*
2 ____
3 ____
4 ____
5 ____
6 ____
7 ____
8 ____

B Pair Work Compare your sentences with a partner. How many different ways are there to say the same thing?

   A *I wrote, "Before free education was available, most people did not read or write."*
   What did you write?

   B *I wrote, "Until free education was available, most people did not read or write."*

C Over to You Think of three more sentences like the ones in B. Use your own ideas and the words *after*, *before*, *when*, *until*, or *as soon as*. Share your sentences with a partner.

Before there were microwave ovens, it took a long time to heat up food.

3 Past with *Used To* and *Would*

Grammar Presentation

Used to and would describe repeated past actions, habits, and situations.	Before we had the Internet, we **used to** go to the library a lot. Before there was refrigeration, people **would** use ice to keep food cool.

3.1 Statements with *Used To*

AFFIRMATIVE

Subject	*Used To*	Base Form of Verb	
I You He/She/It We They	**used to**	**listen**	to the radio.

NEGATIVE

Subject	*Did* + *Not*	*Use To*	Base Form of Verb	
I You He/She/It We They	**did not** **didn't**	**use to**	**watch**	TV.

DATA FROM THE REAL WORLD

Research shows that statements about the past with *didn't use to* are not very common. Instead, you can use the negative form of the simple past.

I didn't watch a lot of TV when I was younger.

3.2 Yes/No Questions and Short Answers with *Use To*

Did	Subject	Use To	Base Form of Verb	
Did	I you he/she/it we they	**use to**	**keep**	food cool with ice?

Short Answers	
Yes, I **did**. Yes, you **did**. Yes, he/she/it **did**. Yes, we **did**. Yes, they **did**.	No, I **didn't**. No, you **didn't**. No, he/she/it **didn't**. No, we **didn't**. No, they **didn't**.

DATA FROM THE REAL WORLD

Research shows that questions with *use to* are very rare. Instead, you can use questions with the simple past.

In those days, did you keep food cool with ice?

3.3 Information Questions with *Used To*

Wh- Word	Did	Subject	Use To	Base Form of Verb	
When **Why** **Where** **How often**	**did**	I you he/she/it we they	**use to**	**keep**	food cool with ice?

Wh- Word	Used To	Base Form of Verb	
Who	**used to**	**keep**	food cool with ice?

3.4 Statements with *Would*

AFFIRMATIVE

	Subject	Would	Base Form of Verb	
In the past,	I you he/she/it we they	**would**	**build**	a fire to heat water.

3.4 Statements with *Would* (continued)

NEGATIVE

	Subject	*Would + Not*	Base Form of Verb	
In the past,	I you he / she / it we they	**would not** **wouldn't**	**bathe**	often.

DATA FROM THE REAL WORLD

Research shows that statements about the past with *wouldn't* are not very common. Instead, you can use the negative form of the simple past.

In the past, they didn't bathe often.

3.5 Information Questions with *Would*

Time Context	*Wh-* Word	*Would*	Subject	Base Form of Verb	
In the past,	**how** **where**	**would**	I you he / she / it we they	**heat**	the water?

Time Context	*Wh-* Word	*Would*	Base Form of Verb	
In the past,	**who**	**would**	**heat**	the water?

DATA FROM THE REAL WORLD

Research shows that *Yes/No* questions with *would* are very rare. Instead, you can use *Yes/No* questions with the simple past.

In the past, did you always get information from the library?

3.6 Using *Used To*

A You can use *used to* for actions that happened regularly in the past. These actions do not happen now.

*My grandmother **used to wash** clothes by hand.*

B You can use *used to* for states that were true in the past. These states are not true anymore.

*Air travel **used to be** very expensive. It is less expensive now.*

C Do not use *used to* for things that happened only once.	In the 1940s, chemists discovered a new way to make ice cream. In the 1940s, chemists ~~used to discover~~ a new way to make ice cream.

3.7 Using *Would*

A You can use *would* for actions that happened regularly in the past.	When my grandparents were children, they **would listen** to the radio every night.
B Before you use *would*, first make the past time clear. Use a time expression, a simple past verb, or *used to*.	In the old days, people **would wash** clothes by hand. They **would hang** them outside to dry. It used to be a day or more before the clothes **would dry**.
C With stative verbs, use *used to*, not *would*, to talk about the past. Some examples of stative verbs are *be*, *love*, *know*, and *want*.	We **used to love** to eat ice cream. We ~~would love~~ to eat ice cream. Ice cream **used to be** a luxury. Ice cream ~~would be~~ a luxury.
D Do not use *would* to talk about things that happened only once.	Last week, Joe **made** green tea ice cream at home. Last week, Joe ~~would make~~ green tea ice cream at home.
E Use full forms in writing. Use contractions in speaking.	In writing: We **would sing** songs or **play** games in the evening. In speaking: We**'d go** to bed early.

🖱 Grammar Application

Exercise 3.1 *Used To*: Statements and Questions

A Complete the article. Use the correct form of *use to* or *used to* and the verbs in parentheses.

The Wisdom of Our Grandparents

College Weekly spoke to Joseph Green, an 87-year-old retired teacher, about the old days.

College Weekly   What _did_ people _use to do_ (do) for
(1)   (1)
fun before there was television?

Joseph Green Well, we ___________________
(2)
(listen) to the radio in the evening.

CW   How ___________ you ___________ (spend)
(3)   (3)
your free time?

JG   Well, because there was no television, we
___________________ (play) games a lot.
(4)

CW   Who ___________________ (play) with you?
(5)

JG   My brothers.

CW   It seems like people ___________________ (have) more free time in
(6)
those days . . .

JG   Not really. In fact, people ___________________ (not have) a lot of free
(7)
time. For example, my parents ___________________ (work) six days
(8)
a week.

CW   What was school like?

JG   We ___________________ (write) with pencils and paper. And when I was
(9)
in college, we ___________________ (take) notes in real notebooks, not
(10)
on notebook computers!

CW   ___________ you ___________ (type) your papers?
(11)   (11)

JG   No, I didn't. Typewriters were too expensive. I ___________________
(12)
(write) all my papers in ink on lined paper. I ___________________ (get)
(13)
so frustrated if I made a mistake because I had to start all over again!

B Write three affirmative sentences and one negative sentence about Mr. Green's life before
computers and TV. Compare your sentences with a partner.

1   *He used to play games in the evenings.* ___________________

2   ___________________

3   ___________________

4   ___________________

5   ___________________

Complete the article about life before electricity. Use *used to* or *would* and the verbs in parentheses, or use the simple past form of the verbs. Sometimes more than one answer is correct.

Voltaic battery

Alessandro Volta ___*invented*___ (invent) the first battery in 1800.
(1)

How ___*did*___ people ___*use to live*___ (live) in the days before electricity?
(2)   (2)

Most people _______________ (burn) oil lamps or candles for light.
(3)

When it got cold, they _______________ (make) open fires to keep
(4)

warm. People _______________ (not travel) long distances. Most people
(5)

only _______________ (visit) neighbors or nearby relatives.
(6)

Before Volta's battery, many scientists _______________ (not think)
(7)

that electricity was useful. And in the early days of electricity, some people

_______________ (think) it was dangerous. They _______________ (be) afraid of
(8)   (9)

it. Some people even _______________ (believe) that electricity had a bad effect on
(10)

society. They _______________ (prefer) the simple life of the past. Soon, however,
(11)

electricity _______________ (make) the world brighter, faster, and more comfortable.
(12)

Electricity in homes and industry _______________ (change) the world in many ways.
(13)

A Imagine that you can talk to a person who lived before there was electricity. Use the words to make questions with *would*. Then add two questions of your own with *would*.

1 how / heat / your house?   *Before electricity, how would you heat your house?*

2 how / light / your house? _______________

3 how / clean / your house? _______________

4 what / do / in the evenings? _______________

5 what / play / with? _______________

6 how / get / to work or school? _______________

7 _______________

8 _______________

B Over to You Now write answers with *would* to the questions. Use your imagination. When you finish, compare your answers with a partner.

We would build a fire to heat our house.

C Group Work Discuss how people used to live before the following inventions changed society. Was life better or worse? Was it safer or more dangerous? In what ways?

- computers
- cold medicine
- cars
- microwave ovens
- airplanes
- TV

A *Before computers existed, students used to write everything down with a pencil or pen.*

B *And they would copy everything again when they revised their papers.*

C *Student life was hard!*

4 Avoid Common Mistakes ⚠ 

1 **Use a subject in the time clause.**

    they

Before ‸ invented electricity, people used candles.

2 **Do not forget the *-d* in *used to* in affirmative statements.**

    used

When I was living in New York, I ~~use~~ to play in a rock band.

3 **Use use *to* (without *-d*) in negative statements and in questions with *did*.**

    use

How did you ~~used~~ to heat your home?

Editing Task

Find and correct six more mistakes in this article from a magazine.

A New Invention

        use

How did people ~~used~~ to wash dishes? People did not used to have dishwashers before invented electricity, so they would wash dishes by hand. But did men and women used to share the dishwashing equally? Not usually. Mostly it was women who did it. Before there was electricity, women use to heat up water on the stove and use it for washing dishes. It took hours and hours, and dishes often broke

5 or chipped.

    In 1886, one woman finally got tired of washing dishes by hand. "If nobody else is going to invent a dishwashing machine," she said, "I'll do it myself." Her name was Josephine Cochrane, a housewife and engineer's daughter who was tired of washing – and sometimes breaking – her favorite dishes after dinner parties. Cochrane worked and worked on her invention until 1893 when finally created a

10 machine that washed dishes. She showed the machine at the World's Fair that year. People operated it by hand, so it was still hard work. After the fair ended, she started a company to make the machines. When first tried to sell dishwashers, only restaurants and hotels bought them from her. However, after electricity became more easily available, her company built electric dishwashers for people to use in their homes. Today, homes around the world have electric dishwashers.

5 Academic Writing

Opinion Writing

Brainstorm 〉 Organize 〉 **Write** 〉 Edit

In Unit 4, you learned how to organize an academic essay and write a general or specific thesis statement. In this unit (5), you are going to complete the first draft of your opinion essay.

Should governments spend more money on space exploration?

My Writing

Exercise 5.1 Planning Your Essay

Work with a partner. Ask and answer the questions.

1 In which paragraph(s) should you give support for your opinion?
2 In which paragraph(s) should you write your conclusion?
3 In which paragraph(s) should you include your opinion about the topic?

Exercise 5.2 Writing Your First Draft

Review your My Writing work in Units 2-4. Complete the opinion essay on page 69 with your ideas and supporting details.

1 Write your thesis statement at the end of the first paragraph.
2 Write two body paragraphs. Include your two strongest arguments.
3 Complete the concluding paragraph.

1	Space exploration used to belong to two countries, the United States and the Soviet Union. They would compete to be the first country to put a satellite into space, the first country to send a human into space, and the first country to reach the moon. However, space exploration is very expensive. For example, between 1981 and 2011, the United States government spent over $192 billion on its space program. That is why in the 1990s, with programs like the International Space Station, countries began to share the costs and benefits. Yet, many people believe that the money governments spend on space exploration should be used for other programs, like health or the environment. On the other hand, supporters argue that it is an important and exciting project that we should spend money on. ____

____

____

2	____

____

____

____

____

3	____

____

____

____

4	In conclusion, I think that governments *should / should not* spend money on space exploration.

____

____

____

____

Past Progressive

Memorable Events

1 Grammar in the Real World

A What were you doing on August 21, 2017? Read the blog. What were the bloggers doing?

B Comprehension Check **Answer the questions.**

1 What were people buying at the store in August 2017?

2 Where was Emily staying when the eclipse happened?

3 What were Steve and his friends doing when the moon blocked the sun?

4 How was Bao feeling when the eclipse happened?

C Notice **Find the sentences in the blog. Circle the correct words.**

1 In 2017, I **studied / was studying** at Clemson University in Greenville, South Carolina.

2 The total eclipse was at 1:17 p.m. in St Louis, but at 10:30 a.m., we **got / were getting** ready!

3 When the eclipse happened, I **packed / was packing** books into boxes.

Do the sentences show an action that was in progress in the past or an action that happened only one time in the past?

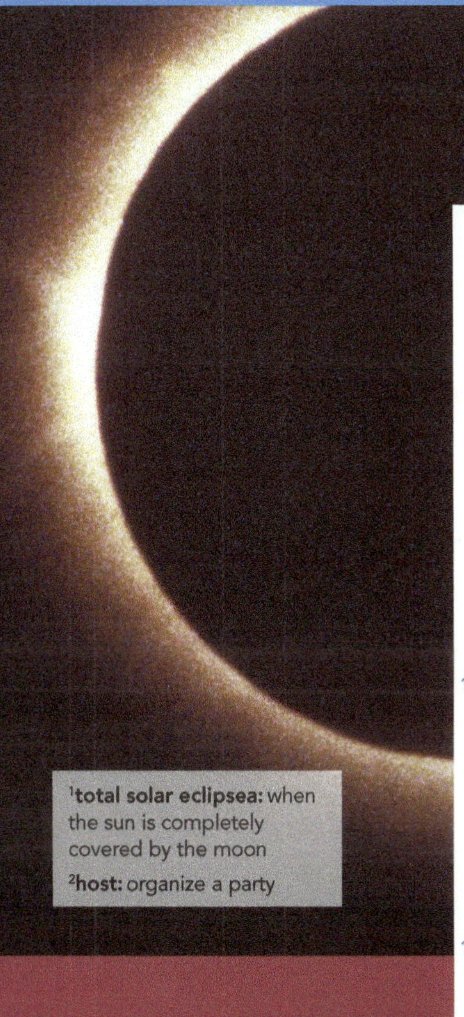

¹**total solar eclipse**ª: when the sun is completely covered by the moon

²**host**: organize a party

The Total **Solar Eclipse**¹ — What were you doing?

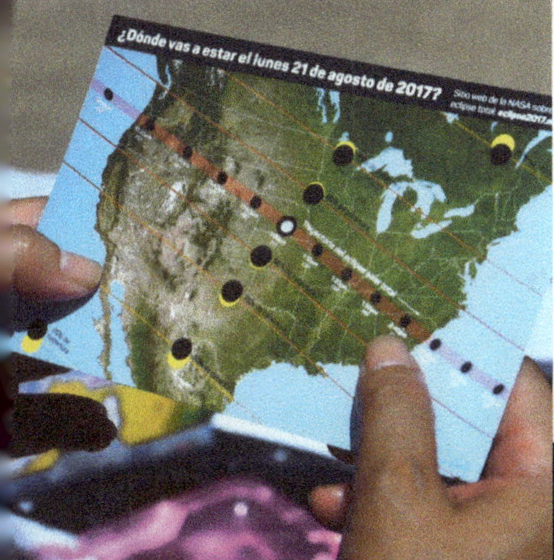

Hey! Do any of our readers remember the solar eclipse in August 2017? Wasn't it awesome? I remember everyone **was running** to the store to buy special eclipse glasses to protect their eyes. It felt like the whole of North America **was waiting** for that magical moment when the moon passed in front of the sun. Eclipse watchers from Oregon to South Carolina **were preparing** to experience the few short minutes when the moon completely blocked the sun's light. Families **were organizing** eclipse parties, people **were traveling** miles to get the best view, and school children **were doing** all kinds of eclipse projects.

Were you waiting outside that day? I was! Most people **weren't working**. They were too busy having fun! So, what **were *you doing*** and where were you **when the eclipse happened**?

3 Responses	leave a comment

Emily: I remember it! I **was staying** with my friends in Missouri **when the eclipse happened**. It was fantastic! We **were standing** in the yard and we **were wearing** our special NASA eclipse glasses. My friend Nathan **was playing** the live NASA event on a big computer screen, too. Oh, yeah, and I remember the total eclipse was at 1:17 p.m. in St Louis, but at 10:30 a.m., we **were getting** ready!

Steve: In 2017, I **was studying** at Clemson University in Greenville, South Carolina so I was lucky! Greenville was right on the path of the eclipse. I **was hosting**² an eclipse party that day. I had over 50 guests. All of us **were taking** pictures **when the moon blocked the sun**. It was amazing.

Bao: Unfortunately, I **was working** on August 21, so I **wasn't having** fun at all! I had a vacation job in a factory. When the eclipse happened, I **was packing** books into boxes. I remember my friend Jorge called me. He and my brother **were watching** the eclipse just down the block from my apartment. **While I was talking** to Jorge, I **felt** sad because I was alone.

2 Past Progressive

Grammar Presentation

The past progressive describes actions that were in progress at a time in the past.	*On August 21, we **were watching** the eclipse.*

2.1 Affirmative and Negative Statements

AFFIRMATIVE

Subject	Was / Were	Verb + -ing	
I He / She / It	**was**	**watching**	the eclipse.
You We They	**were**		

NEGATIVE

Subject	Was/Were + Not	Verb + -ing	
I He / She / It	**was not** **wasn't**	**working**	that day.
You We They	**were not** **weren't**		

2.2 Yes/No Questions and Short Answers

Was / Were	Subject	Verb + -ing	
Was	I he / she / it	**watching**	the eclipse?
Were	you we they		

Short Answers

Yes, I **was**. Yes, he/she/it **was**.	No, I **wasn't**. No, he/she/it **wasn't**.
Yes, you **were**. Yes, we **were**. Yes, they **were**.	No, you **weren't**. No, we **weren't**. No, they **weren't**.

2.3 Information Questions

Wh- Word	Was/Were	Subject	Verb + -ing
What **How**	**was**	I he / she / it	**doing?**
	were	you we they	

Wh- Word	Was/Were	Verb + -ing
Who **What**	**was**	**hosting** a party? **happening** at 1:17 p.m.?

2.4 Using Past Progressive

A Use the past progressive to talk about events in progress at a time in the past.

*They **were watching** the eclipse at lunchtime.*

B Use time expressions with *in*, *at*, *on*, and *last* to talk about events in progress at specific times in the past.

__In 2017__, I was studying in Greenville.
We were traveling a lot __in August__.
I was hosting a party __at 12:00__.
He wasn't working __on New Year's Eve__.
She wasn't working __on August 21__.
They weren't watching TV __last night__.

DATA FROM THE REAL WORLD

Research shows that these are the verbs most frequently used with the past progressive in formal and informal writing and speaking. The verbs in **bold** are very frequent.

say	**wonder**	try	come	take	make
think	**ask**	look	work	watch	drive
talk	do	get	sit	read	wear

Grammar Application

A Complete the interview about New Year's Eve activities. Use the words in parentheses with the past progressive.

New Year's Eve Roundup

The *Morning Sun* asked three people:

"What were you doing last New Year's Eve?"

Sandy L., 25, Personal Trainer

Q What were ___*were*___ (1) you ___*doing*___ (1) (do) last New Year's Eve?

A I was dancing ___*was dancing*___ (2) (dance) and I ___________ (3) (have) a great time.

Q Who ___________ (4) you ___________ (4) (celebrate) with?

A My best friends and I ___________ (5) (celebrate) New Year's Eve at a party.

Amir A., 20, Salesperson

Q What ___________ (6) you ___________ (6) (do) last New Year's Eve?

A I ___________ (7) (not have) fun! I ___________ (8) (sleep) last New Year's Eve!

Q Why ___________ (9) you ___________ (9) (sleep)?

A I was tired! At that time, I ___________ (10) (work) for several hours a day at a department store. The store ___________ (11) (have) a big sale on December 31.

Roberto R., 34, Computer Technician

Q ___________ (12) you ___________ (12) (do) anything fun last New Year's Eve?

A Not really. I ___________ (13) (drive) from New York to Chicago. My wife and I ___________ (14) (move) to Chicago. We ___________ (15) (start) new jobs there.

Q That's too bad. Who ___________ (16) (drive)?

A I ___________ (17) (be). But we ___________ (18) (not feel) bad. In fact, we ___________ (19) (feel) very good about our new life in Chicago.

B Group Work Talk in groups about what you were doing last New Year's Eve. Ask *Yes/No* and information questions to get as many details as you can.

Exercise 2.2 Time Expressions

A Over to You Complete the questions. Circle the correct words. Then answer the questions about yourself.

1 What were you doing **last**/in year?
   I was going to school and working part-time.

2 Where were you living **at**/**in** 2009?

3 What were you doing **on**/**in** the Fourth of July?

4 What were you doing **at**/**on** 9:00 a.m. yesterday?

5 Were you studying English **in**/**last** month?

6 Was your family living in the United States **on**/**in** 2000?

7 Who were you living with **at**/**in** the winter of 2010?

8 Were you working **at**/**on** 6:00 p.m. yesterday?

B Pair Work Compare the words you circled with a partner. Then discuss your answers to the questions.

Exercise 2.3 More Statements and Questions

A Listen to people talking about the most important time in their lives. When was the day or time? What were they doing? How were they feeling? Complete the chart.

Name	Day/Time	What he or she was doing	What he or she was feeling or thinking
1 Wei	*April 25, 2005*	1 2	1 2
2 Nick		1 *getting his driver's license*	1
3 Ana	*the spring of 1999*	1 2	1 *thinking about her family* 2

B Pair Work Now take turns telling your partner about the people in A.

A *On April 25, 2005, Wei was . . .*
B *On . . . , Nick was getting his driver's license. He was feeling . . .*

C Over to You What was an important day or time in your life? What were you doing? What were you thinking or feeling? Tell your partner.

An important day in my life was in July 2008, the first day of my new job. I was starting a new career, and I was feeling very . . .

Using *When* and *While* with Past Progressive

Grammar Presentation

Time clauses with *when* and *while* and the past progressive show something that was in progress; the main clause shows that something happened.

> **The eclipse happened while I was packing** books into boxes.
> **While I was sitting** at my desk, **I got** only one call.

3.1 Past Progressive or Simple Past?

A Use the past progressive for an action in progress in the past.

> On the day of the earthquake, we **were living** in San Francisco.

B Use the simple past for an action that happened one time and was completed.

> On the day of the earthquake, the power **went out.**

3.2 Using Past Progressive with Simple Past with Time Clauses

A Time clauses with *when* or *while* show when events happened.

> MAIN CLAUSE / TIME CLAUSE
> The power went out **while we were riding the elevator**.
>
> MAIN CLAUSE / TIME CLAUSE
> We were riding the elevator **when the power went out.**

B Use *when* or *while* in a past progressive time clause to show an event that was in progress when a second event happened. Use the simple past in the main clause.

> MAIN CLAUSE / TIME CLAUSE
> SECOND EVENT / EVENT IN PROGRESS
> The power **went** out **when/while** we **were riding** the elevator.
>
> TIME CLAUSE / MAIN CLAUSE
> EVENT IN PROGRESS / SECOND EVENT
> **When/While** we **were riding** the elevator, the power **went** out.

C Use *when*, but not *while*, in a simple past time clause to show an event that happened while an event was already in progress. Use the past progressive in the main clause.

> MAIN CLAUSE / TIME CLAUSE
> EVENT IN PROGRESS / SECOND EVENT
> We **were riding** the elevator **when** the power **went** out.
>
> TIME CLAUSE / MAIN CLAUSE
> SECOND EVENT / EVENT IN PROGRESS
> **When** the power **went** out, we **were riding** the elevator.

D Time clauses usually come second. When they come first, remember to use a comma.
Do not use a period after a time clause. It is not a complete sentence.

> We were riding the elevator **when the power went out.**
> **When the power went out**, we were riding the elevator.
> ~~When the power went out.~~ We were riding the elevator.

3.2 Using Past Progressive with Simple Past with Time Clauses *(continued)*

E You can also use time clauses in questions. Notice that the word order does not change.

SUBJECT   VERB
*Were you having fun **when the eclipse happened**?*
*What was he doing **when the earthquake hit**?*
*Where were you sitting **when the power went out**?*

Grammar Application

Exercise 3.1 Past Progressive or Simple Past?

Complete the paragraph about a memorable event. Circle the correct verb.

My most memorable experience _**(was)** / was being_ the solar eclipse of 2009. In the
(1)
summer of 2009, I _traveled / was traveling_ around
(2)
Turkey. One day when I _read / was reading_ the
(3)
newspaper, I _saw / was seeing_ an article about the
(4)
eclipse. I _decided / was deciding_ to go to the town
(5)
of Amasya because the article _said / was saying_ it
(6)
was the best place to see it. I _arrived / was arriving_ in town on the day of the
(7)
eclipse. I _walked / was walking_ down the street when I _saw / was seeing_
(8)   (9)
a group of people in the town square. They _waited / were waiting_ for the
(10)
eclipse to start. I _decided / was deciding_ to join them. Then the eclipse
(11)
started / was starting at around 2:00 in the afternoon. The shadow of the
(12)
moon moved across the sun, and the sky started to get dark. By 3:00, the sun was
completely covered. Everyone was quiet and amazed. Unfortunately, while the eclipse
happened / was happening , my cell phone rang! I was so embarrassed!
(13)

Exercise 3.2 Time Clauses

Correct the punctuation mistakes in these sentences.

1 When the power went out, I was cooking a big dinner.
2 When the eclipse happened Bao was working in a factory.
3 When the power went out we were riding home on the subway.
4 While we were standing in a doorway the ground started to shake.
5 When the earthquake hit she was driving across the bridge.
6 Asha was standing in the town square. When the sky got dark.
7 Rob was shopping. When the lights went out.
8 While we were working. The hurricane hit.

A Complete the reader stories. Use the past progressive or simple past form of the verbs in parentheses.

Reader Stories: A Day I Will Never Forget

I will never forget the 1989 San Francisco earthquake.
My wife and I _____were eating_____ (eat) at a restaurant
(1)
when the earthquake _________________ (hit).
(2)
We _________________ (wait) for our food when the waiter
(3)
_________________ (shout), "It's a big one!
(4)
Get under the table!" We _________________ (stay) under
(5)
the table and _________________ (eat) our dinner while the ground _________________ (shake).
(6) (7)

– Samir N., Oakland, California

I will never forget Hurricane Newton. It wasn't dangerous,
but it was very exciting. I _________________ (walk)
(8)
on the beach when a lifeguard _________________
(9)
(tell) me to go home. When I _________________
(10)
(get) home, my mother _________________ (wait)
(11)
for me. She _________________ (make) dinner when
(12)
the electricity _________________ (go) out.
(13)
We _________________ (stay) inside and _________________ (play) games by candlelight while
(14) (15)
the storm _________________ (crash) all around us.
(16)

– Luisa F., Acapulco, Mexico

B Use the words to write questions about the stories in A. Use the past progressive.

For Samir N.

1   What / do / ?   _What was Samir doing when the earthquake hit?_

2   Where / eat / ?   ____

3   What / eat / ?   ____

For Luisa F.

4   What / do / ?   ____

5   Where / walk / ?   ____

6   What / mother / do / ? ____

C Group Work Talk about a memorable event in your life. What happened? What were you doing? Ask and answer questions about the event. Use information questions.

A *My most memorable experience was the snowstorm of 2010.*
B *What were you doing when it started snowing?*
A *When it started snowing, I was . . .*
C *Then what did you do?*

4 Avoid Common Mistakes ⚠

1 **Use the correct form of *be* in the past progressive.**
   were
They ~~was~~ watching fireworks on New Year's Eve.

2 **Use the correct word order in information questions in the past progressive.**
   were the people
Where ~~the people~~ were standing?

3 **Use the past progressive for an event in progress.**
   went   *were riding*
The power ~~was going~~ out while they ~~rode~~ the elevator.

4 **A time clause by itself is not a complete sentence.**
We stayed in the car while the ground was shaking.
We stayed in the car. ~~While the ground was shaking.~~

5 **If the time clause comes first in a sentence, use a comma.**
While they were looking at the map, they found their hotel.

Editing Task

Find and correct nine more mistakes in this excerpt of an interview with some people who remember the moon landing in 1969.

Interviewer *were you*
Where ~~you were~~ when *Apollo 11* landed on the moon?

Maria Well, in the summer of 1969 I was nine. I was living in Mexico. On July 20, I was playing on
5 the beach with some friends. My parents was listening to the radio. When the speaker was announcing the landing.

Interviewer What you were doing when the astronauts landed on the moon?

Tom At that time, my wife and I moved from
10 Chicago to San Diego. To save money, we stayed in campgrounds every night. We listened to the car radio at our campsite when the astronauts stepped on the moon. That night, while we was lying on the ground we looked up at the moon. We were being amazed!

Memorable Events **79**

Opinion Writing

Brainstorm 〉 Organize 〉 Write 〉 **Edit**

In Unit 5, you completed an opinion essay for the prompt below. In this unit (6), you are going to revise and edit your essay.

Should governments spend more money on space exploration?

My Writing

Exercise 5.1 Revising Your Ideas

1 Work with a partner. Use the questions below to give feedback on your partner's essay.
- Which of your partner's ideas seem strongest to you?
- Which of your partner's ideas need to be explained more clearly?
- What could your partner add or remove to make the essay stronger and easier to understand?
- Do you agree or disagree with your partner's opinion?

2 Use the feedback from your partner to revise your essay.

Exercise 5.2 Editing Your Writing

Use the checklist to review and edit your essay.

Did you answer the prompt completely?	
Did you use academic essay organization?	
Did you write a specific thesis statement that tells what the essay is about and gives your point of view?	
Did you write topic sentences that connect to your thesis statement in your body paragraphs?	
Did you include arguments for or against government spending money on space explorations?	
Did you use evidence and examples to support your opinions?	
Did you summarize your main points and include your opinion in the concluding paragraph?	

Exercise 5.3 Editing Your Grammar

Use the checklist to review and edit the grammar in your essay.

Did you use the simple present correctly?	
Did you use present progressive correctly?	
Did you use the simple past correctly?	
Did you use the past progressive correctly?	
Did you use stative verbs and "opinion" words or phrases instead of the imperative to introduce your points of view?	
Did you use time clauses correctly?	
Did you use *used to* and *would* correctly?	
Did you avoid the common mistakes in the charts on pages 25, 53, 67, and 79?	

Exercise 5.4 Writing Your Final Draft

Apply the feedback and edits from Exercises 5.1 to 5.3 to write the final draft of your essay.

1 Grammar in the Real World

A What information about yourself do you want to keep private? Read the article from a website. What are some ways you can protect your personal information?

B Comprehension Check Match the kind of ID theft with the way to avoid it.

ID thieves . . .

1 take information from your garbage. _____

2 steal your credit card number online. _____

3 "phish" for information. _____

But you can . . .

a only pay on secure websites.

b not respond to an unsolicited e-mail.

c shred your bills before you throw them away.

C Notice Find the sentences in the article and complete them with *a* or *an*. If no word goes in the blank, write **X**.

1 Identity theft is the act of using someone's personal information without

_____X_____ permission.

2 ID thieves go through your garbage and look for __________ papers.

3 They "phish" for __________ information.

4 Phishing is sending __________ e-mail that asks you for your personal information.

5 The e-mail looks like it is from __________ bank.

Which of the nouns are things you can count? Which are things you cannot count? Which noun is plural?

IDENTITY THEFT

Keep your identity private! Here are some facts about identity (ID) theft.

What Is Identity Theft?

Identity theft is the act of using someone's personal **information** without **permission**. ID thieves use the **information** to buy things. They also use it to get
5   credit cards or to open other types of accounts. Personal **information** includes your name and address. It also includes your Social Security number or credit card numbers. You can lose **money** because of ID theft. ID theft also causes **damage** to your reputation. Sometimes, people cannot get **work** or loans for school because of ID theft.

10   ### How Do Thieves Steal Your Identity?

■ ID thieves go through your garbage and look for papers with **information** about you, such as bills.

■ They steal your credit card number when you are buying something. This can happen with online shopping or in stores.

15   ■ They "phish" for **information**. Phishing is sending an e-mail that asks for your personal **information**. The e-mail looks like it is from a bank or credit card company. It often asks you to go to a website and give your personal **information**.

How Can You Avoid ID Theft?

20   ■ Shred[1] bills and other documents that have personal **information** before you throw them away.

■ If you shop online, only shop at well-known shopping sites. Only pay on secure[2] Web pages. URLs on secure pages begin with "https." (The s means "secure.")

■ Never answer an unsolicited[3] e-mail. This is especially true if
25   the e-mail looks like it is from a bank or a credit card company.

Follow this advice, and you can protect yourself from ID theft.

[1] **shred:** cut into very small pieces
[2] **secure:** safe
[3] **unsolicited:** not asked for

Count Nouns and Noncount Nouns

Grammar Presentation

Nouns are the names of people, places, and things. You can count most nouns (*an e-mail, three e-mails*); you cannot count certain nouns (*information, money*).

*A **website** gave us **information** about ID theft.*

2.1 Count Nouns

Count nouns refer to things you can count with numbers. They have a plural form.

*I do not have a credit card **account**.*
*An ID thief opened two **accounts** in my name.*
*The **bank** on First Street is closed.*
*There are three **banks** on Oak Street.*

2.2 Noncount Nouns

Noncount nouns refer to things you *cannot* count with numbers. They have only one form.

*ID theft causes **damage** to your reputation.*
*The computer records how much **money** you spend.*
*I need some **advice**.*

2.3 Using Count Nouns

A Singular count nouns always have a determiner before them. Determiners are words like *a, an, the, that, this, my,* or *our.*

*I have **a brother**.*
I have ~~brother~~.
***This computer** is fast.*
~~Computer~~ is fast.

B You can use plural count nouns with or without a determiner. However, do not use *a* or *an* with plural nouns.

***Computers** are not very expensive nowadays.*
***These computers** are not very expensive.*
*Credit **cards** are convenient.*
*I can't find **my** credit **cards**.*
I can't find ~~a credit cards~~.

2.4 Using Noncount Nouns

A	Do not use plural forms like *-s* with noncount nouns.	They gave us **information** about ID theft. They gave us ~~informations~~ about ID theft.
B	Do not use numbers with noncount nouns.	She gave me **advice** about using my credit card. She gave me ~~two advices.~~
C	Do not use *a / an* with noncount nouns.	Because of ID theft, he can't get **work**. Because of ID theft, he can't get ~~a work~~.
D	You can use other determiners (*my*, *some*, *this*, etc.) with noncount nouns.	They found **some information** on the Internet. **Her advice** was useful.
E	Use a singular verb form with noncount nouns.	**Safety is** important to everyone. There **was information** about ID theft online.
F	Some noncount nouns also have a countable meaning.	**Coffee** is delicious. (coffee as a drink) We ordered two **coffees**. (two cups or orders of coffee) They hired someone with **experience**. (knowledge about a job) He has had a lot of interesting **experiences**. (things that he did or that happened to him) She needed some **paper** to print on. (material for writing or printing on) She threw away some important **papers**. (individual documents)

Noncount Noun	Count Noun
coffee	coffees
experience	experiences
paper	papers

DATA FROM THE REAL WORLD

Some common noncount nouns in speaking and writing are:

advice	equipment	information	music	research	stuff
bread	evidence	knowledge	news	rice	traffic
cash	fun	luck	permission	safety	water
coffee	furniture	milk	progress	security	weather
damage	health	money	publicity	software	work

Exercise 2.1 Count or Noncount?

A Complete the chart. Check (✓) *Count* or *Noncount*. Then write the plural form of the count nouns.

Noun	Count	Noncount	Plural Form
1 passport	✓		*passports*
2 document			
3 information			
4 research			
5 equipment			
6 computer			
7 software			
8 credit card			
9 identity			
10 safety			
11 privacy			
12 e-mail			

B Complete the article. Where needed, write *-s*, *-es*, or *-ies* to make nouns plural. Write **X** if a plural form is not needed.

ID thieves use other people's identity _*ies*_ without their (1) permission_ **X** _ . Some ID thieves look in the garbage for (2) information_____ about you. Others use software_____ and (3) (4) high-tech equipment_____ to steal your identity. (This is why Internet (5) security_____ is so important on home computer_____ today.) In (6) (7) addition, some ID thieves just steal your bag. These thieves do not just take your money_____ . They also steal document_____ like your driver's license and one or (8) (9) more of your credit card_____ . ID thieves love these! (10)

If you want to protect your privacy_____ and avoid identity theft, do not carry these (11) things in your wallet, pocket, or purse:

- Your Social Security card or number.
- Your passport. If someone steals this, they could use it to commit a serious crime. These criminals threaten everyone's safety_____ . (12)
- Your computer, e-mail, and other password_____ . A lot of people keep this (13) information in their wallets, but it is a bad idea!
- Your birth certificate. With a little research_____ about you, a thief can use your birth (14) certificate to get a driver's license, credit cards, and even bank loans.

C Pair Work Think about an ID card you have (for example, your student ID card or your driver's license), and discuss it with your partner. When do you use this card? What kind of information does it have about you? How easy is it to steal or copy the information on it?

Exercise 2.2 Count and Noncount Meanings

Complete the sentences. Use the correct form of the nouns in the box. Then write *C* if the noun is a count noun or *NC* if it is a noncount noun.

crime	experience	life	paper

1 Marc had a bad _____ *experience* _____ with ID theft. It damaged his reputation.   _C_

2 Now he can't get a job, even though he has a lot of _______________ in his field.   _____

3 How did it happen? There were _______________ in Marc's garbage that had a lot of personal details about him.   _____

4 In addition, he put his passwords down on _______________ instead of memorizing them.   _____

5 Marc is not alone – there is a lot of Internet _______________ nowadays.   _____

6 Some _______________ affect us financially, but ID theft can hurt us emotionally, too.   _____

7 _______________ is difficult for Marc right now.   _____

8 We all have difficult times in our _______________ , but we can learn from our mistakes.   _____

Exercise 2.3 More Count Nouns

A Write these count nouns in the correct categories.

backpacks	CDs	jeans	soccer balls	sweaters
basketballs	computer games	movies	sofas	tables
briefcases	desks	shirts	suitcases	tennis rackets

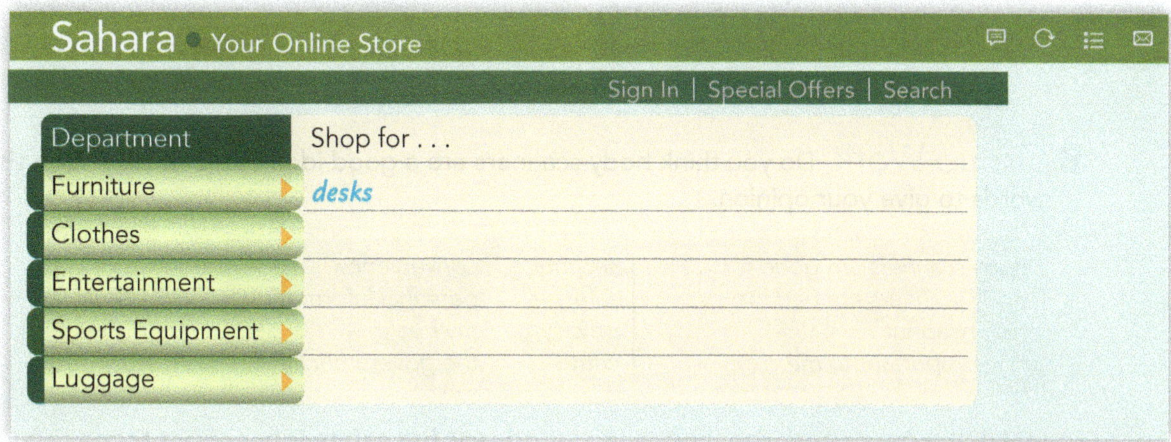

B Pair Work Now ask and answer questions with a partner about where things are in the store.

A *Where do you shop for sofas?*
B *You shop for sofas in the furniture department.*

A Complete the conversation about full-body scanners (machines that show what is on a person's body) with the correct form of the words in the box.

airport	fun	person	publicity	traveler
evidence	~~news~~	progress	traffic	

A There was a report on the _______*news*_______ last night about
 (1)
 those full-body scanners at _________________ . People were
 (2)
 complaining about them. Do you know anything about them?

B Not much, but there's a lot of _________________ about them
 (3)
 these days in the media. I know some people are worried about
 the health issues. I mean, is the technology safe?

A Well, so far, there's no _________________ that body scanners
 (4)
 are dangerous. There's no real proof. In fact, I was reading
 somewhere that they're pretty safe.

B Hmm. Maybe they're better than what we had before. I guess
 we're making _________________ in keeping airports safe, but
 (5)
 what about the privacy issues?

A Right! Scanners can give some pretty personal information about _________________ .
 (6)
 They're like an X-ray. They can show exactly what's on your body.

B And there are millions of _________________ these days! With all the _________________
 (7)   (8)
 at airports nowadays, security is taking a lot longer.

A Yeah. I used to like going to the airport, but I guess you aren't supposed to have
 _________________ at the airport nowadays!
 (9)

B Group Work Do you think body scanners are a good idea or a bad idea? Use these words to give your opinion.

Body scanners are good for . . .	security	convenience
Body scanners are bad for . . .	safety	personal information
I worry about . . .	privacy	my health
. . . is important to me.	crime	the government

I think they're a good idea. I worry about privacy, but safety is important to me.

3 Noncount Nouns: Determiners and Measurement Words

Grammar Presentation

<table>
<tr><td>You can use certain determiners and measurement words with noncount nouns.</td><td>Can you give me **some advice** about spyware programs?
She told me two interesting **pieces of news**.</td></tr>
</table>

3.1 Noncount Nouns with Determiners

<table>
<tr><td>**A** Use *a lot of, some,* and *a little* with noncount nouns in affirmative statements.</td><td>There was **a lot of milk** in the refrigerator.
I have **some** important **information** for you.
Could I have **a little cream** in my coffee, please?</td></tr>
<tr><td>**B** Use *much, a lot of,* and *any* with noncount nouns in questions.</td><td>Was there **much furniture** in the apartment?
Is there **a lot of traffic** at 5:00 p.m.?
Are you making **any progress** with your English these days?</td></tr>
<tr><td>**C** Use *some* and *a little* for questions that are offers and requests.</td><td>Would you like **some tea**?
Would you like **a little sugar** in your coffee?</td></tr>
<tr><td>**D** Use *not much, not a lot,* and *not any* with noncount nouns in negative statements.</td><td>There's **not much juice** left in your glass.
She does**n't** earn **a lot of money** in her present job.
We did**n't** do **any work** yesterday.</td></tr>
<tr><td>**E** Do not use *much* or *a little* with count nouns.</td><td>We don't have **much time** left.
We don't have ~~much hours~~ left.
There's **a little coffee** in the cup.
There's ~~a little cups~~ on the table.</td></tr>
</table>

F Do not use *many* or *a few* with noncount nouns.	There is **not much news** today. There is ~~not many news~~ today. I sold **some furniture** that I didn't need. I sold ~~a few furniture~~.
G You can use *a lot of*, *some*, and *any* with both count and noncount nouns.	There is **a lot of** Internet **crime** nowadays. They caught **a lot of** ID **thieves** last year. There's **some** new **furniture** at the apartment. We bought **some** new **chairs**. We don't have **any** new **equipment**. There aren't **any** new **computers** at the school.

A Use *too many* with count nouns and *too much* with noncount nouns to say "more than you want."	**Too many people** came to the lecture on Internet privacy. *Some of them had to stand.* There is **too much information** about us on databases. *It's scary!*
B Use *enough* with count and noncount nouns to say "the amount you need."	We have **enough eggs** in the refrigerator. We have **enough information** on the problem. We don't have **enough potatoes**. We don't have **enough milk**. *We need to buy some.*

A Containers

a **box** of	cereal pasta	a **bottle** of	water juice
a **package** of	sugar rice coffee	a **glass** of	milk juice water
a **can** of	soup tuna	a **carton** of	milk juice

Portions

a **piece** of	cake bread pie candy	
a **slice** of	pizza bread cake cheese turkey	
a **scoop** of	ice cream sorbet	

3.3 Noncount Nouns with Measurement Words *(continued)*

Measurements			Shapes		
a **gallon** of	milk gas	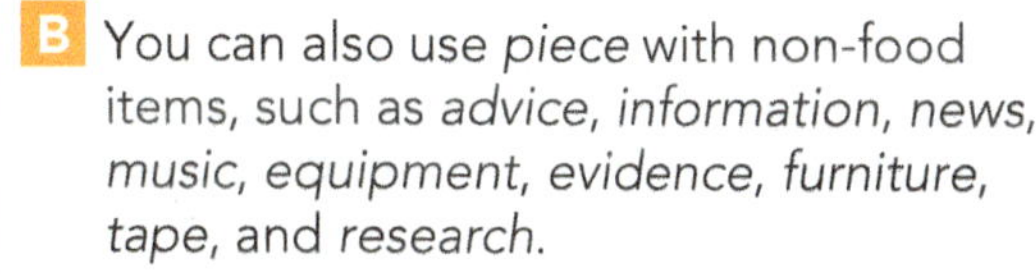	a **bar** of	soap chocolate	
a **pound** of	butter sugar coffee meat		a **loaf** of	bread	
a **cup** of	sugar milk coffee tea		a **sheet** of	paper	
			a **tube** of	toothpaste	

B	You can also use *piece* with non-food items, such as *advice, information, news, music, equipment, evidence, furniture, tape,* and *research.*	He told us **an** interesting **piece of news**. They gave us **a** helpful **piece of advice**.
C	Measurement words can be singular or plural.	I bought **a pound of butter** and **three loaves of bread**.

Grammar Application

Exercise 3.1 Determiners and *Too* and *Enough*

A Complete the web article. Circle the correct words.

What Are Cookies? by Sue Wilder

(**Many**) / **Much** computer security experts are concerned about the use of cookies on the Internet. A "cookie" is a piece of information stored in your computer. It contains information on all the Internet sites that you look at. **A lot of / Much** websites send a cookie to your computer when you visit them. Companies with websites can get **many / a lot of** information about consumers with cookies. For example, an online store sends a cookie that gives the store **much / some** details about who you are. The next time you visit the store, it remembers your details.

There is **a lot of / many** concern about cookies because they are a privacy issue. However, **some / much** experts do not think that there are **some / any** problems to worry about. These experts say cookies do not have **any / much** harmful effects on your computer; that is, they do not contain **a few / any** viruses.

You can change a setting on your computer to block cookies. However, one study showed that **not many / a few** computer users do this.

B Complete the comments on the article in A with *too much*, *too many*, or *enough*.

Comments (3)

Tom S., Canada: The writer spent ______*too much*______ time on cookies. She didn't spend
____________ (2) ____________ time on social networking sites. ____________ (3) ____________ computer users think those
sites are private, but they're not.

Amy G., New York: I agree with Tom. Not ____________ (4) ____________ computer users understand how social
networking sites work. Some of those sites give out ____________ (5) ____________ information. There isn't
____________ (6) ____________ privacy!

Maria R., Houston: It's not the site's fault if you put up ____________ (7) ____________ silly pictures of yourself!
And you can set your profile to "private." It only takes a minute, so everyone has ____________ (8) ____________ time
to do that.

A Match the measurement words and the nouns.

1 a piece of ___*b*___   **a** rice   5 a cup of _________   **e** chocolate

2 a package of _________   **b** cake   6 a bar of _________   **f** paper

3 a glass of _________   **c** pizza   7 a scoop of _________   **g** coffee

4 a slice of _________   **d** milk   8 a sheet of _________   **h** ice cream

B Complete the article about privacy issues and shopping. Use the
correct form of the words in the box. Then listen and check your answers.

bar	box	carton	~~loaf~~	pound
bottle	can	gallon	package	tube

A lot of supermarket shoppers have store club cards these days. Club cards give you lower
prices or points for shopping. To get the lower prices, you swipe your card every time you
make a purchase. The card tells the store who you are and what you buy. Here is an example.
Shopper 1 buys three ______*loaves*______ of bread, two ____________ (2) ____________ of juice, a
____________ (3) ____________ of milk, a ____________ (4) ____________ of toothpaste, a ____________ (5) ____________

of rice, a _______________ of soap, and two _______________ of cereal each week.
(6)   (7)
What does that tell the store? It probably tells the store that he has a big family, and he probably
has children. Shopper 2 buys seven _______________ of water, seven _______________ of
(8)   (9)
tuna, and a _______________ of turkey each week. What does this tell the store? Shopper 2 is
(10)
probably single, and she is probably dieting or is concerned with her health. How does the store
use this information? It sends advertising to the shoppers with specific information about the
products that they buy. This gets them back into the store to buy more products.

C Group Work   **What did you buy this week? Write three sentences on a piece
of paper. Do not write your name! Read the papers in groups and try to guess who
wrote them.**

This person bought three loaves of bread, so it might be Nicki.

4 Avoid Common Mistakes ⚠

1   **A singular count noun needs a determiner.**
a
I do not have ᵥcard for this store.

2   **Do not use *a/ an* with a noncount noun.**
You need ~~a~~ permission to use my credit card.

3   **Do not use a noncount noun in the plural.**
information
The supermarket has personal ~~informations~~ about shoppers.

4   **Do not use *many* or *too many* with a noncount noun.**
a lot of
There was ~~many~~ Internet crime last year.

5   **Do not use *much* with a noncount noun in affirmative statements.**
a lot of
She had ~~much~~ cash in her wallet when somebody stole it.

Editing Task

Find eight more mistakes in this article about Internet spyware.

a
Spyware is ᵥtype of computer software. Someone sends it to computer
without your knowledges or permissions. It takes control of your computer. It
can make your computer run slowly or even crash. Spyware often records an
information about your computer use. It gives the information to advertisers or
5   other people who want to collect informations on you. Many spyware sneaks
into your computer when you are downloading and installing programs from
the Internet. One way to prevent a spyware is to put security settings on your
Internet browser. Set your browser to a medium or higher setting. There is also
much software you can buy that blocks spyware.

5 Academic Writing

Expository Writing

Brainstorm > Organize > Write > Edit

In this writing cycle (Units 7-9), you are going to write a report that answers the prompt below. In this unit (7), you will analyze an article and brainstorm ideas about the topic.

Choose a new area of technology or invention to analyze. Write a report about its advantages and disadvantages, and include a prediction in the conclusion.

Exercise 5.1 Preparing to Write

Work with a partner. Discuss the questions.

1 What kind of technology is important to you in your life now? Why?
2 Are there disadvantages to this kind of technology? What are they?
3 In the future, what kind of problems could technology solve?

Exercise 5.2 Focusing on Vocabulary

Read the definitions. Complete the sentences with the correct form of the words in the box.

> **artificial** (adj) not natural, made by people
> **benefit** (n) advantage; positive result; (v) to help or give an advantage to
> **convenience** (n) something that makes life or a process easier
> **congestion** (n) a situation when something is blocked or stopped
> **organ** (n) part of a human or animal that has a special purpose
> **power** (n) energy, usually electricity or gas, used to provide heat, light, etc.
> **process** (n) a series of actions to reach a result
> **progress** (n) movement toward an improved situation

1 Designing new technology is often a long ____________. It can take years until it works well.

2 New technology sometimes creates problems, but there are usually ____________ to people, too.

3 Most modern cities have serious traffic ____________ because there are too many cars on the road.

4 Many cities are making environmental ____________ with better public transportation, like cleaner buses and safer subways.

5 An electronic bus pass is a ____________ for riders because it is so easy and fast.

6 Electric cars make the air cleaner because they get ____________ from electricity, not gasoline.

7 In medicine, _______________ legs and arms are now so advanced that people use them to run marathons and to climb mountains.

8 With special equipment, doctors can now see a patient's _______________, like the heart, to look for signs of disease.

The **World** Of **Tomorrow**

Every generation develops new technology that has both positive and negative effects. In the past 30 years, for example, the Internet has become part of daily life. However, along with more information, faster communication, and greater **convenience**,
5 there are issues with privacy, identity theft, and online harassment. Now, what comes next? What will the world of tomorrow look like? Will it be easier or more difficult? Many people are confident that technology is going to help solve some of today's most challenging problems. Other people worry that new technology may solve
10 old problems but create new ones, like the Internet has. While it is difficult to predict the world of tomorrow, **progress** today in the areas of transportation, production, and safety will probably change the future.

When we dream about the future of transportation, many of us
15 believe that we will be able to exit our garages and take to the skies in our own personal flying cars. In fact, companies like Terrafugia and AeroMobil are already developing them. The advantages of flying cars are obvious. They would allow full freedom of movement. We could fly at 300 miles per hour, avoiding traffic
20 lights, busy roads, and speeding tickets. However, some people point to the disadvantages of flying cars. They claim that there are certain to be problems with controlling traffic. If the cars become popular, there is likely to be more **congestion** in the air. Another big problem is mechanical failure. What will happen if the cars break
25 down? These are problems we must solve when flying cars become a reality.

The way we make, buy, and sell things is also going to change. For example, most people print out electronic documents on sheets of paper at work or school, and many people are probably aware
30 of 3D printing, a **process** by which three-dimensional objects are created. 3D printers build an object using layers of liquid plastic, metal, or other materials. They build up the layers line by line like a normal printer until the object is complete. Car companies like BMW and Volkswagen already use 3D printers to make life-size models
35 of car parts, and medical technology companies have already used 3D printing to make body parts, such as **artificial** ears. Some

people print their own small objects at home, such as jewelry and toys, with 3D printers. However, 3D printing has the
40 ability to change the future. It can create something as large as a house in a few days at a low cost. In addition, scientists are conducting experiments to "print" biological tissue. Before long, it might
45 be possible to use 3D printing to create affordable housing, print **organs** for transplants, or even make food.

Finally, the future of personal health and safety is bright. Imagine wearing a real Ironman suit. Several companies are trying to build a practical robot "exoskeleton." This is a suit of robot arms
50 and legs that follows the wearer's movements. It allows the wearer to lift heavy objects, walk long distances, and even punch through walls! There are obvious military advantages for this technology, but there are also **benefits** for people with disabilities. The suit could help people walk again after disease or injury. However, the obvious
55 disadvantage at the moment is the cost. Even a simple exoskeleton can cost hundreds of thousands of dollars. Another problem is battery life. This type of suit needs a lot of **power**; at the moment, the batteries last only about 15 minutes. One other problem is that a badly programmed robot suit could injure the wearer if the robot suit
60 bent the leg or arm the wrong way, for instance.

The future is clearly exciting. One day we might be able to fly to work, print out a new pair of shoes, or lift a car above our heads, but there are still a lot of problems to solve before any of these products become part of normal life. However, companies are making
65 progress in all three areas.

Read the text on page 95. Work with a partner. Ask and answer the questions.

1 Will flying cars solve traffic problems? Why or why not?
2 How can 3D printers be used by medical doctors?
3 To which two groups of people could the robot exoskeleton be useful?
4 Does the author believe that technology is always a benefit to people?

Exercise 5.4 Noticing the Grammar and Structure

Complete the tasks. Compare your answers with a partner.

1 Underline the thesis statement. Circle all the non-count nouns in it.
2 Match each invention in the body paragraphs to a non-count noun in the thesis statement.

  a robot suit   b flying car   c 3D printer

3 Circle one advantage and put a box around one disadvantage of each invention.
4 How does the writer organize the information in paragraphs 2-4?
5 Find and highlight two uses of the determiner *a lot of* in paragraphs 4-5. What kind of noun follows it?

Using A T-Chart

A T-chart is a kind of graphic organizer. It is useful for examining two sides or aspects of a topic, such as advantages and disadvantages or pros and cons.

Exercise 5.5 Applying the Skill

Choose one invention in the text, and complete the T-chart. Add at least one advantage and one disadvantage to the T-chart.

Invention: ____

Advantages	Disadvantages

My Writing

Exercise 5.6 Brainstorming Ideas

Work with a partner. Write down one modern invention in each area of technology in the chart. Do research online if necessary.

medicine	
home	
space	
transportation	
entertainment	
computers	

Exercise 5.7 Identifying Advantages and Disadvantages

Choose one of the inventions from Exercise 5.6 to write about in your report. Write at least three advantages and three disadvantages of the invention in the T-chart below.

Invention: ______________________________

Advantages	Disadvantages

Exercise 5.8 Writing a Paragraph

Write a paragraph about the invention you chose. Include:
- a topic sentence with a description of the invention
- its advantages and disadvantages
- a concluding sentence with a prediction

Exercise 5.9 Editing Your Writing

Use the checklist to edit your paragraph.

Did you use a noncount noun to refer to a general idea and then give details about that idea?	
Did you use the correct determiner with count and noncount nouns?	
Did you avoid the common mistakes in the chart on page 93?	

8 Articles

The Media

1 Grammar in the Real World

ACADEMIC WRITING

Expository writing

A Where do you get the news? Read the web article about how people get their news from a website. What are some ways that people get news online?

B Comprehension Check **Answer the questions.**

1 How does Christina Jackson get the news?
2 What is changing about the way people get the news?
3 The article says news is becoming an online social activity. What are some examples of this?
4 What are some very popular news subjects on the Internet right now?

C Notice **Read the sentences from the article and answer the questions.**

1 "They go to **a** news site and list the type of stories they want to read. They tell **the** news site if they want pictures or video."

   In the first sentence, do we know which site this is? Is the site in the second sentence the same one?
2 "Many people do not read **a** daily newspaper anymore."

   Do we know which newspaper the writer is talking about?
3 "They still have more access to the news they want, thanks to **the** Internet."

Do we know what the article refers to by "Internet"? Is this part of our general knowledge?

GETTING The NEWS

How do you get **the** news? Do you get it from TV, **the** Internet, **the** radio, or **the** newspaper? For many people, this is changing.

Take Christina Jackson, **an** office manager in Dallas, for example. Each morning, she checks her phone for news headlines. Then she
5   checks **a** social networking site and her e-mail to see what news stories her friends are discussing. In other words, friends are becoming **the** new news editors.

A recent study analyzed how people get their news. It found that news is becoming **an** online social activity. Seventy-one percent of
10   adults get their news online, and many of them leave comments for other people to read. They write their reactions to news stories on social networking sites, and they e-mail their friends links to interesting stories on news sites.

The study also showed that people like to customize their news.
15   For example, they go to **a** news site and list **the** type of stories they want to read. They tell **the** news site if they want pictures or video, and they also get news stories sent to them by e-mail. A lot of people go to **a** wide range of sites to get their news. Fifty-seven percent visit between two and five different news sites each day. Some popular news subjects
20   online are **the** weather, health, business, and international events.

Even though many people do not read **a** daily newspaper anymore, they still have more access to **the** news they want, thanks to **the** Internet.

2 Articles

Grammar Presentation

<table>
<tr>
<td>

Articles are used with nouns.
The indefinite article is *a* or *an*.
The definite article is *the*.

</td>
<td>

A recent study analyzed how people get *the* news.
The study found that news is becoming *an* online social activity.

</td>
</tr>
</table>

2.1 Using *A* and *An*

A Use *a / an* with singular count nouns. It means "one."	*A study* analyzed news trends.
Use *a* with consonant sounds. Use *an* with vowel sounds.	*I went to a website.* *I wrote an e-mail.*
B *A / An* can go before a noun or an adjective and a noun.	*It's a study.* *It's a new study.* *It's an interesting study.*
C Do not use *a / an* with plural nouns or noncount nouns.	*I watch (some) TV news shows every day.* *I watch a̶ TV news shows every day.*
You can use no article or *some* with plural or noncount nouns instead.	*Wei gets (some) information from the Web.* *Wei gets a̶n̶ information from the Web.*
D Use *a / an* with a person, place, or thing when you and your listener are not familiar with it or when the specific name of it is not important.	*I go to a news site each day.* (We do not know which news site it is.) *Raul bought a newspaper yesterday.* (We do not know which newspaper it is.)

2.2 Using *The*

A Use *the* with singular nouns, plural nouns, and noncount nouns.	*The study showed Internet news habits.* *The news stories were interesting.* *The information was useful.*
B *The* can go before a noun or an adjective + noun.	*I read the news online every morning.* *Did you hear the big news? Tom got married!*

2.2 Using *The (continued)*

C Use *the* with people, places, and things that are familiar to you and your listener. For example, when:

1 The noun is unique – there is only one (*the sun*, *the moon*, *the Internet*).

*People walked on **the moon** in 1969.* (We know that there is only one moon.)

2 The noun is part of your and your listener's everyday world or general knowledge (*the dog*, *the newspaper*).

*I read **the newspaper** every day.* (The newspaper is part of our everyday life.)

3 There is additional information that explains which noun you are talking about (*the building on the left*, *the computer in the lab*).

*I watch **the news show** that's on at 11:00 p.m.* (It is a specific news show, the one that is on at 11:00 p.m.)

D People often use *a / an* the first time they speak or write about a new noun, and then use *the* every time after that.

***A recent study** analyzed how people get their news.* (We do not know which study it is.)

***The study** found that not many people read newspapers.* (Now we know that it is the study you just mentioned.)

 Grammar Application

Exercise 2.1 *A or An?*

Complete the sentences about people's media habits. Circle the correct words.

1 **A** / **An** recent study showed **a / an** change in media habits.

2 Sara Cameron, a business student, used to read **a / an** newspaper every day, but now she visits **a / an** Internet news site several times a day.

3 Last night, her friend Rachel sent her **a / an** interesting news story from **a / an** business blog.

4 Rachel also put **a / an** link to **a / an** news video in **a / an** e-mail to all her friends.

5 Rachel used to write articles for **a / an** fashion magazine, but now she posts articles on **a / an** online fashion blog.

6 Last month, Sara bought **a / an** book at **a / an** used bookstore. Yesterday, she downloaded **a / an** ebook instead.

7 When she misses **a / an** episode of her favorite TV show, she watches it on **a / an** TV website the next day.

Look at the pictures. What are the people saying? Circle the correct answer.

1 a Did you see a movie?
  b Did you see the movie?

2 a My laptop's on a chair.
  b My laptop's on the chair.

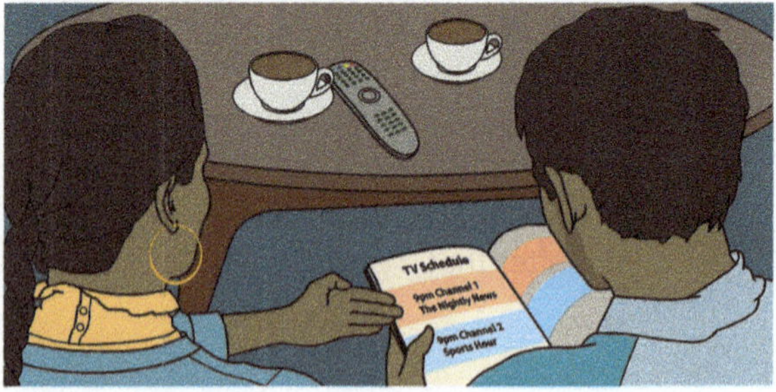

3 a I want to buy a phone.
  b I want to buy the phone.

4 a Let's watch a news show.
  b Let's watch the news show.

A Read an excerpt from a report on jobs in new media. Write *a*, *an*, *the*, or Ø (no article).

Public relations (PR) firms create ____Ø____ publicity for companies. For example,
(1)
__________ PR person writes __________ interesting story about __________ company
(2)   (3)   (4)
and tries to get __________ story into a newspaper. PR firms also try to get people on
(5)
TV or on __________ radio to talk about the company. PR firms like to use these media.
(6)
However, today, they also get their stories into new media, for example, on __________
(7)
social networking sites or in __________ blogs. PR firms often hire young people to help
(8)
them do this. For example, while Ali Lewis, a 25-year-old from Boston, was in college,
he wrote __________ popular blog about the media. __________ public relations firm
(9)   (10)
read his blog and asked him to come in for __________ job interview. Ali is __________
(11)   (12)
good writer, and he understands how new media work, so they gave him __________
(13)
job. In his new job, Ali helps companies work with social networking sites and blogs.

B Now listen to the report and check your answers.

Exercise 2.4 *The:* Only One or General Knowledge

People often use *the* with these nouns. There is only one of these nouns (e.g., the *moon*), or it is clear which one is meant.

the government	the media	the past	the environment	the moon
the president	the Internet	the future	the weather	the sky
the public	~~the radio~~		the world	the sun
	the press		the Earth	

A Complete the blog and follow-up comments with a word from the word box above. Sometimes, more than one answer is possible.

The News Today

February 11 by Claire Sanchez

I'm so bored with the news these days! Everything in the media – including TV, the Internet, magazines, and newspapers, and even ___*the radio*___ (1) – is about celebrities. It seems that the only stories that we see in the media are about celebrities and their personal problems! There are a lot of serious issues in ______________ (2) today, and we don't see much in ______________ (3) about them. What's your opinion?

3 Comments

Emily: I agree. For example, climate change is a serious issue. We need more stories about how global warming is affecting the environment. ______________ (4) is in danger, and the public isn't interested. I mean, it's great to see the blue sky and ______________ (5) every day, but ice is melting in the Arctic! Why aren't people interested in this?

NewsBoy: I agree, too. There isn't enough news about education, in my opinion. In ______________ (6), when I was a kid, schools had enough money and classes weren't crowded. Today, it's getting very hard to get into a class at the community college. ______________ (7) won't be better, unless we do something in the present.

Erkan: Actually, ______________ (8) was talking about education on TV last night, NewsBoy. But even though the president thinks we need more money for education, that doesn't mean that ______________ (9) is doing anything about it. I don't think ______________ (10) really cares about education. I mean, think about the average person – your neighbors, for example. Do they really care about crowded college classes?

B Group Work **Discuss these questions in groups.**

1 What's a recent news story that you were really interested in? Why did it interest you?

2 What kind of news stories do you hate reading? Why?

3 What do you think is the best (or worst) way to get the news?

3 Generalizing: More about Articles

Grammar Presentation

| Generalizations are true statements about all or most members of a group. | *Teens usually get their news from the Internet.* (= Almost all teens do this; this is true in general.) |

3.1 Using Articles in Generalizations and Definitions

A To make generalizations, you can use:

1 a plural noun with no article
2 a noncount noun with no article
3 *a/an* or *the* + a singular count noun

Young people don't read newspapers.
Information on new media habits is available.
A good journalist covers all sides of an issue.

B Do not use *the* with a plural count noun or a noncount noun when you make generalizations.

Society
~~The society~~ needs people with ~~the~~ good communication skills.

C You can also use quantifiers like *most*, *a lot of*, and *some* in generalizations.

Most Internet users visit more than one news site each day.
A lot of teenagers get the news from the Internet.
Some people get the news on their phones.

D You can use *a/an* with definitions to say what something is.

A PR firm creates publicity for companies.

Grammar Application

Exercise 3.1 Generalizations

Complete the report on a survey. Circle the correct words.

A recent study analyzed the media habits of American teens. The study showed that **the/Ø** American teens are not giving up TV for new media. In fact, they are watching more
(1)
TV than before. For **the/Ø** TV viewers aged 13–20, the top show was *American Idol* in the
(2)
year of the survey. This was the same for **the/Ø** parents, too. The survey found that teens
(3)
also play **the/Ø** video games, and not always **the/Ø** violent games.
(4)   (5)
According to the study, **a/Ø** typical U.S. teen remembers **the/Ø** TV
(6)   (7)
advertisements well and does not have a negative attitude toward them. **Most/The**
(8)
young people also love the Internet, but they spend less time on it than **the/Ø** adults.
(9)
They download **the/Ø** music and spend about two or three hours a day listening to it.
(10)

Complete the definitions. Use *a*, *an*, or Ø (no article) and the correct form of the words in the box.

adult	parent	senior	tween
minor	preteen	~~teenager~~	twenty-something

1 ___*A teenager*___ is a young person between 13 and 19 years old.
2 ___________________ is a person over the age of 18.
3 According to the law, ___________________ is a person below the age of 18.
4 ___________________ are people with children.
5 ___________________ are people over the age of 65.
6 ___________________ is a person between the ages of 20 and 29.
7 ___________________ is like a preteen – a child aged 8 to 12 years old. It's a new word in marketing.
8 ___________________ are young people under the age of 13.

4 Avoid Common Mistakes ⚠

1 **Use *a/an* the first time you mention a new idea.**

Do you have ⌃ social networking site?   *(a)*

2 **Use *the* with a noun when there is only one or when the noun is part of your and your listener's everyday world or general knowledge.**

⌃ Internet is a good source of news.   *(The)*

3 **Use plural nouns without *the* in generalizations.**

~~The online~~ news consumers go to many different websites.   *(Online)*

4 **Use noncount nouns without *the* in generalizations.**

~~The communication~~ is changing.   *(Communication)*

Editing Task

Find and correct 10 more mistakes in this article on microblogging.

   Microblogging is ⌃ way of keeping in touch with other people. The people write   *(a)*
microblogs for their friends and families. They use microblogging sites to publish
information about their activities. It is an economical way to give a lot of information to
a lot of people.

5   Microblogs are very useful method of communicating for companies, too.
The companies advertise their products with microblogs. They send the information in
short messages to customers.

   In education, some teachers use microblogging with the students. Students write down
all their study activities, and teachers send the advice. Some people use audio blogs in the
10 education. They record the spoken messages and upload them to a microblogging site.

   People first started using microblogs in 2005. By 2007, there were 111 microblogging
sites around world. The microblogs are becoming more and more popular.

5 Academic Writing

Expository Writing

Brainstorm > Organize > Write > Edit

In Unit 7, you read an article and brainstormed ideas in a T-chart for the prompt below. In this unit (8), you are going to start organizing your ideas and learn how to write an introductory paragraph.

Choose a new area of technology or invention to analyze. Write a report about its advantages and disadvantages, and include a prediction in the conclusion.

Writing an Introductory Paragraph

The first, or introductory, paragraph of an academic report or essay usually has three parts: a hook, background information, and a thesis statement.

The **hook** is a statement or question at the beginning of the paragraph. Its purpose is to get the reader interested in the topic and to want to keep reading. A good hook can be a thought-provoking question, a surprising fact or statistic, a request to the reader to imagine a situation, an interesting observation, or a relevant quotation.

The next time you read a news story, you might be reading something that was written by a robot.

Background information provides context to help readers understand the topic of the report or essay. It can include definitions of important terms, historical information, data and statistics, or a general explanation of the topic.

In the mid-2010s, media outlets began using software to write news stories. The news items were mostly about sports and finance because they include a lot of statistics, which are easy to report.

The **thesis statement** is usually the last sentence of the introduction. It includes the topic and the writer's point of view about the topic. A good thesis statement also tells the reader how the report or essay will develop.

Robots may be efficient, accurate, and cost-effective news writers, but they cannot replace the creativity, curiosity, or judgment of human journalists.

Exercise 5.1 Applying the Skill

In Unit 7, you read the article "The World of Tomorrow." Re-read the introductory paragraph below. Then complete the tasks.

Every generation develops new technology that has both positive and negative effects. In the past 30 years, for example, the Internet has become part of daily life. However, along with more information, faster communication, and greater convenience, there are issues with privacy, identity theft, and online harassment. Now, what comes next? What will the world of tomorrow look like? Will it be easier or more difficult? Many people are confident that technology is going to help solve some of today's most challenging problems. Other people worry that new technology may solve old problems but create new ones, like the Internet has. While it is difficult to predict the world of tomorrow, progress today in the areas of transportation, production, and safety will probably change the future.

1 Underline the hook. What type of hook does the writer use? Is it effective?

2 Put a box around the background information. What kind of background information is it?

3 Double underline the thesis statement. How many body paragraphs do you think there will be? Will the writer focus more on the advantages or disadvantages?

My Writing

Exercise 5.2 Planning Your Introductory Paragraph

Review your notes and work in My Writing in Unit 7. Plan your essay's introductory paragraph.

1 Write notes about the hook.

2 Write notes about the background information.

3 Write notes about the thesis statement.

Exercise 5.3 Writing Your Introductory Paragraph

Use your notes from Exercise 5.2. Write an introductory paragraph for your essay. Make sure the thesis statement shows the reader what your body paragraphs will be about.

Exercise 5.4 Editing Your Writing

Use the checklist to edit your paragraph.

Did you use an indefinite article with unfamiliar count nouns or not specific ones?	
Did you use any definitions in your paragraph?	
Did you use a definite article with specific, familiar, or unique count and noncount nouns?	
Did you avoid the common mistakes in the chart on page 105?	

Pronouns; Direct and Indirect Objects

Challenging Ourselves

1 Grammar in the Real World

A What challenges do you face in your life? Read the online article about ways people challenge themselves. What are some reasons to challenge yourself every day?

B Comprehension Check Answer the questions.

1 According to the text, what are some reasons to challenge yourself?

2 How does challenging yourself help you when you have real problems?

3 If you want to challenge yourself, what are some steps to follow?

C Notice Read the sentences from the article and answer the questions.

1 "Mari is afraid to speak in public, so **she** challenges **herself** by taking a public speaking class."

Who does *she* refer to? ____

Who does *herself* refer to? ____

2 "Ken wants to improve **his** critical thinking skills."

Who does *his* refer to in this sentence? ____

Challenging Ourselves

We all face challenges in **our** lives. For example, people lose **their** jobs, or **they** deal with health problems. These challenges are difficult for all of us. However, if **you** challenge **yourself**, even when **your** life is going well, **you** can be ready to handle tough situations in the future. **You** will become more confident and more creative. **You** will also improve **your** problem-solving skills.

Challenging **yourself** means trying new things. These things will help **you**, but **they** may also be difficult or scary. People have **their** own needs and goals, so other people's challenges may be different from **yours**. Here are some examples:

- Alison wants to be more fit. To challenge **herself, she** works out an extra half hour each day.

- Dan wants to improve **his** performance at work. He challenges **himself** by volunteering to do difficult tasks that no one else wants to do.

- Mari is afraid to speak in public, so **she** challenges **herself** by taking a public speaking class.

- Ken wants to improve **his** critical thinking skills. **He** now reads articles with opinions that are different from **his**.

Do **you** want to challenge **yourself**? Follow these three easy steps:

1 Write down **your** goal. Give **your** plan a start and a finish date.

2 Tell people about **your** goal. This helps **you** stick to **your** plan.

3 Go one step further than **you** originally planned. For example, do **you** want to save $25 a week to buy a car someday? Then save $30.

Take on small challenges every day. Small challenges give people strength. **They** help people handle life's *big* challenges when **they** happen.

2 Pronouns

Grammar Presentation

Pronouns replace or refer to nouns.	(= MARI) (= MARI) **Mari** is afraid to speak in public, so **she** challenges **herself** by taking a public speaking class.

2.1 Pronouns

Subject	Object	Possessive Determiner + Noun	Possessive	Reflexive	Reciprocal
I	me	my + noun	mine	myself	
you	you	your + noun	yours	yourself	
he	him	his + noun	his	himself	
she	her	her + noun	hers	herself	each other
it	it	its + noun	—	itself	one another
we	us	our + noun	ours	ourselves	
they	them	their + noun	theirs	themselves	

2.2 Using Pronouns

A Use subject pronouns to replace nouns in the subject position.	**Alison** wants to be more fit. **She** is taking an exercise class.
B Use object pronouns to replace nouns in the object position.	Sara loves **exercise classes**. She takes **them** three times a week.
C Use a possessive pronoun to replace a possessive determiner + singular or plural noun. The possessive pronoun agrees with the subject that it replaces.	**My exercise class** is at night. **Hers** is on the weekend. (hers = her exercise class) **Amy's classes** meet in the afternoon. **His** meet in the morning. (his = his classes)
D Use reflexive pronouns when the object of the sentence is the same as the subject. Use them in the object position.	**I** taught **myself** to speak Japanese. **Ken** challenges **himself** by reading different opinions. **The students** didn't hurt **themselves** in the exercise class.

2.2 Using Pronouns *(continued)*

E Use *by* + a reflexive pronoun to mean "alone" or "without any help."

*My son can ride a bike **by himself**.*
(He does not need any help.)

*Lara works out **by herself**.*
(She works out alone.)

F Use reciprocal pronouns when two or more people give *and* receive the same action or have the same relationship.

*Mari and I have the same challenges. We help **each other**.*
(I help Mari, and Mari helps me.)
*Tom and his sisters e-mailed **one another** about the news.*
(Each person e-mailed the other people.)

G You can use *one* to replace a singular noun. Use *ones* to replace a plural noun.

*I need an **exercise class**. That **one** looks good.*

A *The white **running shoes** are nice.*
B *I like the black **ones**.*

🌐 *Each other* is about four times more frequent than *one another*.

Exercise 2.1 Pronouns

A Complete the interview. Circle the correct pronouns.

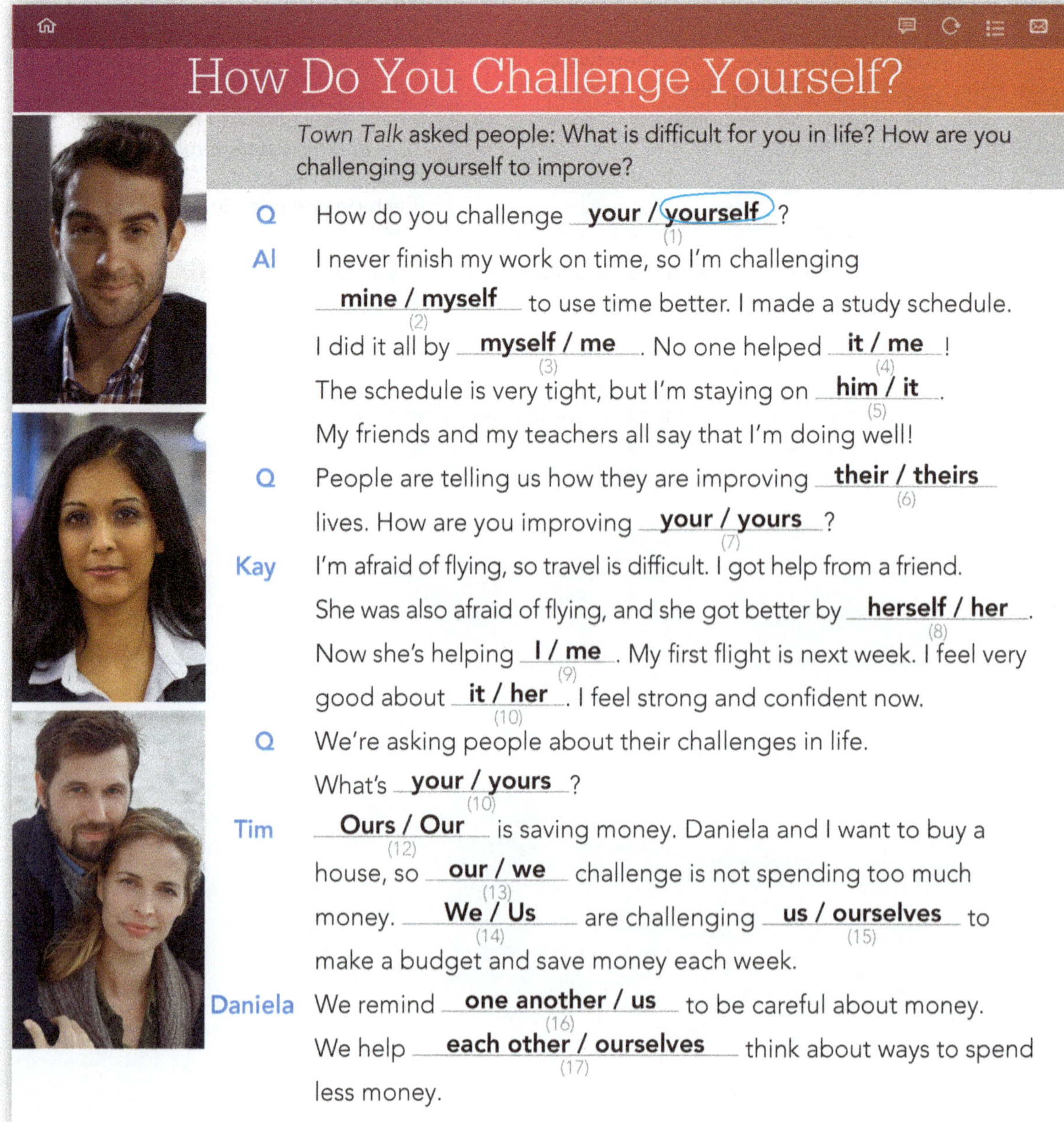

B Pair Work Discuss these questions with a partner.

1 What is difficult for you?

2 What do you challenge yourself to do?

A *I'm afraid of public speaking. I'm challenging myself to speak in class whenever I can. How about you?*

B *I'm challenging myself . . .*

Exercise 2.2 *One and Ones*

Complete the conversations. Use *one* or *ones*.

1 A Do you want the large box of cereal?

   B No. I'm saving money. I want the small ____*one*____ .

2 A Which exercise class are you taking?

   B The _______________ at 3:00 p.m. looks good.

3 A I'm making a budget. Can I borrow your calculator?

   B Sorry, I don't have _______________ .

4 A Which sports do you like to do?

   B I like the challenging _______________ , like skiing and rock climbing.

5 A Being a parent is challenging! I need some books to help me.

   B Sure. The _______________ on the shelf over there are very useful.

6 A Do you want to return these running shoes?

   B Yes. The _______________ that I ordered were white.

7 A Do you want to sign up for a credit card with our store?

   B No. I don't want _______________ . I'm challenging myself to get out of debt.

8 A I need to go downtown. Which bus stop should I go to?

   B The _______________ on Oak Street.

Exercise 2.3 Prepositions with Reflexive Pronouns

DATA FROM THE REAL WORLD

Research shows that reflexive pronouns frequently follow these verbs with *for*, *to*, and *about*:
do (something) *for*, make (something) *for*
talk to + (someone)
talk about, think about, feel + adjective + *about* (something / someone)

*I **made** a schedule **for myself**.*
*Sometimes I **talk to myself**.*
*Tim never **thinks about himself**.*
*She **feels good about herself**.*

A Complete the article about controlling your nerves in an uncomfortable situation. Circle the correct preposition.

Do You Get "the Jitters"?

When people do challenging activities, they get nervous. Sometimes this is called "the jitters." Getting nervous is a normal reaction. Like an athlete before an event, maybe you get the jitters before a class presentation or a test. Here are some tips from successful students to help you control the jitters when you have to take a test or speak in front of the class.

- Be well prepared. For example, for a test, make a study schedule **for / to** (1) yourself and stick to it. For a presentation, make an outline **about / for** (2) yourself and memorize it.

- Be positive. Think **to / about** (3) yourself and how well prepared you are. Talk **for / to** (4) yourself before the event. Tell yourself that you are smart and well prepared.

- Focus on the task. If you are taking a test, focus on the test. If you are speaking, think about the topic of your talk. Don't think **about / for** (5) yourself during the event.

- Reward yourself. After the event, feel good **for / about** (6) yourself! You did something very challenging! Now, do something nice **for / about** (7) yourself. Make a nice meal **for / to** (8) yourself, or go out with friends and celebrate!

B Pair Work Discuss these questions with a partner.

1 How do you prepare for a challenging activity? What do you think about?

2 How do you reward yourself afterward?

I prepare by practicing a lot with my friends. I think about how much I practiced, and I try not to think about myself. I also make a schedule for myself. …

3 Direct and Indirect Objects

Grammar Presentation

Objects are nouns that receive the action of a verb. Some sentences have two objects after the verb: an indirect object (IO) and a direct object (DO).	IO DO They gave **the winner an award**.

3.1 Using Direct and Indirect Objects

A The direct object is the person or thing that receives the action of the verb.

                            DO
The teacher gave the student **a test**.
(What did the teacher give? A test.)

B The indirect object is the person or thing that receives the direct object.

                     IO   DO
The teacher gave **the student a test**.
(The student received the test.)

C You can use indirect object + direct object.

                 IO   DO
The teacher gave **the student a test**.

You can also use direct object + preposition + indirect object.

           DO PREP   IO
The teacher gave **a test to the student**.

These sentences have the same meaning.

Do not use *to* and *for* with indirect object + direct object.

~~The teacher gave to the student a test.~~

D The pronouns for indirect objects are *me, you, him, her, it, us,* and *them*.

              IO   DO
The teacher gave **her** a test.

You can replace both the direct and the indirect objects with pronouns when you use direct object + preposition + indirect object.

            DO   IO
The teacher gave a test **to her**.

            DO   IO
The teacher gave **it to her**.
(it = the test; her = the student)

Do not replace both the direct and the indirect objects with pronouns when you use indirect object + direct object.

            IO DO
The teacher gave ~~her it~~.

Grammar Application

Exercise 3.1 Direct and Indirect Objects

A Read the text. For each numbered sentence, write *DO* above the direct object and *IO* above the indirect object. Then label the sentences *IO + DO* (indirect object + direct object) or *DO + PREP + IO* (direct object + preposition + indirect object).

Vu Tran wanted to go to college, but he did not have any money. However, Vu had a very helpful counselor in high school, Mrs. Ramirez.

1 Mrs. Ramirez gave Vu some good advice.   *IO + DO*

2 Mrs. Ramirez gave Vu the names of 10 scholarship organizations.   ______________

3 Vu and Mrs. Ramirez sent the completed applications to the scholarship organizations.   ______________

4 A few months later, Vu told Mrs. Ramirez the good news.   ______________

5 Five of the 10 organizations offered a scholarship to Vu.   ______________

6 Vu chose one organization, and it sent a check to his college.   ______________

Today, Vu is a successful computer technician. He overcame a great challenge with help from Mrs. Ramirez.

B Rewrite each sentence in A. Change the IO + DO sentences to DO + PREP + IO sentences. Then change the DO + PREP + IO sentences to IO + DO.

1 *Mrs. Ramirez gave some good advice to Vu.*

2 ______________

3 ______________

4 ______________

5 ______________

6 ______________

Exercise 3.2 *To* and *For* with Direct Objects

 **DATA FROM THE REAL WORLD**

Research shows that the following verbs and prepositions are frequently used together in sentences with the pattern: verb + direct object + preposition + indirect object.

verb + DO + *to* + IO *e-mail, give, lend, offer, owe, read, sell, send, show, teach, tell* *To* emphasizes the direction of the action.	*I **e-mailed** pictures **to** you.* *The teacher **gave** a test **to** the student.* (The test went from the teacher to the student.)
verb + DO + *for* + IO *bake, buy, cook, do, find, get, keep, leave, make, order, save* *For* means that the subject does the action to please or help the other person or thing.	*I got tickets **for** my friends.* *The students baked a cake **for** the teacher.* (The students baked a cake to please the teacher.)
verb + DO + *to* / *for* + IO *bring, take, write* These verbs use either *for* or *to*.	*He took a schedule **for** his friend.* (He took it to give to his friend as a favor.) *He took a schedule **to** his friend.* (He carried or gave it to his friend.)

A Complete the text with *to* or *for*.

Is it possible to change the way you think? Sometimes. Take Ken, for example. Ken had very strong opinions about a lot of things. One day, Ken's teacher, Mrs. Green, gave an exam __*to*__ the class. When Mrs. Green showed the test results
(1)

__________ Ken, he was shocked. The results showed that he didn't always base his
(2)

ideas on correct information. Ken then decided to challenge himself and Mrs. Green helped Ken. First, she found a website __________ Ken. It published articles on ideas
(3)

that were different from Ken's. Ken discussed the articles with Mrs. Green. Mrs. Green also made quizzes __________ Ken on the articles he read. In addition, Mrs. Green
(4)

found a critical thinking skills class __________ Ken. He also e-mailed some reports on
(5)

the class __________ Mrs. Green. Today, Ken has excellent critical thinking skills.
(6)

B Pair Work Listen to the text. There is additional information about Ken. Write down three new things you hear. Then tell your partner.

1 ____

2 ____

3 ____

A *Ken was a biology student at a community college.*

B *Right. And the exam was about . . .*

Complete the answers in the conversations with the correct indirect object pronoun for the underlined word. Then rewrite each answer using a different pattern.

1 **A** Where did <u>Ken</u> get that course schedule?

   B Mrs. Green gave the schedule to _*him*_ .   _*Mrs. Green gave him the schedule.*_

2 **A** What did Mrs. Green give <u>Ken</u>?

   B She gave __________ an exam. ____

3 **A** What did Mrs. Green find for <u>Ken</u>?

   B She found a critical thinking skills class for __________ . ___________________________

4 **A** What did Mrs. Ramirez do for <u>Vu</u>?

   B She wrote __________ a letter of recommendation. _______________________________

5 **A** Did Vu mail the applications to <u>the scholarship organizations</u>?

   B Yes, he e-mailed __________ the applications. __________________________________

6 **A** Did the scholarship organization send some of the scholarship money <u>to Vu's parents</u>?

   B No, it didn't mail the money to __________ . _________________________________

7 **A** Did your school give <u>you and your sister</u> scholarships?

   B No, our school gave __________ a loan. _____________________________________

8 **A** Can you give <u>me</u> $200 for books this semester?

   B No, but I can give __________ $100. _______________________________________

A Write six sentences about nice things that people have done for you or given to you.

1 _*My brother gave me some money for my birthday.*_

2 ____

3 ____

4 ____

5 ____

6 ____

B Pair Work Exchange information with a partner. Ask questions as you talk.

A *My brother gave me $20 for my last birthday.*

B *That's nice. My brothers don't give me presents, but we go out together on our birthdays.*

4 Avoid Common Mistakes ⚠

1 Do not confuse subject and object pronouns.

She gave the schedule to Ken and ~~I~~. (me)

2 Do not use *to* or *for* in sentences with the pattern verb + indirect object + direct object.

Tom gave ~~to~~ his brother a skateboard.   Tom bought ~~for~~ his brother a skateboard.

3 Some verbs take *to*. Some verbs take *for*.

I e-mailed the assignment ~~for~~ you. Did you get my message? (to)

I made a cake ~~to~~ you. (for)

4 In sentences with verb + indirect object + direct object, do not replace both the direct and the indirect objects with pronouns.

The teacher gave ~~her it~~. (her the test)

Editing Task

Find and correct eight more mistakes in this story about a personal challenge.

Lara was afraid of heights. The fear caused many problems for ~~she~~ (her). Her life was
very difficult. For example, her was very uncomfortable on airplanes. She also did not
like to take elevators in tall buildings. Lara's husband gave to her some advice.
He told to Lara a secret: If she deals with her fears, she can improve in all areas of her
5 life. Then her husband found a skydiving class to her. He found a schedule online,
and he gave her it. Then he gave Lara money to pay for the class. He also bought the
equipment to her. Lara took the class. It was hard, but she challenged herself.
After Lara finished the class, her husband gave a present for her. He baked for her
a cake, and they celebrated together.

5 Academic Writing

Expository Writing

Brainstorm > Organize > Write > Edit

In Unit 8, you wrote an introductory paragraph for the prompt below. In this unit (9), you are going to learn how to introduce advantages and disadvantages, and write, revise, and edit your report.

> *Choose a new area of technology or invention to analyze. Write a report about its advantages and disadvantages, and include a prediction in the conclusion.*

Introducing Advantages and Disadvantages

Writers often use prepositional phrases at the start of a new sentence to introduce the advantages and disadvantages of a subject.

Exercise 5.1 Understanding the Skill

Read the phrases below. Write *A* for advantage and *D* for disadvantage.

________ 1 The main **advantage of**…

________ 2 One **disadvantage of**…

________ 3 One of the biggest **concerns with**…

________ 4 A real **benefit of**…

________ 5 The **problem with**…

________ 6 One **point against**…

________ 7 The main **argument in favor of**…

________ 8 The main **argument against**…

________ 9 The **main worry about**…

________ 10 One **good thing about**…

Exercise 5.2 Applying the Skill

Review your work in My Writing in Unit 7. Write two sentences about the advantages and two sentences about the disadvantages of the invention in your report. Use a different phrase from Exercise 5.1 in each sentence.

1 ____

2 ____

3 ____

4 ____

My Writing

Exercise 5.3 Writing Your First Draft

Review your work in My Writing in Unit 7 and your introductory paragraph in Unit 8. Write two body paragraphs and a concluding paragraph to complete your report.

Exercise 5.4 Revising Your Ideas

1 Work with a partner. Use the questions below to give feedback on your partner's report.

- Which of your partner's ideas seem the strongest to you?
- Which of your partner's ideas need to be explained more clearly?
- What could your partner add or remove to make the report stronger and easier to understand?

2 Use the feedback from your partner to revise your report.

Exercise 5.5 Editing Your Writing

Use the checklist to review and edit your report.

Did you answer the prompt completely?	
Did you write a hook and background information in the introductory paragraph?	
Did you write an effective thesis statement?	
Do the topic sentences in your body paragraphs connect to your thesis statement?	
Did you write about advantages and disadvantages in your body paragraphs?	
Did you use evidence and examples to support your statements?	
Did you summarize your thesis and main points in your concluding paragraph?	

Exercise 5.6 Editing Your Grammar

Use the checklist to review and edit the grammar your report.

Did you use count and non-count nouns correctly?	
Did you use the indefinite article with unfamiliar count nouns or not specific ones?	
Did you use the definite article with specific, familiar, or unique count and noncount nouns?	
Did you use pronouns to connect your sentences and ideas?	
Did you avoid the common mistakes in the charts on pages 93, 105, and 119?	

Exercise 5.7 Writing Your Final Draft

Apply the feedback and edits from Exercises 5.4 to 5.6 to write the final draft of your report.

10 Present Perfect

Discoveries

1 Grammar in the Real World

A Where do you think new medicines come from? Read the article about a scientist who looks for new medicines. Where does Dr. Smith find new medicines?

B **Comprehension Check** Who went to these places? According to the article, did they find medicines or chemicals there? Check (✓) the correct boxes. Sometimes more than one answer is correct.

	Did Dr. Smith go there?	Did other scientists go there?	Did people find medicines or chemicals there?
1 the Amazon	☐	☐	☐
2 the Arctic Ocean	☐	☐	☐
3 Africa	☐	☐	☐
4 the Pacific Ocean	☐	☐	☐
5 an underwater volcano	☐	☐	☐

C **Notice** Find the sentences in the article and complete them.

1 We _________________ chemicals all around the world.

2 I _________________ around the world twice.

3 I _________________ more than 50 countries for my work.

4 About two years ago, we _________________ a submarine inside an underwater volcano.

In which sentence do we know when the action happened? In which sentences is the time indefinite?

ACADEMIC WRITING

Comparison-and-contrast writing

Interview with Jane Smith, Ph.D.,

Marine Biologist[1]

[1]**marine biologist:** someone who studies plants and animals that live in the ocean
[2]**expedition:** a long journey with a special purpose, e.g., to discover something
[3]**submarine:** a boat that travels underwater

So, Dr. Smith, what exactly do you do?

We look for new medicines. We go to the ocean and discover chemicals in marine organisms – deep-sea animals and plants. We use these chemicals to develop drugs to treat human diseases.

5 **That's amazing. I didn't know medicines came from under the sea! Tell me more.**

Over the years, scientists **have** also **found** a lot of important drugs on land. For example, they **have developed** useful drugs from plants and animals in the Amazon rain forest in Brazil. Our work is similar. However, 10 we look for medicines in the ocean.

Where exactly do you find these chemicals?

We **have discovered** chemicals all around the world. Scientists **have found them** in warm water and in cold water, like in the Arctic Ocean. We**'ve found** them in shallow water and in very deep water, sometimes 15 tens of thousands of feet under the surface.

It sounds like you get to travel a lot for your work. Where have you been?

I**'ve been** around the world twice. My team **has led** underwater expeditions[2] in Africa, the Caribbean, the Pacific Ocean, off the coast 20 of South America, and in Asia. I**'ve been** very lucky with this job! I**'ve visited** more than 50 countries for my work.

What are some of the most exciting things you have seen or done?

I**'ve made** hundreds of very deep dives and **had** some exciting adventures. For example, about two years ago, we took a submarine[3] 25 inside an underwater volcano. However, we didn't know it was a volcano. Suddenly, the volcano erupted. The submarine shot up 200 feet a minute! That was really exciting!

 # Present Perfect

Grammar Presentation

The present perfect describes past events that are important in the present, but the specific time that the events happened is not important or is unknown.

*We **have found** chemicals all over the world.*

(We found them sometime in the past, and this is still important now.)

2.1 Statements

Subject	Have/Has (+ Not)	Past Participle	
I You We They	**have** **have not** **haven't**	**visited**	50 countries.
He She It	**has** **has not** **hasn't**		

Contractions	
I have	**I've**
You have	**You've**
We have	**We've**
They have	**They've**
He has	**He's**
She has	**She's**
It has	**It's**

2.2 Yes/No Questions and Short Answers

Have/Has	Subject	Past Participle	
Have	I you we they	**found***	new medicines?
Has	he/she/it		

Short Answers	
Yes, I **have**.	No, I **haven't**.
Yes, you **have**.	No, you **haven't**.
Yes, we **have**.	No, we **haven't**.
Yes, they **have**.	No, they **haven't**.
Yes, he/she/it **has**.	No, he/she/it **hasn't**.

Found is an irregular past participle. Irregular Verbs: See page A3.

2.3 Information Questions and Answers

Wh- Word	Have/Has	Subject	Past Participle		Answers
Where	**have**	I	**traveled**?		You **have traveled** around the world.
Why	**have**	you	**gone**	to the Amazon?	I **have gone** to look for medicines.
What	**have**	we	**discovered**?		We**'ve discovered** chemicals in plants.
How	**have**	they	**studied**	life under the sea?	They**'ve studied** it in submarines.
How often	**has**	he/she/it	**traveled**	in a submarine?	He**'s traveled** in a submarine many times.

Wh- Word	Has	Past Participle		Answer
Who	**has**	**been**	to Africa?	Dr. Smith **has been** to Africa.

2.4 Using Present Perfect

A	Use the present perfect to talk about past events that are still important now.	*People **have discovered** medicines in the Amazon.* (This began in the past and is important now.)
B	Use the present perfect to describe actions or events that happened once or repeatedly at indefinite times in the past.	*She **has traveled** to Mexico.* *She **has traveled** around the world many times.* (We don't know exactly when she did these things.)
C	Use the present perfect to give the number of times something happened up to now.	*I**'ve been** to Africa twice.* (Before now, I went there two times.)
D	Use the present perfect to give lists of past experiences.	*I**'ve been** to France, Spain, and England.*
	You can also use the present perfect with "been" to mean "go and come back again."	A *Where **have** you **been**?* B *I**'ve** just **been** to the store.* (I went to the store and have come back again.)
E	Use *ever* in present perfect questions to ask if something happened at any time in the past.	A *Have you **ever traveled** to Africa?* B *Yes, I have. / No, I haven't.* A *Have you **ever been** inside a volcano?* B *Yes, I have. / No, I haven't.*

Grammar Application

Exercise 2.1 Statements

Complete the sentences about a biotech company, a company that develops medicines. Use the present perfect form of the verbs in parentheses.

A number of drug companies ___*have found*___ (find) medicines in the rain forest. (1) In fact, over 120 medicines ___________ (come) from rain forest plants. Some companies (2) ___________ (get) information about these plants from the local people. In many cases, (3) the people ___________ (live) there for hundreds of years, and they know all about the (4) plants. However, they ___________ (not receive) money or other benefits for their help. (5) Some drug companies ___________ (not think) about the rights of the local people who (6) help them. Also, some companies ___________ (not take) care of the local environment. (7)

One drug company, Rain Forest Biotech, ___________ (take) steps to improve (8) things. Rain Forest Biotech ___________ (develop) a new way to find drugs and respect (9) the people and land at the same time. Rain Forest Biotech also ___________ (set) up (10) programs to help the local people they work with.

Exercise 2.2 Questions and Answers

A Complete the interview with the president of Rain Forest Biotech. Use the present perfect form of the verbs in parentheses. Then listen and check your answers.

Chris Green My guest today is Dr. Marty Robles. Dr. Robles is the president of Rain Forest Biotech. Rain Forest Biotech has made some exciting discoveries in the rain forests of the Amazon. Dr. Robles, you have an exciting company, and you ___*'ve had*___ (have) (1) an exciting life, too, I think. Tell us a little bit about your life. How many times ___________ you (2) ___________ (be) to the Amazon? (2)

Dr. Robles I ___________ (make) 100 trips to the (3) Amazon region.

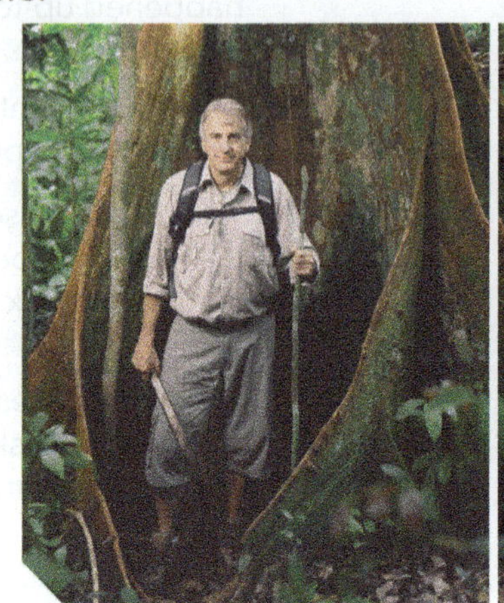

Chris Green	Who _____________ (go) with you?
Dr. Robles	My team.
Chris Green	And who else _____________ you _____________ (work) with there?
Dr. Robles	Well, I _____________ (meet) many traditional healers on my trips. These people _____________ (teach) me how they use local plants to cure diseases. I _____________ (learn) a great deal about their lives and about their land, too.
Chris Green	_____________ you _____________ (be) to Africa?
Dr. Robles	No, I _____________ (not be) to Africa, but my team _____________ (visited) New Guinea, and I _____________ (do) research in Australia.

B Listen again. What else do you learn about Dr. Robles? Circle the correct words.

1 Dr. Robles has traveled to rain forests in **Central America** / **Central Asia**.

2 His team has discovered medicines for **heart** / **brain** disease.

3 He's brought his children with him on **some** / **all** of his expeditions.

Exercise 2.3 More Questions

A Unscramble the words to make questions.

1 lived / have / How many / places / different / you / ?

   How many different places have you lived?

2 Chicago / you / in / lived / Have / ?

   ____

3 Where / traveled / you / have / ?

   ____

4 Have / New York City / visited / you / ever / ?

   ____

5 with / Who / you / traveled / have / ?

   ____

6 your family / you / helped / has / How / ?

   ____

7 Has / advice / you / your family / life / given / about / ?

   ____

8 learned / have / this class / in / you / What / ?

   ____

B Pair Work Ask and answer the questions in A with a partner. Give true answers about yourself. Ask follow-up questions and add extra information.

> **A** *How many different places have you lived?*
>
> **B** *Two.*
>
> **A** *Where have you lived?*
>
> **B** *I've lived in El Salvador and the United States.*
>
> **A** *Have you ever visited . . . ?*

3 Present Perfect or Simple Past?

Grammar Presentation

<table>
<tr>
<td>The present perfect describes events that happened at an indefinite time in the past and may still be happening in the present. These events are still important or still have an effect in the present. The simple past is for finished events that happened at a specific time in the past.</td>
<td>She has visited the rain forest many times. She went there last year.</td>
</tr>
</table>

3.1 Present Perfect or Simple Past?

A Use the present perfect for things that happened at an indefinite time (or times) in the past.	*She **has been** to Costa Rica.* *Scientists **have discovered** medicines in the Amazon.*
Use the simple past for things that happened at a specific time (or times) in the past.	*She **went** to Costa Rica in 2010.* *Scientists **discovered** a new medicine in the Amazon last year.*
B Use the present perfect for things that have happened in an unfinished time period (e.g., *today, this morning, this year*).	*He **has traveled** to Africa twice this year.* (This year is not finished. He may travel there again.) *I **have visited** three cities for my current job.* (My job is not finished. I may visit more cities for it.)
Use the simple past for things that happened in a time period that is finished (e.g., *yesterday, last night, a year ago*).	*He **traveled** to Indonesia twice last year.* (Last year is finished. He cannot go to Indonesia again in that time period.) *I **visited** three cities for my old job.* (That job is finished. I can't travel for it again.)

3.1 Present Perfect or Simple Past? *(continued)*

C Use the present perfect to introduce a topic, and then use the simple past to give the details.

We've had a lot of exciting experiences. For example, we took a submarine into an underwater volcano last year.

Grammar Application

Exercise 3.1 Present Perfect or Simple Past?

A Complete the article about Amanda Lewis, an astronaut. Circle the correct verbs.

She **has wanted** / **wanted** to be an astronaut when she
(1)
was a child. She **has grown up** / **grew up** in Texas and
(2)
has studied / **studied** biology and engineering at the University
(3)
of Texas. After college, she **has been** / **was** a pilot in the Navy.
(4)
She **has joined** / **joined** NASA in 1999 and **has become** / **became**
(5)   (6)
an astronaut. Since then, she **has orbited** / **orbited** the Earth
(7)
230 times and **has gone** / **went** on three spacewalks in the last
(8)
mission. She also participates in science experiments as part
of her job, and she **has studied** / **studied** the effects of radiation
(9)
on plants for the past six months. The most exciting thing she
has seen / **saw** as a pilot is the Northern Lights. She **has seen** / **saw**
(10)   (11)
them on a mission last year.

B Pair Work Compare your answers with a partner. Discuss the time that the actions in each sentence happened. Decide if the time is definite or indefinite, finished or unfinished.

A Complete the text with the present perfect or simple past form of the verbs in parentheses.

SCIENCE TALK

Three scientists answer the question, "What is the most interesting or exciting thing you have seen or done in your work?"

ERICA SALAZAR, Marine Archaeologist

I _____*have seen*_____ (see) a lot of amazing things under (1)
the sea. For example, in 2013, my team _________________ (2)
(discover) some Roman ships in the Mediterranean. The ships
probably _________________ (sink) around 100 BCE. (3)

JOE COSTA, Biologist

I _________________ (have) some very exciting experiences (4)
in the Amazon rain forest. On a trip last year, a local person
_________________ (tell) us about a plant for treating stomach (5)
problems. My stomach _________________ (be) upset, and I _________________ (6) (7)
(try) a traditional healer's plant. I _________________ (feel) better immediately! (8)

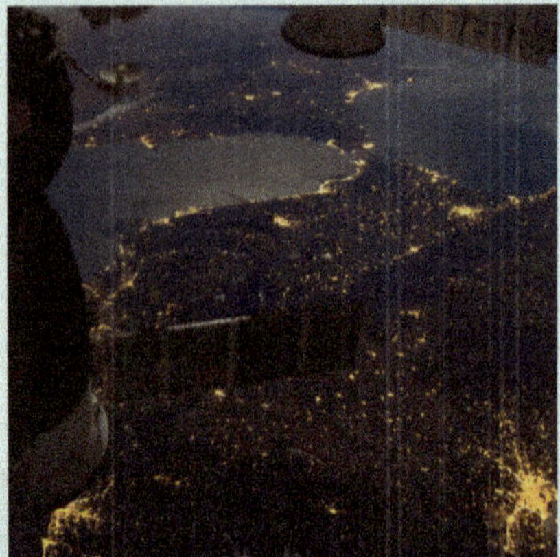

JENNY LEE, Astronaut

We _________________ (see) many wonderful sights from the (9)
International Space Station. On our last mission, we
_________________ (look) out a window and (10)
_________________ (see) a meteor shower. (11)
Some of the meteors _________________ (hit) the station. (12)
It _________________ (be) spectacular! (13)

B Over to You What is one exciting or interesting thing you have seen or done in your life? Tell your partner. Use the present perfect to begin, and give the details in the simple past.

A *I've had a lot of exciting adventures. For example, last summer I climbed Mount Whitney.*

B *The most interesting thing I've seen is an eclipse. I saw it when I was a child.*

4 Avoid Common Mistakes ⚠ 

1 **Use the correct word order in present perfect information questions.**
has he
Where ~~he has~~ gone?

2 **Use the correct form of the past participle in the present perfect.**
found
I have ~~finded~~ many useful plants in the Amazon.

3 **Use the simple past for finished actions or events.**
graduated
She has ~~graduated~~ from the University of Texas in 2011.

4 **Use the simple past to say exactly when something happened.**
went
They ~~have gone~~ on an expedition last year.

5 **Use the present perfect for actions or events in the indefinite past that are still important now.**
have gone
I ~~went~~ to three different countries on my trip so far.

Editing Task

Find and correct nine more mistakes in this interview with a rain forest explorer.

Claire Smith How did you decide to become a rain forest explorer?

Bettie Silva I ~~have been~~ *was* interested in the rain forest when I was a child. I have grown up in Brazil, and I heard many stories about the rain forest regions in my country as a child.

5 **Claire Smith** When did you go on your first expedition?

Bettie Silva I have gone on my first expedition in 2005. I have seen a lot of amazing sights on that first trip.

Claire Smith Where have you gone on your first trip?

Bettie Silva I went to rain forests in the Amazon and in Asia.

10 **Claire Smith** Who you have traveled with?

Bettie Silva I've traveled with teams of scientists and other explorers at different times.

Claire Smith Have you ever had any dangerous experiences in the rain forest?

Bettie Silva Yes. Sadly, I have loosed team members. For example, last year, a poisonous snake has bitten one of my group members. But I had many wonderful
15 experiences on trips so far, too. I have helped scientists discover new medicines, and I have meeted many interesting local people.

5 Academic Writing

Comparison-and-Contrast Writing

Brainstorm > Organize > Write > Edit

In this writing cycle (Units 10-12), you will complete a comparative essay that answers the prompt below. In this unit (10), you will look at an essay and learn how to use a Venn diagram to brainstorm.

Compare and contrast the whale shark and the tiger shark.

Exercise 5.1 Preparing to Write

Work with a partner. Discuss the questions.

1 What are three wild animals and plants in your home country? Describe them.

2 Are there any wild animals or plants in your country from another place? How did they get there? Do they cause any problems?

3 Have you ever visited a rainforest, jungle, or similar place? Describe your experience.

4 What animals live in rainforests? Should governments protect them?

Exercise 5.2 Focusing on Vocabulary

Read the definitions. Then complete the sentences with the correct form of the words in bold.

> **common** (adj) happening often or existing in large numbers
>
> **cruel** (adj) causing pain or suffering on purpose
>
> **disease** (n) illness; a serious health condition that requires care
>
> **fatal** (adj) causing death
>
> **major** (adj) most serious or important
>
> **native** (adj) used to describe animals and plants that are from and still live in a particular place
>
> **survive** (v) to continue to live after difficulties or possibly almost dying

1 The coyote, a wild member of the dog family, has become so __________ in the western United States that it sometimes appears in city streets and parks.

2 Plastic is often __________ to sea birds. Nearly ten million have died from eating plastic bags and other plastic garbage in the past ten years.

3 Rabies was a deadly __________ to humans and animals until scientists discovered a vaccine in 1885.

4 Many people believe that it is __________ to keep animals in zoos, where they cannot move around freely.

5 Scientists have identified habitat loss as the ___________ cause of animal and plant extinction in the Amazon.

6 Several types of frogs have ___________ since the time of dinosaurs, but they are now disappearing because of human activity and climate change.

7 There are many unique species that are ___________ to the island of Madagascar, including more than 80 kinds of snakes.

Losing the Battle for Survival

Invasive species are plants and animals that arrive in an area where they are not **native**, usually due to human activity. For example, a species of shellfish might attach itself to the outside of a ship traveling between countries and enter a new environment in this way. Invasive species are often able to grow quickly in their new homes because they have no natural enemies. As a result, they may replace or damage native plants and animals that live in the same environment. One example is the case of gray and red squirrels in Great Britain.

Red squirrels were once a **common** sight in British forests and countryside. Then, in the 1870s, gray squirrels were introduced from North America because rich people thought the squirrels looked fashionable on the grounds of their large homes. Since then, the grey squirrel population in Great Britain has grown whereas the number of red squirrels there has decreased. Today, only about 140,000 red squirrels remain, mostly in Scotland. In contrast, gray squirrels are now extremely common and seen as **major** pests due to the damage they cause to plants and houses. As a result, the red squirrels have been protected, but the gray squirrels can be legally trapped and destroyed.

At first sight, the two species of squirrels are physically similar. That can make it difficult to see why one is doing well and the other is suffering. They both have a long tail, which helps them balance when jumping from tree to tree. In addition, both kinds of squirrels have the same large eyes, small ears, and powerful back legs.

On the other hand, the two types of squirrels are different in body size and weight. The red squirrel has a typical head-and-body length of approximately 7.5 to 9 inches (19 to 23 centimeters), a tail length of 6 to 8 inches (15 to 20 centimeters) and a body weight of 9 to 12 ounces (250 to 340 grams). The gray squirrel is larger than the red squirrel. The head and body measure between 9 and 12 inches (23 and 30 centimeters), and the tail is between 7.5 and 10 inches (19 and 25 centimeters) long. Adult gray squirrels are also heavier, weighing between 14 and 21 ounces (400 and 600 grams). This size allows them to store more fat and helps them to **survive** hard winters, which could be **fatal** to their smaller cousins.

Three more differences explain why red squirrels have lost out in the competition with gray squirrels. First, red squirrels live high up in the trees, whereas gray squirrels spend more of their time on the ground. This means that loss of forest habitat has been more difficult for the red squirrel population. Another reason is that gray squirrels are more intelligent and can adapt to new situations more easily than red squirrels. For example, they have been able to survive in an urban environment because of their ability to use food provided by humans. A third problem for the red squirrel has been **disease**. Both squirrels carry the parapox virus. The virus does not seem to affect gray squirrels, but it has been fatal to red squirrels.

In conclusion, there does not seem to be much that scientists can do to help red squirrels survive in Great Britain. Some politicians support destroying populations of gray squirrels, but many British people have complained that this is **cruel**. Scientists have successfully reintroduced some red squirrels from other countries, and the animals could be protected in places where there are no gray squirrels, such as the Isle of Wight. However, some people have questioned whether red squirrels should be protected at all. Worldwide, they are not an endangered species. Considering the evidence, saving the red squirrel may be a waste of British government money. Government conservation funding should instead be spent on other endangered species.

Read the text on page 133. Work with a partner. Discuss the questions.

1 Which animal is an invasive species in Great Britain? How did it get there?
2 How are the red squirrel and gray squirrel similar? How are they different?
3 Why has the gray squirrel successfully survived in Great Britain?

Exercise 5.4 Noticing the Grammar and Structure

Complete the tasks. Compare your answers with a partner.

1 Underline the simple past verbs in paragraph 2. Why does the writer use this form?
2 Circle the present perfect verbs in paragraph 2. Why does the writer use this form?
3 Reread the first sentence of paragraphs 3–5. What is each paragraph about? Why does the author organize the paragraphs in this order?

Using Venn Diagrams to Compare and Contrast

In comparison-and-contrast essays, writers look at the similarities and differences between two topics in order to present a conclusion. They often use a graphic organizer called a Venn diagram to brainstorm and organize these similarities and differences.

A Venn diagram consists of overlapping circles. The special characteristics of one topic are on the left side. The special characteristics of the second topic are on the right side. The shared characteristics (similarities) are in the middle.

Exercise 5.5 Applying the Skill

Work with a partner. Complete the Venn diagram about red and gray squirrels.

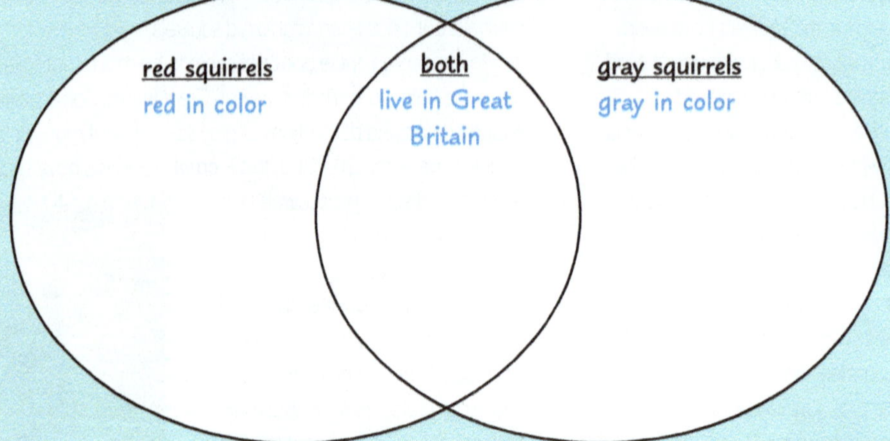

Combining Sentences

Good writers combine sentences to add variety and clearly show the relationship between two ideas.
When combining two sentences, you can usually take out some words and avoid repetition.
In positive sentences, use **and**; in negative sentences, use **or**.

Tropical rainforests, like the Amazon, are very warm **and** quite humid.

Temperate forests do not have freezing temperatures **or** extremely high temperatures.

But and **whereas** are used to contrast two sentences. *Whereas* is more formal than *but*.

Temperate rainforests get 140-160 inches of rainfall each year, **whereas** a tropical rainforest can get over 400 inches.

Recently, the Amazon has experienced serious fires, **but** the cooler Hoh Rainforest has not.

If two things have the same characteristic, use **both...and...**

Both temperate rainforests **and** tropical rainforests are now endangered.

If they do not have a particular characteristic, use **neither...nor...**

Neither temperate rainforests **nor** tropical rainforests are found in Antarctica.

Exercise 5.6 Applying the Skill

Use words from the skills box to combine the pairs of sentences.

1 Tropical rainforests are located near the equator. Temperate rainforests are found in the northern or southern part of the Earth.

2 Tropical rainforests have a lot of flowers. Tropical rainforests have millions of insect species.

3 Tourism has increased in the Amazon. Tourism has also increased in the Hoh.

4 Temperate rainforests do not have a lot of light because there are so many huge trees. Tropical rainforests also do not have a lot of light.

My Writing

Exercise 5.7 Writing a Paragraph

Use the Venn diagram in Exercise 5.5 to write a paragraph about the similarities and differences between red and gray squirrels. Use at least one example of the present perfect tense. Combine sentences to add variety, avoid repetition, and show the relationships between ideas.

1 Grammar in the Real World

A In your opinion, what has been the most important scientific discovery? Read the article from a science magazine. What are some mysteries that science has not yet solved?

B Comprehension Check **Answer the questions.**

1 What is one theory about why birds do not get lost when they migrate?
2 How do we know earthquake lights exist?
3 How many bees have died since the 1980s?
4 What are some situations in which people yawn?

C Notice **Read the sentences from the article and answer the questions.**

1 "They have not figured out the cause **yet**."

   Did scientists figure out the cause? Does the writer think that they will figure it out in the future?

2 "They have **already** given the problem a name: Colony Collapse Disorder."

   Did scientists give the problem a name?

3 "Why do we yawn? Scientists **still** have not solved this mystery."

Did scientists solve the mystery? Does the writer want them to solve it?

Unsolved MYSTERIES

Humans have learned many things over the years. For example, we have discovered DNA, and we have cured many diseases. We have visited the moon and sent robots to Mars. However, scientists **still** have not solved these mysteries.

5 **Bird migration[1]** How do birds travel thousands of miles over land and sea without getting lost? Scientists have **never** understood this. There are some theories. One idea is that birds have magnetic particles[2] in their brains to help them find their way. However, science has **never** proven this.

10 **Earthquake lights** Blue and white lights flash in the sky just before an earthquake occurs. People have reported this for hundreds of years. Photographs from the 1960s prove the lights exist, but researchers **still** have not found the cause. One explanation is that the lights are gas escaping from openings in the earth.

15 **Disappearing bees** Scientists have **recently** said that billions of bees have died since the 1980s. Why? They have not figured out the cause **yet**. However, they have **already** given the problem a name: Colony Collapse Disorder.

Yawning Why do we yawn? Scientists **still** have not solved this
20 mystery. People yawn when they are tired, but they also yawn in other situations, such as during exercise. Another mystery is why yawning is "contagious" – we yawn when other people yawn.
In fact, you may have **just** yawned from reading this sentence!

These and other mysteries are a challenge for scientists. Although
25 we have not **yet** solved them, we are making progress every day.

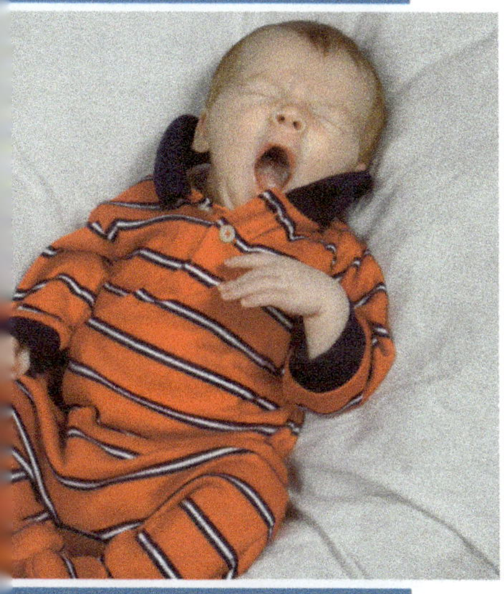

[1]**migration:** movement from one place to another
[2]**particles:** a technical term for very small pieces

2 Adverbs with Present Perfect

Grammar Presentation

<table>
<tr>
<td>Adverbs already, still, and yet with the present perfect show how a past event relates to the present.</td>
<td>He has already given a name to the disease, but he has not discovered the cause yet. He still has not found a cure for it.
(This is the situation right now, up to this point in time.)</td>
</tr>
</table>

2.1 Adverbs with Present Perfect

A Use *already* when something happened sooner than expected.	*Scientists have* **already** *given the disease a name.* *It is only 8:00 p.m., but they have* **already** *gone home.*
Use *already* in affirmative statements and in questions. It usually comes before the past participle.	PAST PARTICIPLE *Have they* **already** *solved the problem?*
B Use *yet* with things that have not happened. It often means you expected something to happen or expect something to happen soon.	*There are many mysteries scientists have not figured out* **yet**.
Use *yet* in negative statements and in questions. It usually comes at the end of the sentence.	*Have they discovered the cause* **yet**?
C Use *still* with things that have not happened. It often means you want something to happen, but it has not.	*Scientists are* **still** *looking for an explanation.*
Use *still* in negative statements, but avoid it in questions. It usually comes before *have / has*.	*It is past midnight, and she* **still** *has not gone home.*
D Use *never* and *not ever* to mean "not at any time" or "zero times." They usually come before the past participle.	PAST PARTICIPLE *Scientists have* **never** *understood the cause.* *They have***n't ever** *understood the cause.* *(These sentences have the same meaning.)*
You can use *ever* in Yes / No questions.	*Have you* **ever** *thought about these mysteries?*
E Use *just*, *lately*, and *recently* when something happened a short time ago. *Just* usually comes before the past participle. *Lately* usually comes at the end of a sentence. *Recently* can go in either position.	PAST PARTICIPLE *We have* **just** *discovered a new type of fish.* *She has been sick* **lately**. *Scientists have* **recently** *studied the issue.* *Scientists have studied the issue* **recently**.

Grammar Application

Exercise 2.1 *Already, Yet,* and *Still*

Complete the statements about earthquake prediction with the present perfect form of the verbs in parentheses. Then check the correct statement about the action.

	The action has happened.	The action has not happened.
1 People _**have not been**_ (not be) able to predict earthquakes **yet**.	☐	☑
2 However, many people ___________ **already** ___________ (notice) that animals behave strangely before an earthquake.	☐	☐
3 The United States Geological Survey (USGS) ___________ **already** ___________ (do) a few studies on animal behavior and earthquakes.	☐	☐
4 However, the USGS ___________ (not prove) that animals can predict earthquakes **yet**.	☐	☐
5 As a result, Western scientists **still** ___________ (not be) able to develop a warning system for earthquakes.	☐	☐
6 However, Asian scientists ___________ **already** ___________ (determine) the connection between animal behavior and earthquakes.	☐	☐
7 In fact, Chinese researchers ___________ **already** ___________ (use) animal behavior to save many people during earthquakes.	☐	☐
8 Many people think that we **still** ___________ (not do) enough animal studies in the West.	☐	☐

A Complete the article about cow behavior. Circle the correct adverb.

Have you ever noticed that groups of cows all face the same way? Scientists have **ever / (never)** been able to explain this. Satellite
(1)
photos have **recently / yet** shown that cows
(2)
around the world all face either north or south. Scientists have **already / still** not learned why
(3)
cows do this. One theory involves magnets. The Earth is like a huge magnet, and magnets

point to the north. Studies have **already / yet** shown that this helps some small animals, such as
(4)
bats, find their way. In addition, researchers have **never / already** found that fish and whales have
(5)
tiny magnetic particles in their brains. Therefore, some researchers have **recently / yet** guessed
(6)
that cows also have magnetic particles in their brains. However, they have not found any proof
already / yet. They **still / lately** have not done any tests to see if cows have magnetic particles in
(7)   (8)
their brains.

B Now listen and check your answers.

Put the adverb in parentheses into the correct place in these sentences about the mystery of aging. Sometimes more than one answer is possible.

still
1 Medical researchers ∧ have not discovered the causes of aging. (still)

2 We have seen that humans are living longer and longer. (already)

3 However, we have not seen many people live beyond the age of 100. (still)

4 So far, humans have not lived past the age of 130. (ever)

5 Researchers have begun to understand the processes that occur in the body as we age. (just)

6 Scientists have discovered chemicals in the body that tell it to start aging. (recently)

7 Many people wonder what we can do to extend our lives, but science has not found the answers. (yet)

8 Some say that eating a low-calorie diet can extend life, but science has not proven this. (still)

Exercise 2.4 Questions and Answers

A Unscramble the words to make questions. Use the present perfect form of the verbs and add *have* or *has* where needed. Sometimes more than one answer is possible.

1 scientists / another planet like Earth / yet / find / ?

   Have scientists found another planet like Earth yet?

2 already / we / what planets / send spaceships to / ?

____

3 find / ever / people / a cure for the common cold / ?

____

4 what medicines / recently / discover / researchers / ?

____

5 people / already / where / look / for new medicines / ?

____

6 figure out why we dream / yet / anyone / ?

____

7 any scientists / recently / in the news / be / ?

____

8 you / wonder about a scientific mystery / ever / ?

____

B Group Work Discuss the questions in A. Try to give extra information and ask follow-up questions.

   A *Have scientists found another planet like Earth yet?*
   B *I don't know. If they've already found a planet like Earth, I want to visit it!*
   C *I don't think they've found a planet like Earth yet. But one is probably out there somewhere.*

Grammar Presentation

For and *since* with the present perfect describe the length of time that an action or event from the past continues into the present.	She has not exercised **for** more than 30 years. She has not exercised **since** 1987.

3.1 *For* and *Since*

A Use the present perfect with *for* and a period of time (*20 years, three days, an hour, a long time*) to show the length of time of an action or event.	He has lived here **for 20 years**. They have studied this problem **for a long time**.
B Use the present perfect with *since* and a point in time in the past (*2009, last year, May 15*) to show when an action or event started.	Humans have kept bees **since 4000 BCE**. We have known about Colony Collapse Disorder **since the 1990s**.
C You can also use *since* before a clause.	I have eaten chocolate **since I was a child**.
D You can use *for* and *since* in negative sentences to show when something happened for the last time.	We **have not gone** to the moon **since** the 1970s. (The last time we went there was the 1970s.) There **has not been** an eclipse **for** five years. (The last eclipse was five years ago.)
E You can ask about periods of time with *How long . . . ?*	A **How long** have you lived here? B For four years. A **How long** has this been a problem? B Since the 1980s.

 **DATA FROM THE REAL WORLD**

In conversation, people often omit *for* with these verbs: *live, work, be, know* (a person), and *play*.	Say: "She's lived here a long time."
In conversation, people also often say *in* instead of *for* in negative statements.	Say: "I haven't exercised **in** years."
Always use *for* in writing.	Write: *She has lived here **for** a long time.* Write: *I have not exercised **for** years.*

▸ Grammar Application

Exercise 3.1 *For or Since?*

A Complete the paragraph from an article about another scientific mystery: people who have bad lifestyle habits but live very long lives. Circle the correct words.

Experts have agreed **(for)** / since many years that exercise, a good diet, and other
(1)
healthy lifestyle habits lead to a long life. However, why do some people with bad

lifestyle habits live long lives? Scientists do not know. Take Sarah Baines, for example.

She is 99 years old, and she is in good health. However, Sarah has had unhealthy habits

for / since her entire life. For example, Sarah has not exercised **for / since** she was a
(2)   (3)
child. She has smoked **for / since** 75 years, **for / since** she was a young woman.
(4)   (5)

Sarah also loves to eat. She has not been on a diet **for / since** 1952. She does not
(6)
like vegetables, and she has not eaten any salads **for / since** the last 40 years. She also
(7)
loves fatty food. She has eaten high calorie meals such as steak, potatoes with butter,

and ice cream almost every day **for / since** her entire life. In addition, Sarah does not
(8)
get much sleep. She has not gone to bed before midnight **for / since** she was 13 years
(9)
old. This lifestyle is incredibly unhealthy, and Sarah often does not feel well, but she is

stubborn and will not change.

B Pair Work Compare your lifestyle habits with Sarah's. Try to use *for* and *since*.
Tell a partner.

A *I've exercised three times a week since 2015. How about you?*
B *I haven't exercised for many years, but I've eaten healthy food since I was a child.*

A Complete the interview with Mel Green, who is 85 years old. Use the present perfect form of the verbs in parentheses. Write *for* or *since* before each time expression.

Andy Jones We're at the Corner Café, and I am speaking with the chef and owner, Mel Green. Mel is 85 years old today. He's in excellent health. He has a sharp mind, and he still works! Happy birthday, Mel! So, tell us a little about your long life. Have you lived here a long time?

Mel Green Well, I *'ve lived* (live) in California _______________ 50 years, (2)
and I _______________ (be) here in San (3)
Miguel _______________ 1972. (4)

Andy Jones How do you spend your days?

Mel Green I work! I _______________ (work) as a chef _______________ 1945. (5) (6)

Andy Jones How long _______________ you _______________ (own) the Corner Café? (7) (7)

Mel Green I _______________ (own) this restaurant _______________ 1980. (8) (9)

Andy Jones What else do you do?

Mel Green I love to learn languages. I _______________ (learn) Spanish, and I speak (10)
a little Chinese, too.

Andy Jones Wow!

Mel Green Yeah. Now I can speak Spanish with some of my customers.

Andy Jones What _______________ you _______________ (do) to stay healthy (11) (11)
_______________ so many years? (12)

Mel Green I _______________ (not do) anything special to stay healthy, but I (13)
_______________ (not eat) sweets _______________ I was in (14) (15)
my twenties.

Andy Jones What are some of your other lifestyle habits?

Mel Green I get up early. I _______________ (get) up at 5:00 a.m. every morning (16)
_______________ about 30 years. (17)

Andy Jones What about exercise?

Mel Green I _______________ (not exercise) _______________ a long time, but my (18) (19)
work keeps me active. I'm on my feet all day.

Andy Jones What are your recommendations for a long life?

Mel Green Keep busy!

B Find one place in the interview in A where you can omit *for* and circle it. Then find one place where you replace *for* with *in* and write *in* above *for*.

C Pair Work   Ask about your partner's life and answer questions about your life. Use the questions in A or your own ideas. Use the present perfect and time expressions with *for* and *since*.

A *How long have you lived here?*
B *I've lived here (for) a long time.*

A *How do you spend your days?*
B *I work. I've worked at a repair shop since last year.*

A *Do you work out at the gym?*
B *Yes, but I haven't worked out in/for months.*

4 Avoid Common Mistakes ⚠

1 **Use *never* in affirmative statements, not negative statements.**
Science has ~~ever~~ *never* been able to explain this.

2 **Use *ever* in negative statements, not affirmative statements.**
They have not ~~never~~ *ever* been able to explain this.

3 **Use the correct word order with adverbs and present perfect.**
~~Just he~~ *He* has *just* returned from his trip.

4 **Use *since* with a point in time in the past. Use *for* with a period of time.**
I have not exercised ~~since~~ *for* three years. I have not exercised ~~for~~ *since* last month.

5 **Do not use *for* or *since* with the simple present or present progressive.**
We ~~study~~ *have studied* this problem for 30 years. We ~~are studying~~ *have studied* this problem since the 1960s.

Editing Task

Find and correct eight more mistakes in this article about blushing.

Max is a drama major. Today, he is presenting a scene from a play in one of his classes. He ~~is taking~~ *has taken* acting classes since he was a child. He is acting, in front of people since many years, and he has been in the drama department since three years. He has ever felt uncomfortable on the stage. However, for some reason, Max just has

5   forgotten his lines, and his face has become red. Max is blushing.

Many people blush when they are embarrassed, but science has not never been able to explain why we blush. Researchers know how we blush: The nervous system causes the blood vessels in our face to dilate. This increases blood flow to the face, and this makes it look red. Researchers know for many years that teenagers blush more

10   than adults do, but still there has not been much research on blushing.

5 Academic Writing

Comparison-and-Contrast Writing

Brainstorm > Organize > Write > Edit

In Unit 10, you looked at an essay and brainstormed ideas in a Venn diagram. In this unit (11), you are going to look at topic sentences and start organizing your ideas to answer the prompt below.

Compare and contrast the whale shark and the tiger shark.

Exercise 5.1 Preparing to Write

Work with a partner. Ask and answer the questions.

1 Have you ever seen a shark? If so, describe the situation.
2 Do you enjoy nature programs about sharks? Why or why not?
3 What are your feelings about sharks? Have your views changed since you were a child?

Exercise 5.2 Comparing Topics

Read the information. Work with a partner. Ask and answer the questions.

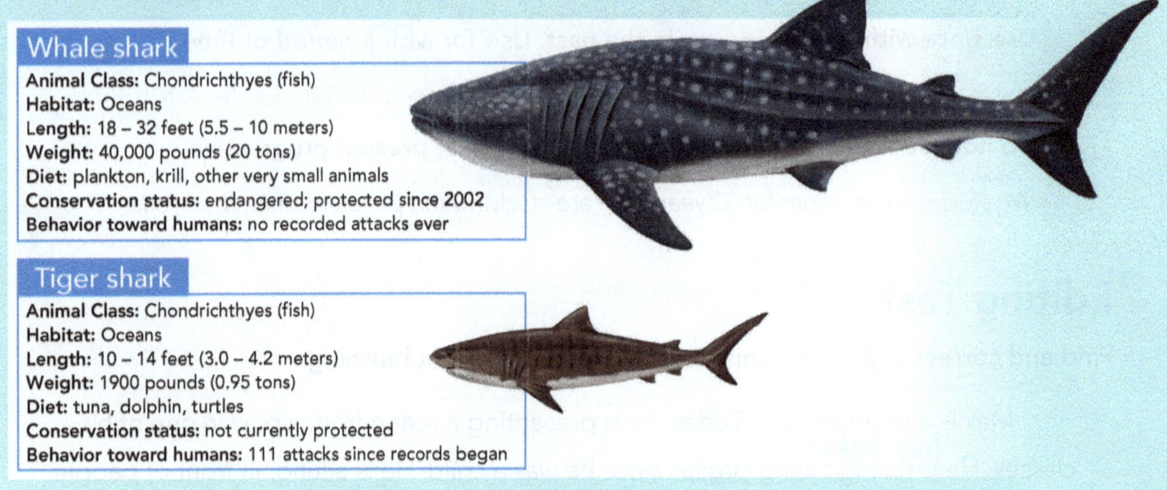

1 Which shark is smaller? Which shark is heavier?
2 Which shark eats large animals? Which shark eats small sea creatures?
3 Which shark is protected? How long has it been protected?
4 Which shark has never attacked humans? Which shark has attacked humans many times?

Exercise 5.3 Using a Venn Diagram

Work with a partner. Draw a Venn diagram to find similarities and differences between the sharks.

Topic Sentences

A **topic sentence** is usually the first sentence of a body paragraph. It introduces the main idea of the paragraph. The topic sentence is a general statement; it should not be too specific. The other sentences in the paragraph support it.

A general statement:

At first sight, the two species of squirrels are physically similar.

A general statement + the topics of the supporting sentences:

On the other hand, the two types of squirrels are different in **body size** and **weight**.

Exercise 5.4 Applying the Skill

The paragraph below is missing a topic sentence. Work with a partner. Choose two possible topic sentences for the paragraph. Explain your choices.

__________ Both honey bees and bumblebees live in colonies with a queen bee and worker bees. Neither honey bees nor bumblebees will attack people for no reason. However, like most animals, they will protect their nests and both kinds of bees will sting a person who comes too close.

    a Honey bees and bumblebees are similar in several ways.

    b Honey bees and bumblebees are similar in social structure and protective behavior.

    c People are often afraid of bees, but there is no reason to be.

My Writing

Exercise 5.5 Planning Your Body Paragraphs

Use your Venn diagram in Exercise 5.3 to answer the questions.

    1 How many similarities and differences are there between the sharks?

    2 Which body paragraph will be longer?

    3 What will the main idea of each body paragraph be?

Exercise 5.6 Writing Topic Sentences

Write two possible topic sentences for each of your body paragraphs:

- Write one general statement.
- Write one general statement + the topics of the supporting sentences.

12 Present Perfect Progressive

Cities

1 Grammar in the Real World

A What do you like about big cities? What don't you like? Read the online article about problems caused by the growth of cities. How is city life improving?

B Comprehension Check Answer the questions.

1 Why do people migrate to cities?
2 What happens when cities grow too fast?
3 Who has found solutions to some of these problems? What are the solutions?
4 What examples of green buildings and green belts does the article mention?

C Notice How does the writer express these ideas in the article? Write the sentences from the article.

1 Environmental problems are now worse than they were.

____

2 Urban planners started creating green belts in cities, and they are still doing this.

____

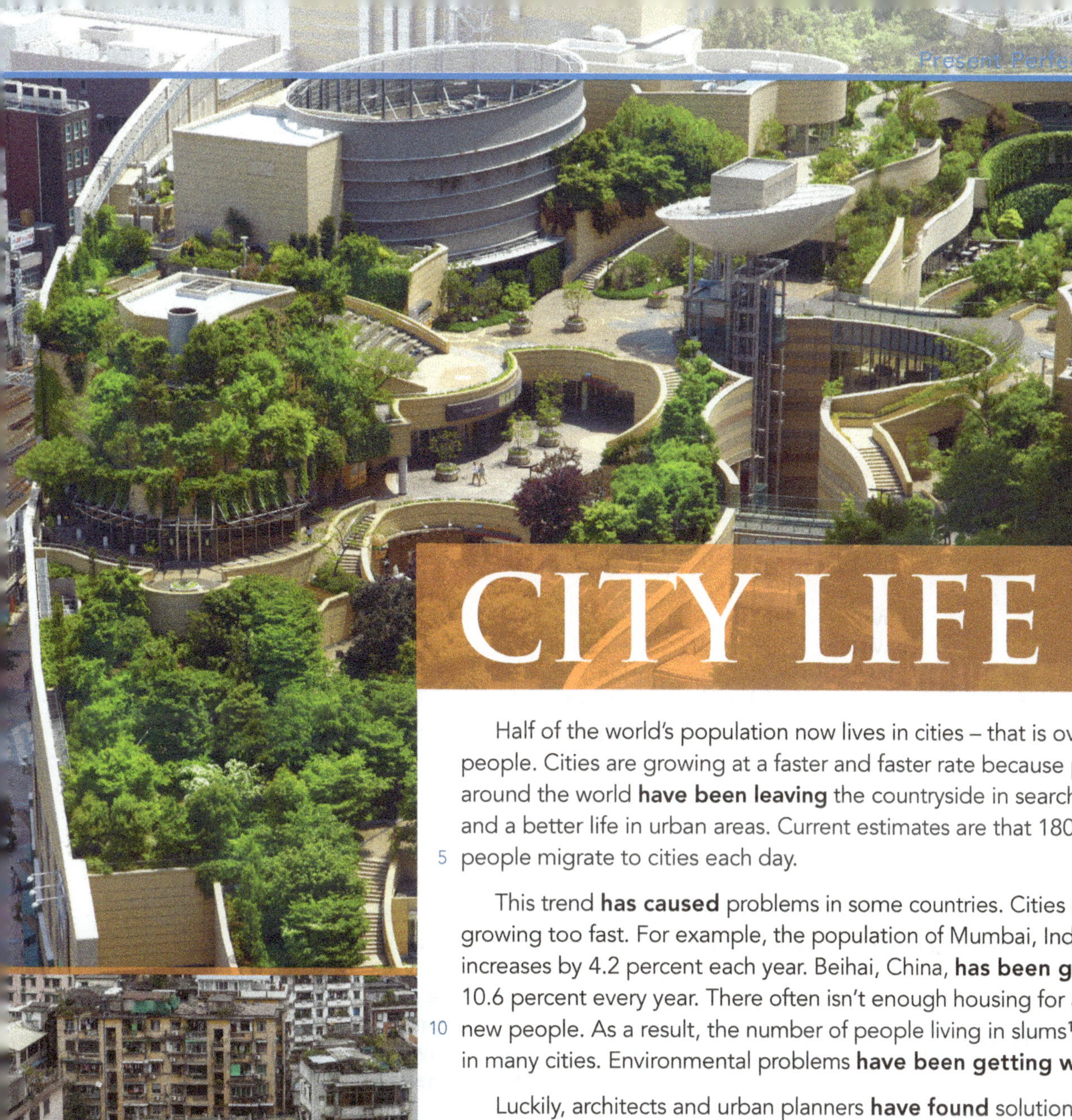

CITY LIFE

Half of the world's population now lives in cities – that is over 3 billion people. Cities are growing at a faster and faster rate because people around the world **have been leaving** the countryside in search of jobs and a better life in urban areas. Current estimates are that 180,000
5 people migrate to cities each day.

This trend **has caused** problems in some countries. Cities are growing too fast. For example, the population of Mumbai, India, increases by 4.2 percent each year. Beihai, China, **has been growing** by 10.6 percent every year. There often isn't enough housing for all of the
10 new people. As a result, the number of people living in slums[1] **has risen** in many cities. Environmental problems **have been getting worse**, too.

Luckily, architects and urban planners **have found** solutions to some of these problems. In many cities around the world, architects **have designed** "green" buildings. They use solar power, and they use
15 less water.

In addition, urban planners **have been creating** green belts in cities. Green belts are large pieces of natural land that offer fresh air and places for recreation for people in cities. Planners **have reclaimed**[2] green belts, too. In Seoul, South Korea, for example, planners uncovered a small river
20 in the middle of the city that was under a highway and built a park on both sides of the river.

These ideas **have not solved** all of the problems of big cities. There is still not enough housing, for example. Also, green buildings and green belts are too expensive for some cities. However, these
25 ideas **have made** life better for many people around the world.

[1]**slum:** a poor and crowded area of a city

[2]**reclaim:** take something back

Present Perfect Progressive

Grammar Presentation

The present perfect progressive usually shows something that started in the past and continues into the present time.

*Environmental problems **have been getting worse**.* (This started in the past and continues into the present time.)

2.1 Statements

Subject	*Has / Have* (+ Not)	*Been*	Verb + *-ing*	
I You We They	**have** **have not** **haven't**	**been**	**working** **migrating** **living**	here.
He She It	**has** **has not** **hasn't**			

Contractions		
I have	→	I**'ve**
You have	→	You**'ve**
We have	→	We**'ve**
They have	→	They**'ve**
He has	→	He**'s**
She has	→	She**'s**
It has	→	It**'s**

2.2 Yes / No Questions and Short Answers

Has / Have	Subject	*Been*	Verb + *-ing*
Have	I you we they	**been**	**working?**
Has	he / she / it		

Short Answers	
Yes, I **have**.	No, I **haven't**.
Yes, you **have**.	No, you **haven't**.
Yes, we **have**.	No, we **haven't**.
Yes, they **have**.	No, they **haven't**.
Yes, he / she / it **has**.	No, he / she / it **hasn't**.

2.3 Information Questions

Wh- Word	*Has / Have*	Subject	*Been*	Verb + *-ing*
Where **When** **Why** **How**	**have**	I you we they	**been**	**working?**
How long	**has**	he / she / it		

2.3 Information Questions *(continued)*

Wh- Word	Has / Have	Been	Verb + -ing	
What	**has**	**been**	**happening?**	
Who			**migrating**	to cities?

2.4 Using Present Perfect Progressive

A Use the present perfect progressive for actions and events that started in the past and continue into the present time or for actions that have just stopped.

*Environmental problems **have been getting** worse.*
*We**'ve been talking** about these problems for years.*

B Use the present perfect progressive with *for* and *since* to show the duration of an action or event.

Remember: Use *for* + a length of time and *since* + a specific time.

*I**'ve been living** here for a year.*
*He **hasn't been working** since last May.*

C Use the present perfect progressive for actions or events that are new, temporary, or changing.

*He**'s been staying** with a friend until he finds his own apartment.*
*We**'ve been talking** about the news all day.*

D Use the present perfect progressive with time expressions and adverbs, such as *this week / month / year*, *these days*, *nowadays*, *recently*, and *lately*.

*The city planners have been working hard **this week**.*
*A lot of people have been coming into the cities **lately**.*

Do not use the present perfect progressive with time expressions that describe finished time periods, such as *last year* or *three days ago*.

*The city **built** a lot of new housing last year.*
The city ~~has been building~~ a lot of new housing last year.

Exercise 2.1 Statements

Complete the blog post on city improvements. Use the present perfect progressive form of the verbs in parentheses.

Jen's Bay City Blog

New Report Has Good News on City Improvements
May 25

If you're like most Bay City residents these days, you ___*have not been feeling*___ (not feel) happy about garbage
(1)
pickup, safety, transportation, and the libraries for a long time. However,

a new report from the city this week has some good news. According

to the report, people ________________________________ (notice)
(2)
a lot of improvements lately. Here are just a few:

• The garbage collection service

________________________________ (pick) up
(3)
trash on time. In addition, the garbage collection service

________________________________ (not leave) garbage
(4)
around the pickup areas. I haven't noticed this one on my block, but I'm glad some of you have.

• People ________________________________ (feel) safer in the park at night. This is because
(5)
more police ________________________________ (patrol) the park after dark. This is one that
(6)
I've definitely experienced. I walked through the park the other night, and it felt much better.

• Public transportation ________________________________ (improve). People
(7)
________________________________ (not complain) about rude bus drivers lately. I guess
(8)
those lucky people aren't on my bus line!

• The libraries ________________________________ (stay) open on weeknights. As a result,
(9)
more families and working people ________________________________ (use) them. I
(10)
haven't been to the library recently, but I want to check this out.

What do you think? Leave a comment below with your opinion!

Exercise 2.2 Questions and Answers

A Complete an interview with a city planner. Use the present perfect progressive form of the verbs in parentheses in the questions. Write *for* or *since* in the answers.

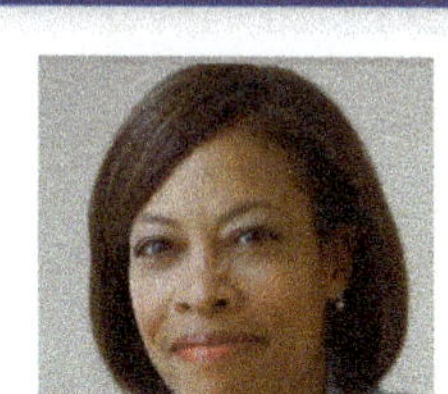

Bay City News Talks to . . . Lisa Daniel

By Pedro Martin

Lisa Daniel is the chairperson of the Bay City Planning Committee. Bay City News spoke to her about her job and the future of the city.

Q Lisa, how long __*have*__ (1) you __*been working*__ (1) (work) as a city planner?

A I've been doing this __*since*__ (2) 2003.

Q And __________ (3) you __________ (3) (work) on the city's planning committee for Bay City long?

A Not really. I've been working as a Bay City planner __________ (4) three years.

Q What __________ (5) the planning committee __________ (5) (focus) on lately?

A Well, we've been looking at environmentally friendly design __________ (6) last year.

Q That sounds interesting. __________ (7) the planning committee __________ (7) (develop) new green belts in our city?

A Yes. We've been increasing green belts around the city __________ (8) 2005. For example, we've been tearing down old, unused warehouses and turning the land into parks.

Q __________ (9) you __________ (9) (address) some of the environmental issues that all cities are facing?

A Yes. We've been traveling to other cities __________ (10) the past two years and studying environmental projects.

Q Where are there some interesting environmental projects these days?

A Well, Berlin, for example.

Q What __________ (11) (happen) there?

A Berlin has been doing some very interesting work adding trees and plants to the tops of buildings in the last few years.

Q Is Bay City growing like other big cities?

A Absolutely. Bay City's population has been increasing __________ (12) 1990. It has caused some problems, but we have been keeping housing costs low __________ (13) the city passed the new rent laws.

B Pair Work Make a list of some of the problems in your town or city. Then, with a partner, write five questions about the problems to ask a member of your town or city planning committee.

- high housing costs
- crowded public transportation
- pollution

Has the city been growing a lot recently?
What improvements have you been talking about?

3

Present Perfect Progressive or Present Perfect?

Grammar Presentation

The present perfect progressive focuses on an ongoing action or event, which may or may not be finished. The present perfect often suggests that the action or event is complete.	*Planners **have been reclaiming** green belts all over the city.* (They may still be doing this.) *Planners **have reclaimed** green belts all over the city.* (They are not doing this anymore.)

3.1 Present Perfect Progressive or Present Perfect?

A	Use the present perfect progressive for an action or event that started in the past and may or may not be finished yet.	*Urban planners **have been creating** green belts in cities.* (They aren't finished. They may still be doing this.)
	You can use the present perfect for an action or event that is finished.	*Urban planners **have created** green belts in cities.* (They have finished. The green belts are done.)
B	Use the present perfect progressive to focus more on the *activity* of the action or event.	***I've been writing** a paper on city planning.* (focus on the activity of writing)
	Use the present perfect to focus on the *results* of the action or event.	***I've written** a paper on city planning.* (focus on the completed paper)
C	Use the present perfect progressive for situations that are new or temporary (only for a short time).	*It takes time to find housing in the city, so **I've been staying** with my aunt and uncle.* (I am doing this for a short time only.)
	Use the present perfect for situations that are permanent (last for a long time).	*He**'s lived** in the same house for 30 years.* (This is a permanent situation.)
D	Use the present perfect, not progressive, when you say how much or how many times something has happened.	*The planners **have visited** Berlin three times.* *They **have built** three green apartments in Brooklyn.*
E	With *get, go, increase, live, study,* and *work,* you can often use either form. The progressive suggests the action or event is new or temporary.	*We **have lived** here for 20 years.* *We **have been living** here for two months.*

3.1 Present Perfect Progressive or Present Perfect? *(continued)*

F Do not use the progressive form with stative verbs such as *be, believe, hate, know, like,* and *understand.*

They *have known* about the problem for many years.

They have ~~been knowing~~ about the problem for many years.

DATA FROM THE REAL WORLD

The present perfect is much more common than the present perfect progressive, especially in writing. When you have a choice of forms in writing, use the present perfect if you need to sound more formal.

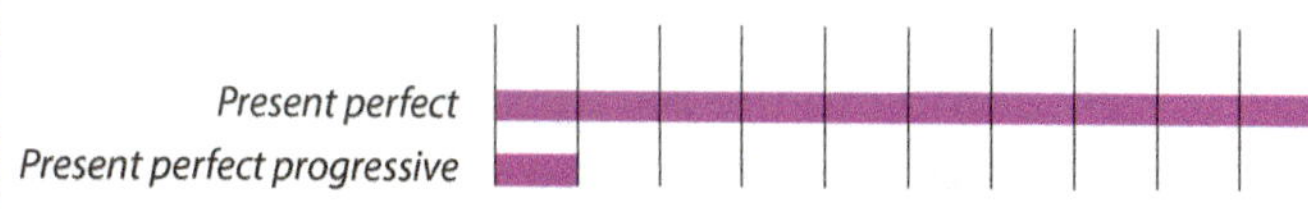

Less formal: *I've been living* here since 2008.
More formal: *I have lived* here since 2008.

Grammar Application

Exercise 3.1 Present Perfect Progressive or Present Perfect?

A Check (✓) the sentences that you can rewrite in the present perfect progressive. Then do B with a partner.

1 Environmental problems in our city have increased. ☑

____

2 For example, air pollution has been a big problem. ☐

____

3 We have known about the causes of air pollution for many years. ☐

____

4 Studies have shown that green belts reduce air pollution. ☐

____

5 Planners have talked about creating more green belts in our city. ☐

____

6 They have studied the effects of green belts in other cities for the past year. ☐

____

7 For example, planners have reclaimed two green belts in New York City. ☐

____

8 As a result, air quality has improved by 10 percent. ☐

____

B **Pair Work** Compare your answers in A with a partner. Discuss the reason
for each of your answers. Then rewrite the sentences you checked. Use the
present perfect progressive.

A *You can rewrite number 1 in the present perfect progressive.
"Environmental problems have been increasing."*

B *Right. But you can't rewrite number 2 because be is . . .*

Exercise 3.2 Present Perfect, Present Perfect Progressive, or Both?

A Complete the paragraphs about a student's description of her neighborhood.
Write the form of the verbs in parentheses – either the present perfect or the
present perfect progressive.

There have been a lot of changes in my
neighborhood in the last year. Some changes
____*have been*____ (be) good. For example,
(1)
four new restaurants ________________
(2)
(open). The city ________________ (build) a
(3)
new children's playground, and it should be
ready next month. They ________________
(4)
also ________________ (build) some green
(4)
apartments – they finished them six months
ago. A lot of new people ________________ (move) in already.
(5)

Unfortunately, some things ________________ (get) worse. About six stores
(6)
________________ (close) down, just on my street. Two of my favorite stores
(7)
________________ (go) out of business. Also, crime ________________ (increase).
(8)   (9)
Thieves________________ (break) into the deli on my street twice in the last
(10)
six months. I guess both good and bad things can happen at the same time.

B Now listen and check your answers. You can use both present perfect progressive and the
present perfect for two of the verbs in A. Which ones?

C **Pair Work** Compare your neighborhood with the one in A. Talk with a partner
about the good changes and the bad ones. Use the present perfect or the present perfect
progressive.

A *We've had some good changes in my neighborhood. For example, the city has built a new
park. How about you?*

B *The city has started a farmers' market right in my neighborhood. We've been getting great
fresh fruit and vegetables straight from the farm right down the street.*

 4 Avoid Common Mistakes ⚠ 

1   **Use *have* when forming the present perfect progressive.**
have
They been creating green belts in cities.

2   **Use *has* with singular third-person subjects (*he, she, it*). Use *have* with other subjects.**
has
This city ~~have~~ been getting more expensive in the last few years.

3   **Use the present perfect with stative verbs. Do not use the present perfect progressive.**
known
Experts have ~~been knowing~~ about the problem for many years.

4   **Use the present perfect progressive, not the present progressive, with *for* and *since*.**
have been
Environmental problems ~~are~~ getting worse here for many years.

Editing Task

Find and correct eight more mistakes in this interview with a green architect.

have
Kyle Jones   Urban planners and architects ∧ been remodeling city buildings to make them more energy efficient. This been making life in our city kinder to the environment. It have also been making life healthier for city residents. Today, we are asking the architect Vinh Hu about his work. Mr. Hu, how long you been designing green buildings?

5   **Vinh Hu**   Oh, a long time. We're designing these buildings for almost 20 years. We've been believing for a long time that green buildings are an important way to improve city life. We've also been knowing for a long time that most people prefer green apartments. In the future, no one will want to live in a building that isn't environmentally friendly.

10   **Kyle Jones**   What you been working on lately?

Vinh Hu   We've been building two new apartments on Murray Street.

Kyle Jones   Yes, I am watching those apartments go up for a while. What makes them green?

Vinh Hu   They use solar energy for heat.

Kyle Jones   Very interesting! Thank you, Mr. Hu.

Comparison-and-Contrast Writing

Brainstorm > Organize > Write > Edit

In Unit 11, you studied topic sentences and ways to compare topics. In this unit (12), you are going to write the body paragraphs of an essay for the prompt below, and then revise and edit it.

Compare and contrast the whale shark and the tiger shark.

My Writing

Exercise 5.1 Writing Your First Draft

Read the introduction (paragraph 1) and conclusion (paragraph 4) of an essay that compares whale sharks and tiger sharks. Write two body paragraphs to complete the essay. Write about the similarities in paragraph 2. Write about the differences in paragraph 3. Use your Venn diagram and your My Writing work from Unit 11.

All Sharks Are Not the Same

(1)   For many people a shark fin in the water at the beach is a scary sight. Perhaps that is one reason that humans kill 100 million sharks a year. However, there are 440 species of sharks, and many of these are quite different in size, diet, and behavior. In fact, sharks are an important part of the ocean's food chain, and fewer sharks in our oceans is a problem, not a benefit. The whale shark and the tiger shark are two examples of shark species found in the major oceans of the world. Understanding their similarities and differences may help us enjoy the ocean safely and maintain the health of our planet.

(4)   Overall, it is clear that the whale shark is a much larger animal, but it is a gentle giant, whereas the smaller tiger shark is a hungry meat eater. However, both animals play important parts in the ocean environment. For example, tiger sharks keep the oceans clean by eating dead whales and fish. As a result, people and nations should cooperate to protect these and other species of shark.

Exercise 5.2 Revising Your Ideas

1 Work with a partner. Use the questions to give feedback on your partner's paragraphs.

- Which of your partner's ideas seem the strongest to you?

- Which of your partner's ideas need to be explained more clearly?

- What could your partner add or remove to make the paragraphs stronger and easier to understand?

2 Use the feedback from your partner to revise your paragraphs.

Exercise 5.3 Editing Your Writing

Use the checklist to review and edit your paragraphs.

Did you answer the writing prompt completely?	
Did you use a topic sentence to introduce each body paragraph?	
Did you write about the similarities in the first body paragraph?	
Did you write about the differences in the second body paragraph?	
Did you combine any sentences to add variety, avoid repetition, and show clear relationships between topics?	

Exercise 5.4 Editing Your Grammar

Use the checklist below to review and edit the grammar in your paragraphs.

Did you use the present perfect and simple past correctly?	
Did you use adverbs with the present perfect correctly?	
Did you avoid the common mistakes in the charts on pages 131, 145, and 157?	

Exercise 5.5 Writing Your Final Draft

Apply the feedback and edits from Exercises 5.2 to 5.4 to write the final draft of your paragraphs.

Adjectives

A Good Workplace

1 Grammar in the Real World

A What makes a good workplace? Read the poster about workplace rights. What are some rights that workers have?

B Comprehension Check **Answer the questions.**

1 Why is it important to know your rights on the job?
2 What are two fair treatment rights that workers have?
3 What are two safety rights that workers have?
4 Who do you report unsafe conditions to?

C Notice **Find the sentences in the poster and complete them.**

1 _________________ employers follow the laws.

2 You have a right to _________________ treatment on the job.

3 You also have a right to a workplace that is not _________________ .

4 You have the right not to feel _________________ or _________________ at work.

Look at the words you wrote. Which words do they describe?

KNOW YOUR RIGHTS ON THE JOB

In the United States, you have **legal** rights to **fair** treatment in the workplace. You also have rights to safe conditions at work. **Ethical**[1] employers follow the laws, but some employers do not, so you should know what your rights are on the job.

FAIRNESS

5   You have a right to **fair** treatment on the job. Women, men, **young** people, and **old** people all have **equal** rights. Discrimination is **illegal**. For example, women and men have the right to **equal** pay for the **same** job.

    You also have a right to a workplace that is not **hostile**.[2] If your co-workers treat you badly because of your race or the place you come from, this is **illegal**.
10   You have the right not to feel **embarrassed** or **humiliated**[3] at work.

    Report **hostile** behavior at work to the Equal Employment Opportunity Commission (EEOC). It is your **legal** right.

SAFETY

    Workers have the right to a **safe** workplace. These are some examples of
15 **unsafe** or **unhealthy** conditions.

- working near **toxic**[4] chemicals
- working with **dangerous** machines
- **slippery** floors
- **sharp** objects
- **loud noise**

    You have the right to **free training** courses on the **safety** issues in your
20 workplace. For example, you have the right to get training on how to use **dangerous** machines.

    If you see **dangerous** or **unsafe** conditions at work, report them to your supervisor or the Occupational Safety and Heath Administration (OSHA). Your company cannot fire you for reporting problems. Everyone has the right
25 to a **safe**, **fair** workplace.

---

[1]**ethical:** good, correct, moral
[2]**hostile:** unfriendly, showing strong dislike
[3]**humiliate:** make you feel ashamed, lose respect for yourself
[4]**toxic:** poisonous

Grammar Presentation

Adjectives describe nouns – people, places, things, and ideas.

Ethical employers follow the laws.
(*Ethical* describes *employers*.)

Discrimination is **illegal.**
(*Illegal* describes *discrimination*.)

2.1 Using Adjectives

A Adjectives usually go before nouns, not after.

Women and men have the right to **equal** pay.
Women and men have the right to ~~pay equal~~.
Workers have **legal** rights to **fair** treatment.
Workers have ~~rights legal~~ to ~~treatment fair~~.

B However, adjectives can go after *be* or after linking verbs like *become, look, feel, sound, smell, taste, seem,* and *appear.*

My company *is* an **ethical** employer.
That job **looks safe**.
The boss **seems nice**.

C Adjectives do not have plural forms. Do not add *-s.*

This is your **legal** right. These are your **legal** rights.
These are your ~~legals~~ rights.
Ethical employers create an **ethical** workplace.
~~Ethicals~~ employers create an ethical workplace.

D Use *an* (not *a*) before an adjective that starts with a vowel sound with a singular count noun.

An ethical employer means **an e**thical workplace.
~~A~~ ethical employer means . . .
Don't use **an u**nsafe machine without training.
Don't use ~~a~~ unsafe machine . . .

2.2 Using Nouns as Adjectives

A You can use some nouns as adjectives before other nouns.

Do not make these plural.

Workers have **safety** rights. They also have **health** rights.
They also have ~~healths rights~~.

B To describe the age or duration of a noun, you can use expressions like *15-year-old* or *six-month* as adjectives before the noun. Notice that the age and time nouns (e.g., *year*) are always singular, never plural.

Fifteen-year-old teenagers work in some restaurants.
~~Fifteen years old~~ teenagers work in some restaurants.
I want to take a **six-month** course in green office design.
I want to take a ~~six months course~~.

2.3 Using More Than One Adjective

Opinion	Size	Quality	Age	Shape	Color	Origin	Material	Type
beautiful nice	big long	free safe	old young	round square	blue red	Canadian Thai	cotton leather	evening training

When you use two or more adjectives before a noun, use the order in the chart above, from left to right.	AGE ORIGIN NOUN *She drives an* **old** **Japanese** *car* *to work.* COLOR MATERIAL NOUN *He wears* **black** **leather** *boots* *to work.* OPINION AGE TYPE NOUN *There's an* **interesting** **new** **safety** *course* *at work.*

Adjectives: Order Before Nouns: See page A9.

Grammar Application

Exercise 2.1 Word Order

A Rewrite these sentences. Use *be* + adjective.

1 Some factories have unhappy workers. Some workers __*are unhappy*__ .

2 They earn low wages. Their wages __________________ .

3 They have bad working conditions. Their working conditions __________________ .

4 They work long hours. Their hours __________________ .

B Rewrite these sentences. Put the adjective before the noun. Use *a* or *an* where needed.

1 The workers' pay at this company is equal. At this company, the workers get __*equal pay*__ .

2 The bosses are ethical. They are __________________ .

3 The training courses are free. They are __________________ .

4 Our work day is eight hours. We have __________________ .

Exercise 2.2 Using Adjectives

A Listen to Annie telling Nick about her new job. Then complete the conversation with the words in the box.

beige	cotton	great	leather	~~new~~	sport
black	fantastic	interesting	long	running	ugly

Nick I hear you have a ___**new**___ job.
(1)

Annie Yes. I'm a technician at PC Emporium.

Nick That's great. What are your hours?

Annie We work 40 hours a week.

Nick And do you get a vacation?

Annie Yes. Even new employees get a
______________________ vacation – two weeks.
(2)

Nick That sounds ______________________ ! Do they
(3)
train you?

Annie Sure. I'm taking an ______________________ training
(4)
course right now. It goes for three days.

Nick Everything sounds ______________________ !
(5)

Annie Not everything. We have to wear an ______________________ uniform. I wear
(6)
______________________ pants and a ______________________ shirt. The pants are
(7) (8)
______________________ and the shirt is ______________________ . Oh, and black shoes.
(9) (10)

Nick ______________________ shoes?
(11)

Annie No! ______________________ shoes.
(12)

B Listen again and complete the paragraph about the conversation. Sometimes, more than one answer is possible.

Annie has a ___**40-hour**___ work week. She gets a ______________________ vacation
(1) (2)
each year. Right now, she's taking a ______________________ training course. She
(3)
wears ______________________ ______________________ pants, a ______________________
(4) (4) (5)
______________________ shirt, and ______________________ ______________________ shoes to work.
(5) (6) (6)

Exercise 2.3 Adjective Endings

DATA FROM THE REAL WORLD

Here are some common adjective endings with the most common adjectives that use them.

-able	-ful	-ial	-ic	-ical	-ive	-ous
comfortable	wonderful	social	public	medical	expensive	serious
available	beautiful	special	basic	political	positive	ridiculous
reasonable	awful	financial	economic	physical	active	dangerous

A Write the correct adjective endings in the opinion column about working conditions.

On average, American workers get only

two weeks of paid vacation. I think that is ridicu l **ous** .
(1)

There are many beauti_____ places in the United States,
(2)

but no one has time to see them. Vacation time is more

reason_____ in a lot of other countries. For example, the French get about 37 paid
(3)

vacation days, and the Koreans get about 25. American companies give short

vacations for econom_____ reasons. It is expens_____ for the company to pay
(4)   (5)

workers for time off, but short vacations don't help give

employees a posit_____ attitude about their workplaces.
(6)

The working hours in the United States are another

problem. Some Americans have a 50-hour work week. Some

say they do not have time for a soc_____ life. A long work
(7)

week can also be danger_____ . If you work all the time, you
(8)

can have med_____ problems. This is a seri_____ issue.
(9)   (10)

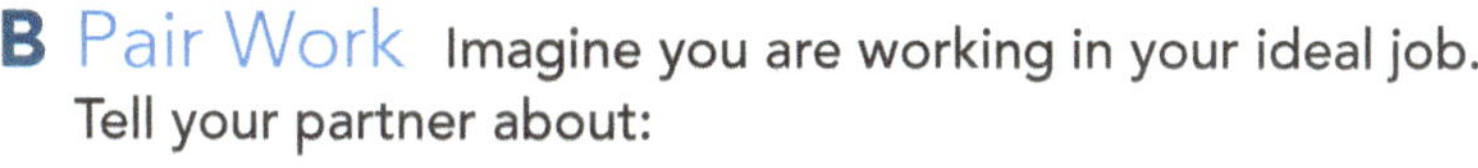

B Pair Work Imagine you are working in your ideal job.
Tell your partner about:

- what you can wear
- the hours you work
- how much vacation you have
- what your co-workers are like

In my ideal job, I don't wear a uniform. I wear casual clothes, like my favorite black running shoes and a sweatshirt. I have a 40-hour work week with no overtime, and I get a four-week vacation every year.

3 More About Adjectives

Grammar Presentation

3.1 Adjectives Ending in -ed and -ing

A Use *-ed* adjectives to describe how a person feels.	*I'm **interested** in workers' rights.* *I get **bored** when I work by myself.*
B Use *-ing* adjectives to say what something or someone is like.	*My new job is **interesting.*** *Working in an office is **boring**.*

A	You usually need a noun or pronoun after an adjective.	*I have a black shirt and a beige* shirt */ a beige* one. *I have a black shirt* and a beige. *I wear nice clothes to work, but I don't wear expensive* clothes */ expensive* ones. *I don't wear expensive.*
B	Adjectives follow a measurement noun (*years, feet,* etc.).	*There are* eighteen-year-old *workers in some of the factories.* *That ladder is over ten* feet high.
C	Adjectives can follow the pronouns *something, anything,* and *nothing.*	*I want to wear* something special *for my first day at work.* *Are you doing* anything interesting *this weekend?*
D	Adjectives can follow the verb *make* + an object.	OBJECT ADJECTIVE *My boss* makes me nervous. OBJECT ADJECTIVE *Chemicals* make some people sick.
E	Do not use these adjectives before a noun: *afraid, alike, alive, alone, asleep, awake, aware.* They usually come after the verb *be.*	*The workers were all still* alive *after the factory explosion.* *He's not* asleep. *He's* awake. *I'm* afraid *of heights.*

DATA FROM THE REAL WORLD

Research shows that these are some of the most common pairs of adjectives ending in *-ing* and *-ed.*

amazing	amazed		exciting	excited
annoying	annoyed		frustrating	frustrated
boring	bored		interesting	interested
confusing	confused		relaxing	relaxed
depressing	depressed		surprising	surprised
embarrassing	embarrassed		worrying	worried

Grammar Application

Exercise 3.1 -ed or -ing?

A Complete the conversations. Choose the correct word.

1 A Have you ever felt __(embarrassed) / embarrassing__ by a joke that someone told at work or at school?

B Yes, I have. Someone joked about my accent. That was __annoyed / annoying__ .

2 A Are you __interested / interesting__ in workers' rights? Or do you think it's a __bored / boring__ issue?

B No, it's a __fascinated / fascinating__ subject. I'm not __bored / boring__ by it at all.

3 A Are you __annoyed / annoying__ by different kinds of discrimination at work?

B Yes, of course. I'm __surprised / surprising__ that it still happens. It's a __depressed / depressing__ situation.

4 A Is your job ever __relaxed / relaxing__ ?

B No, but I don't think work is supposed to be __relaxed / relaxing__ . My job is sometimes __excited / exciting__ , and I like that.

5 A Did you ever wear an __embarrassing / embarrassed__ uniform to school or to work?

B No. I wore a uniform, but it wasn't __embarrassed / embarrassing__ because I liked it.

B Pair Work Practice the conversations with a partner. Then practice them again. This time, give your own answers.

Exercise 3.2 Adjective Patterns

Complete the conversations with *one / ones* and the words in parentheses.

1 A Which pants should I wear, the blue pants or the __brown ones__ ?
(brown)

B The brown pants look better.

2 A How's your job?

B It's OK. There are some nice co-workers and some _______________ .
(less friendly)

3 A Joe has such an interesting job! He always has funny stories to tell.

B That's true. We only have _______________ .
(boring)

4 A Who goes to your restaurant?

B Most of the customers are young professionals, but there are _______________ , too.
(older)

5 A I work for an ethical employer.

B You're lucky. I work for an _______________ .
(unfair)

A Correct the mistakes in these sentences. You may need to add or change words.

1 Many ~~aware~~ people are _aware_ of gender, race, and ethnic discrimination in the workplace.

2 However, many aware people are not of size and age discrimination in the workplace.

3 For example, if a thin woman and an overweight woman apply for the same job, the thin often gets the job.

4 If a tall man and a short man try to get a promotion, the tall often gets the promotion.

5 A recent survey showed that the average Chief Executive Officer (CEO) in the United States is 6 tall feet.

6 Another survey showed that only 3 percent of CEOs in the United States are less than tall 5 feet, 7 inches.

7 Many older afraid workers are of age discrimination.

8 An older employee with a lot of experience can make nervous a young boss.

9 Some laws make illegal age discrimination.

10 For example, after you are 40 years, a law called the Age Discrimination Employment Act protects you.

B Pair Work Have you heard about someone who experienced discrimination? Tell a partner about it.

A Add adjectives to the questions below.

1 Do you want a job where you do something ___________________ every day?

2 In your job, do you ever do anything ___________________ ?

3 Have you met anyone ___________________ at work recently?

4 Did anything ___________________ happen at your job recently?

B Group Work Ask and answer your questions in A. Give extra information in your answer.

A *Do you want a job where you do something exciting every day?*

B *No, actually, I don't. I don't have the energy for that. I want a quiet job where I don't do anything exciting or dangerous.*

Exercise 3.5 Using *Make* + Object + Adjective

A Answer the questions about work or school. Use the words in the box or your own ideas to help you answer the questions.

chemicals	early mornings	interesting work	long vacations
dangerous machines	an ethical boss	late nights	loud noise
discrimination	friendly co-workers	long hours	uncomfortable chairs

1 What makes you happy in the workplace?

____

2 What things about your job make you unhappy?

____

3 What workplace situations make you worried?

____

4 Has anything in your workplace ever made you sick?

____

B Pair Work Discuss your ideas in A with a partner.

4 Avoid Common Mistakes ⚠

1 **Notice the correct spelling of adjectives ending in *-ful* (not *-full*).**
stressful
She has a ~~stressfull~~ job.

2 **Don't confuse these common verbs and adjectives: *interest ≠ interested, relax ≠ relaxed, stress ≠ stressed, worry ≠ worried.***
worried
I'm ~~worry~~ about my job.

3 **Be careful with adjectives that describe ages and length of time before a noun.**
Fifteen-year-old
~~Fifteen-years-old~~ teenagers work in some restaurants.

4 **Remember to put opinion adjectives before others in a list before a noun.**
wonderful little
We work at a ~~little wonderful~~ shop on the weekends.

Editing Task

Find and correct eight more mistakes in this blog on work–life balance.

Balancing Work Life and Personal Life

interested
I have a very busy life. I have a fun job, and I am ~~interest~~ in my work. My boss is fair, and I work for an ethical company. I have friends. My life sounds perfect, right? However, I work a 60-hours week. I can't get all my work done during the day, so I take it home. I do not spend much time with my husband and our little beautiful four-years-old daughter. I also do not see my wonderfull friends. This makes me feel very stress. I am never relax. I know my friends
5 and family are worry about me.

I think I have a problem. I need some balance between my work life and my personal life. I know there are usefull articles with tips for balancing your life. The problem is, I do not have the time to read them!

5 Academic Writing

Argumentative Writing

Brainstorm > Organize > Write > Edit

In this writing cycle (Units 13-15), you will write an argumentative essay for the prompt below. In this unit (13), you will look at an essay and how to develop strong arguments. Then you will start brainstorming and organizing your ideas.

Do you agree or disagree with the following statement? "The fashion industry is harmful to society and the environment." Use reasons and examples to support your answer.

Exercise 5.1 Preparing to Write

Work with a partner. Discuss the questions.

1 What kind of clothes do people usually wear in the workplace? Describe them.
2 Are you interested in fashion? How often do you go shopping for new clothes?
3 Which is more important to you: low price, high quality, or the most current fashion?
4 In what countries are most clothes manufactured? What are the factories like there?

Exercise 5.2 Focusing on Vocabulary

Read the definitions. Then complete the sentences with the correct form of the words in bold.

> **conditions** (n) the physical environment where people live or work
>
> **import** (v) to buy or bring in products from another country for business; (n) a product bought by one country from another
>
> **massive** (adj) very large in size or amount
>
> **multinational** (adj) referring to a business or company that has offices, stores, or factories in several countries
>
> **offshore** (adj) located in another country
>
> **textile** (n) cloth or fabric that is made by weaving (crossing threads under and over each other)

1 Some large ___________ companies have branches in more than a hundred countries.

2 The workers at that factory are well-paid, and their ___________ are safe and comfortable.

3 Egypt produces cotton ___________, which are used to make bedsheets.

4 One company built a ___________ factory that produced 100,000 shirts a month.

5 Many manufacturers use ___________ factories because labor is cheaper in other countries.

6 We ___________ fabric from China, and then we sew and finish the shirts here.

Offshore Production

The world's consumption of fashion is huge. To give just one example, the United States alone **imported** almost 122 billion dollars' worth of **textiles** in 2014. As consumption has risen, prices
5 have fallen. Today, a hand-finished shirt may cost as little as five dollars. To make clothes at these low prices, companies have to keep costs down. They use **offshore** production to do this. Large **multinational** companies outsource[1] their
10 production to developing countries like Egypt or Cambodia, where workers are paid much less than in developed countries. Supporters of outsourcing claim that it helps local economies, but I believe it is harmful for two main reasons.

15 First, overseas workers usually receive very low wages. These workers, many of them women and children, often work 14 hours a day and earn less than a hundred dollars a month. One study of 15 countries found that textile workers earned
20 less than 40% of the money they needed to live on each month. In some countries this figure is even lower. Also, most workers are paid by the piece. This means they might earn only a few cents for making a dress that sells for hundreds of
25 dollars in the United States or Europe. Such low wages are wrong and unfair. As Priya Kapoor, a human rights researcher in Delhi, says, "Garment[2] workers in countries like India and Bangladesh can't afford to pay their basic needs like food and
30 health care. We need to establish a fair wage for the work they do."

The second problem with outsourcing is that working **conditions** in many offshore factories are uncomfortable and unsafe. It is a fact that worker-

35 protection laws like those in developed nations either do not exist or are often not followed. As a result, workers are exposed to chemicals, dust, and unsafe levels of noise from sewing machines. I saw this myself when I visited a clothing factory
40 in Bangladesh in 2015. The noise was so loud that I had to cover my ears. Moreover, factory buildings are often unsafe, and horrible accidents happen. For example, the whole world was shocked in 2012 when a fire that broke out at a
45 garment factory in Dhaka, Bangladesh killed 117 people and injured 200.

I realize some experts, like the economist David Schneider, say that outsourcing benefits local economies by providing jobs at higher
50 wages than local workers can make by working in agriculture. Supporters of outsourcing point out that people in developing countries often line up to take jobs in multinational factories. These arguments may be correct, but in my opinion
55 they do not justify the low wages and dangerous conditions found in many overseas factories today. If multinationals are going to continue to benefit from low costs by using overseas suppliers, I believe they should contribute a
60 much larger share of their **massive** profits to correcting these problems and improving social conditions in the countries where they are located—starting today.

---

[1] **outsource** (v) to have work done by another company, often in another country, rather than in your own company

[2] **garment** (n) a piece of clothing

Read the article. Work with a partner. Ask and answer the questions.

1 According to the article, how do companies reduce the cost of making clothes?
2 What is one difference between offshore factories and those in more developed countries?
3 What two things does the writer think that multinational companies should do overseas?

Complete the tasks. Compare your answers with a partner's.

1 Find and underline the writer's point of view in paragraph 1.

2 How many reasons does the writer mention to support this point of view? How many supporting paragraphs are in the essay?

3 Circle four adjectives that describe wages in paragraph 2. How is the last adjective different from the first three? How do these adjectives support the writer's thesis?

4 Underline the topic sentence in paragraph 3. Highlight two examples that support the main idea.

5 What is the purpose of paragraph 4?

Developing Strong Arguments

In an argumentative essay, a writer states a clear point of view and gives evidence to build an argument and lead the reader to a conclusion.

An argument is an opinion with reasons and evidence to show that the opinion is valid. Successful arguments help the reader understand and recognize the value of the writer's opinion.

Writers use many types of evidence to support arguments, including facts, statistics, expert opinions, quotations, examples, and personal experience.

Work with a partner. Use the reading on page 171 to make notes in the chart below. Include the type of evidence (fact, statistic, etc.) in parentheses.

Main argument:	
Reason 1:	**Reason 2:**
Evidence: (1) (2) (3) (4)	Evidence: (5) (6) (7)
Concluding paragraph Evidence: (8) Final comment:	

My Writing

Exercise 5.6 Brainstorming Ideas and Evidence

Review the writing prompt on page 170. Work with a partner to complete the tasks.

1 Brainstorm a list of arguments *for and against* the statement.
2 Decide if you will argue *for or against* the statement.
3 Brainstorm at least two main reasons for your argument.
4 Discuss possible evidence to support each reason.

Exercise 5.7 Organizing Ideas and Evidence

Organize your ideas and evidence from Exercise 5.6 in the chart below. Use at least three different types of evidence (facts, statistics, expert opinions, quotations, examples, or personal experience).

Main argument:	
Reason 1:	**Reason 2:**
Evidence (1):	Evidence (1):
Evidence (2):	Evidence (2):
Evidence (3):	Evidence (3):

Exercise 5.8 Writing a Paragraph

Choose one of the reasons in your chart and write a paragraph. Include a topic sentence and evidence to support the reason.

Using Descriptive Adjectives

Descriptive adjectives make your writing more specific, clearer, and more accurate.

A **horrible** accident is more specific than an accident.

I believe outsourcing is **harmful** is clearer than I disagree with outsourcing.

A **comfortable** workplace is more specific than a good workplace.

For **financial** reasons is more accurate than for many reasons.

Exercise 5.9 Applying the Skill

Revise your paragraph. Add or replace at least five adjectives to make your writing more specific, more accurate, and clearer.

Adverbs of Manner and Degree

Learn Quickly!

1 Grammar in the Real World

ACADEMIC
WRITING

Argumentative
writing

A Is language learning easy or hard for you? Read the online article about language learning strategies. What are some ways to learn a language, both inside and outside the classroom?

B Comprehension Check Answer the questions.

1 What is a learning strategy?
2 What are two strategies that help you do well in class?
3 Why is it a good idea to get a good night's sleep before a test?
4 What are two strategies that help you communicate?

C Notice Find the sentences in the article and complete them.

1 In class, listen ______________________ and take notes.

2 Make a list of new words and study the list ______________________ .

3 Also, do not stay up ______________________ the night before a test.

4 If you do not understand a word or phrase, ______________________ ask the person to explain.

Do the words in your answers describe people, or do they describe how an action happens?

Learn to Learn a LANGUAGE

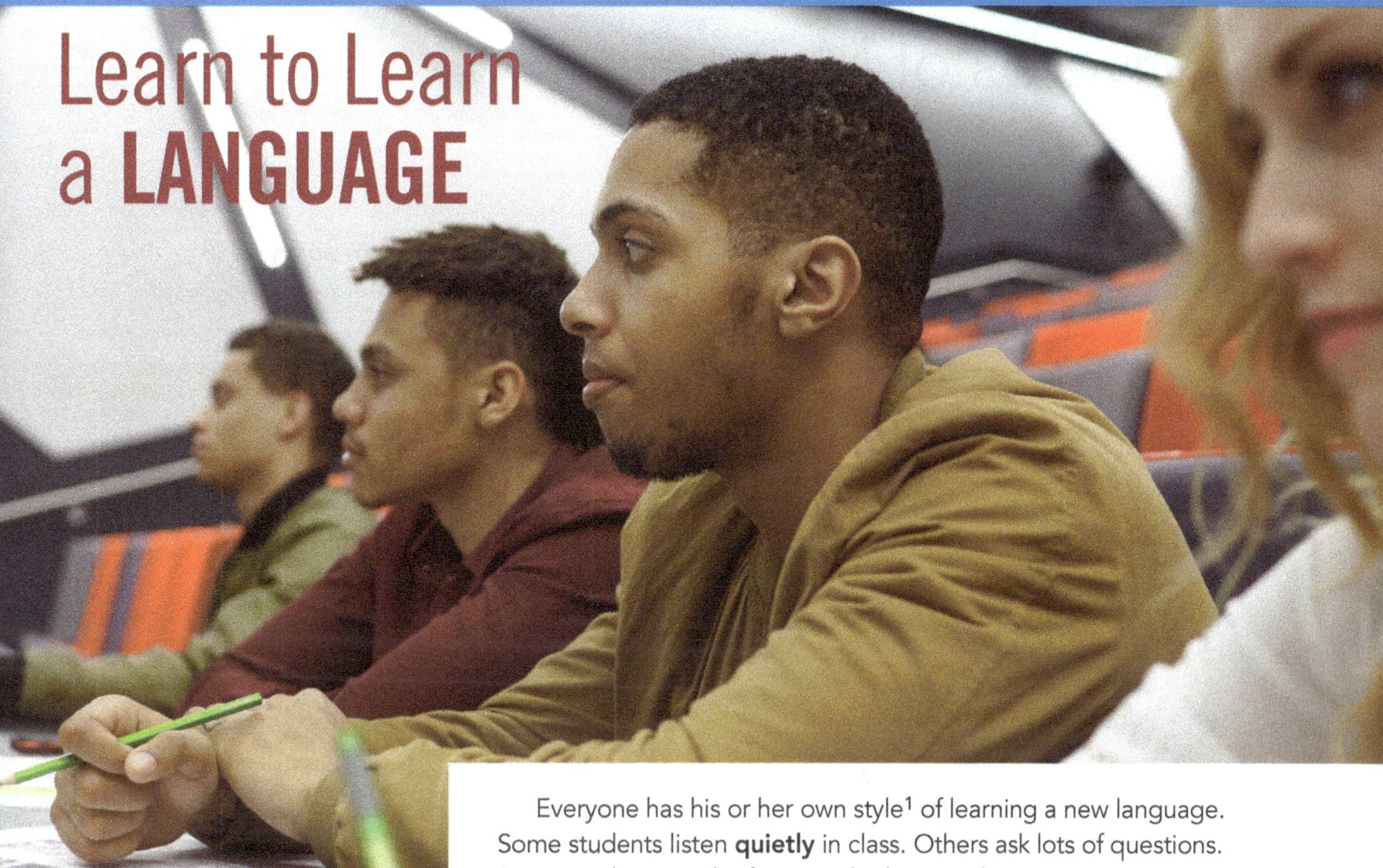

Everyone has his or her own style[1] of learning a new language. Some students listen **quietly** in class. Others ask lots of questions. Some students study **alone**, and others study in groups. However, one thing is true for all learners. You can become a better language
5 learner by using learning strategies. Language learning strategies are techniques[2] that help you learn. There are strategies that help you do **well** in your class, and there are strategies that help you use the language with others.

There are many study strategies for your classes. For example, in
10 class, listen **carefully** and take notes. The first time you read something, skim it. This means you read the material **quickly** and only look for the main points. Then read again and take notes on your reading. Make a list of new words and study the list **regularly**. Do not study for a test at the last minute. Also, do not stay up **late** the night before a test. Instead, get lots of sleep. A good night's sleep helps you think **clearly**.
15

Strategies also help you communicate with people in a new language. Talking to people is a good way to improve listening and speaking. However, some people speak very **quickly**, and they do not speak **clearly. Politely** ask a person to speak **slowly** and **clearly.** This is a useful
20 strategy. It is also a good idea to ask the person to repeat things. If you do not understand a word or phrase, **politely** ask the person to explain.

Learning strategies are good both for your classes and for communication outside of class. They help you to learn a new language **quickly** and **easily**.

[1]**style:** way of doing something that is typical of a person, group, place, or time

[2]**technique:** a specific way of doing a skillful activity

2 Adverbs of Manner

Grammar Presentation

Adverbs of manner describe how an action happens.	*I read **quietly** in the library.* *The teacher says the answers **quickly**.*

2.1 Forming Adverbs of Manner

A Add *-ly* to most adjectives to form adverbs of manner.	quick → quickly *She **quickly** memorized the words.* careful → carefully *Nick read the chapter **carefully**.*
B Some adverbs have the same form as adjectives: *alone, early, fast, hard, high, late, low, right, wrong.*	*He studied **alone**.* (adverb; describes how he studied) *The boy is **alone**.* (adjective; describes the boy)
These adverbs usually go after the verb.	*He ~~alone~~ studied. He studied **alone**.*
C The adverb form of *good* is *well*.	*Tom did **well** on the test.* *Tom did ~~good~~ on the test.* *She speaks English **well**.* *She speaks English ~~good~~.*
Well only goes after the verb.	*We communicate **well**.* *We ~~well~~ communicate.*
D Some adjectives end in *-ly*. They are not adverbs. Examples: *friendly, lively, lovely, silly, ugly.*	*Sara is **friendly**.* (adjective; describes Sara) *She makes **silly** faces in class.* (adjective; describes faces)

2.2 Using Adverbs of Manner

A Most adverbs of manner come after the verb or after the verb + the object. Do not put an adverb between a verb and the object.	*He spells **terribly**.* *She always writes her essays very **carefully**.* *They take ~~carefully~~ tests.*
B Many adverbs of manner can also come before the verb for emphasis.	*She **nervously** looked at the test.*

2.2 Using Adverbs of Manner *(continued)*

C Adverbs of manner usually come between the auxiliary verb (*be, have*) or modal verb (*can, should*) and the main verb.

They are **quietly** waiting for the test results.
He has **suddenly** left the room.
You can **politely** ask a question.

D Do not use adverbs after *be* or linking verbs (*appear, look, feel, sound, seem, smell, taste*). Use an adjective instead.

The test **sounds** easy.
The test sounds ~~easily~~.

Grammar Application

Exercise 2.1 Forming Adverbs

Complete the sentences with the correct adverb forms.

The Learners' Blog

What learning strategies do YOU use? Here's what our readers are using!

Marc J. I have a lot of reading assignments. I read _____*quickly*_____ (quick) through a (1) whole chapter. Then I read it ________________ (careful) a second time. (2)

Lisa L. I'm studying Chinese. I make flash cards for new words, and I study them ________________ (regular). It works! I always do ________________ (3) (4) (good) on tests.

Roberto R. I don't like to study ________________ (alone), so I joined a study group. (5) We study ________________ (hard), but we have a good time, too! (6)

Danielle F. I always go to bed ________________ (early) before a big test. (7) The next day, I think ________________ (clear) and do (8) ________________ (good). (9)

Nick B. When I read a textbook chapter, I skim the headings and ________________ (10) (quick) read the first sentence of each paragraph.

Jin P. There are a lot of hard words in textbooks! If I don't know a word, I read the sentence ________________ (slow) and try to figure out the meaning. (11)

Read a student's blog entry about memory tricks. Decide if each word in **bold** is an adverb or an adjective. Circle the adverbs. Underline the adjectives.

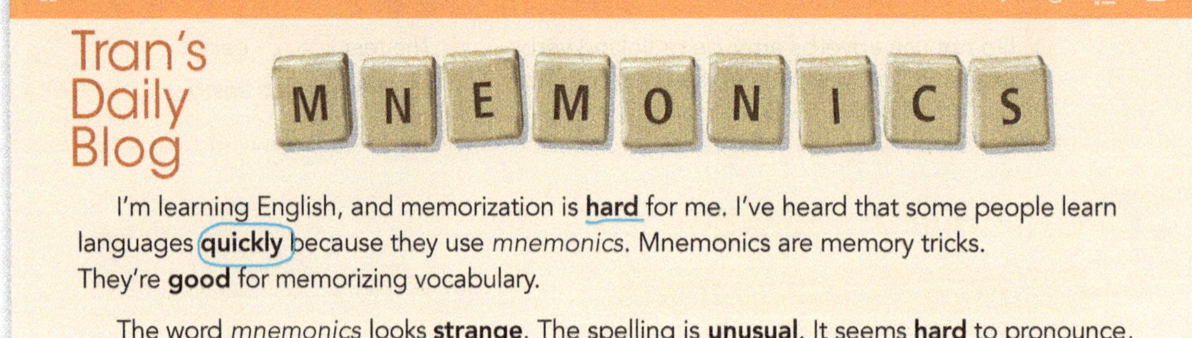

I'm learning English, and memorization is **hard** for me. I've heard that some people learn languages **quickly** because they use *mnemonics*. Mnemonics are memory tricks. They're **good** for memorizing vocabulary.

The word *mnemonics* looks **strange**. The spelling is **unusual**. It seems **hard** to pronounce,
5 too. But you can say it **right** if you forget about the *m* at the beginning – "nuh-mon-iks." Why is there a silent *m* at the beginning? I don't know. Sometimes English spelling is **silly** like that.

There's a friendly vocabulary study group at our Student Learning Center, but I like to study **alone**. In fact, I **easily** found two or three great tricks on a website. Here's one: Link new words with words you already know. Take the word *memory*, for example. You can link *memory* with
10 *remember* in your head. Another trick is to find an **easy** rhyme for a word that looks **hard**, like the word *guess*. It sounds like *mess* or *dress*. If you need a **new** strategy that works **well**, try mnemonics. And let me know if you can find a rhyme for *mnemonics*!

Complete the sentences about preparing for tests. Circle the correct words.

1 Studies show that students who do not sleep **well** / **good** do **poor** / **poorly** on tests.

2 Try to get a **good** / **well** night's sleep before a test.

3 Do not stay up **late** / **lately** the night before a test.

4 It is common to feel **nervously** / **nervous** the night before a big test, so try to relax.

5 Review everything **carefully** / **careful** two nights before a test; that way, you will sleep **sound** / **soundly** the night before the test.

6 The evening before a test, spend your time **peaceful** / **peacefully**: listen to music or take a warm bath.

7 On the morning of the test, eat **proper** / **properly**. For example, some experts recommend a high-protein breakfast like eggs.

8 Drink water **frequently** / **frequent** throughout the day.

Exercise 2.4 Word Order

A Rewrite the sentences. Change the adjectives into adverbs, and put them in the correct place. Sometimes more than one answer is correct.

1 I got up for my 8:00 a.m. class. (early) *I got up early for my 8:00 a.m. class.*

2 Max is taking notes. (neat) _______________________________

3 Tim always studies. (alone) _______________________________

4 She asks questions in class. (polite) _______________________________

5 My teacher pronounces new words. (clear) _______________________________

6 I study hard, so I pass all my tests! (easy) _______________________________

7 Ana has learned some mnemonics. (quick) _______________________________

8 I proofread my paper. (careful) _______________________________

B Over to You Make a list of the strategies you have seen in this unit so far. Check (✔) the ones you use now and the ones you are going to try to use. Add your own strategies to the list if you want. Then compare lists with a partner. Use adverbs of manner.

A *What strategies do you use?*
B *I make flash cards and study them regularly. How about you?*

3 Adverbs of Degree

Grammar Presentation

Adverbs of degree make other adverbs or adjectives stronger or weaker.	*The reading was **quite** confusing.* *The teacher speaks **kind of** softly.*

3.1 Adverbs of Degree

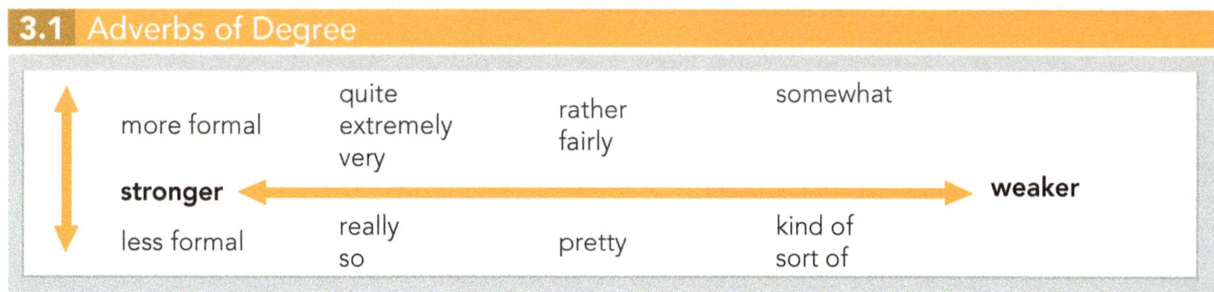

A Adverbs of degree can be used with adjectives or adverbs to make them stronger or weaker.

ADVERB ADVERB
*The teacher speaks **extremely softly**.*

ADVERB ADJECTIVE
*The reading was **extremely difficult**.*

ADVERB ADJECTIVE
*I had a **really wonderful** day!*

B Do not use the weaker adverbs of degree in negative statements.

*Tim did **not** study **very** hard for the test.*
Tim did not study ~~fairly~~ hard for the test.
Ana did not ask ~~somewhat~~ politely.

C Use these adverbs of degree with adjectives or adverbs to give opinions: *amazingly, dangerously, horribly, incredibly, seriously, terribly, wonderfully.*

*She did **amazingly well** on the test.*
*We worked **incredibly hard** on our class project.*
*Your paper is **wonderfully creative**.*

D Use *enough* after an adverb or an adjective to show whether an amount is acceptable.

*I studied hard **enough**.*
(an acceptable amount)

*Your essay seems long **enough**.*
(an acceptable amount)

*I did not study hard **enough**.*
(an unacceptable amount)

*Your essay doesn't seem long **enough**.*
(an unacceptable amount)

E Use *too* before an adverb or an adjective to show whether an amount is more than necessary.

*We studied **too** hard!*
(more than necessary)

*Your essay is **too** long.*
(more than necessary)

*We did not study **too** hard.*
(not more than necessary)

*Your essay is not **too** long.*
(not more than necessary)

Grammar Application

Exercise 3.1 Adverbs of Degree

A Complete the sentences. Circle the adverb of degree that matches the type in parentheses: either weak, strong, or in the middle.

1 My English class is (sort of)/ pretty fun. (weak)

2 The teacher is **really** / **pretty** nice. (strong)

3 My teacher speaks <u>very/kind of</u> quickly. (weak)

4 I listen <u>really/pretty</u> hard, but I don't understand everything. (in the middle)

5 My math class is <u>extremely/somewhat</u> difficult. (weak)

6 I do the assignments <u>pretty/very</u> carefully. (strong)

7 We have a <u>very/rather</u> difficult quiz every Friday. (strong)

8 I study <u>so/fairly</u> hard every night. (strong)

9 I get <u>fairly/quite</u> nervous before every quiz. (in the middle)

10 I'm <u>pretty/really</u> sure I'm going to get a good grade. (in the middle)

B Over to You **Write six sentences about your teachers, your classes, and your schoolwork. Then discuss your sentences with a partner. Use adverbs of degree that are weak, strong, and in the middle.**

A *I'm pretty sure I'm going to get a good grade in English.*

B *Why?*

A *I study very hard before every test.*

Exercise 3.2 Using *Too* and *Enough*

A Match the statement on the left with the correct response on the right. Complete the responses with *too* or *enough* and the adjectives or adverbs in parentheses.

1 I didn't do as well as I expected on the test. _*f*_

2 I have to rewrite my essay. ______

3 I have a big test tomorrow. ______

4 Is my homework OK? It's due soon. ______

5 The group meets at 8:00 a.m. Can you come? ______

6 We have only two days to write a paper. ______

7 The teacher didn't hear my questions. ______

8 We've studied all day. I'm tired! ______

a Yes, we've studied ______________ . (long) Let's go to bed.

b Two days doesn't seem ______________ ! (long)

c Sure. That's not ______________ for me. (early)

d Then don't stay up ______________ (late) tonight!

e Maybe you didn't speak ______________ . (loudly)

f Maybe you didn't study _*hard enough*_ . (hard)

g Maybe it was ______________ . (short)

h Sure. It looks ______________ . You (good) can turn it in.

B Pair Work **Practice the statements and responses in A with a partner.**

DATA FROM THE REAL WORLD

Research shows that the formal adverbs of degree are more common in class papers, presentations, and other formal situations.	The questions were **extremely** difficult. (more formal)
Use the less formal adverbs of degree in conversations with friends, in e-mails, and in other informal situations.	The questions were **really** difficult. (less formal)

Read a formal letter that a student wrote to a professor. Choose the correct adverbs of degree.

Dear Dr. Green,

I am in your Math 101 class. I am really / <u>quite</u> worried about my grades for this class. I am
₍₁₎
<u>pretty / fairly</u> sure that I am not doing <u>very / so</u> well. The work for this class is <u>so / extremely</u> difficult
₍₂₎   ₍₃₎   ₍₄₎
for me. I do the assignments <u>pretty / rather</u> carefully, but I do not understand everything. I study
₍₅₎
<u>quite / so</u> hard for every test. However, I did not study <u>extremely / sort of</u> hard for the last test, and I
₍₆₎   ₍₇₎
know I did not do <u>so / very</u> well.
₍₈₎

Can you give me some advice? I am <u>very / really</u> eager to improve in your class.
₍₉₎

Thank you.

Sincerely,

Matthew Yee

A **Listen to a group of students. They are working on a flier about study skills.**
Complete their conversation with the adverbs of degree that you hear.
Then compare your answers with a partner.

Alison	So, what are some tips for studying and getting good grades?
Dinh	Well, it's important to study _____*really*_____ hard. ₍₁₎
Alison	Right. It's also _______________ important to do all of your ₍₂₎ homework. What do you think, Carlos?
Carlos	Um, my vocabulary notebook is _______________ helpful to me! ₍₃₎
Alison	How does that help?
Carlos	When I want to use a new word, my notebook has sentences to help me remember how to use it.
Dinh	Hmm, I don't know . . .
Carlos	Oh, it works _______________ well, in my opinion. ₍₄₎
Dinh	OK. So, a vocabulary notebook is a _______________ good idea. ₍₅₎

Alison Yes. So we have three tips. Study, do your homework, and keep a vocabulary notebook. What else?

Dinh Asking questions. Ask questions in class. That's _________________ important.
(6)

Carlos Here's another one: I think it's a _________________ good idea to have a study
(7)
group. It's _________________ important to have people to study with and to
(8)
talk about class with, in my opinion.

Dinh I agree. Studying together is _________________ helpful!
(9)

B Group Work Brainstorm ideas for a group about study skills. Use the ideas from the conversation and your own ideas. Then make a flier on a piece of paper. Use formal adverbs in your flier, not the informal ones that the students used.

4 Avoid Common Mistakes ⚠ 

1 **Use an adverb, not an adjective, to describe how something happened.**

carefully
She studied very ~~careful~~.

2 ***Well* is the adverb for *good*.**

well
He did ~~good~~ on the test.

3 **Do not put an adverb between the verb and the object.**

the questions loudly
They answered ~~loudly the questions~~.

4 **In negative statements, only use strong adverbs.**

very
They did not study ~~fairly~~ hard.

5 **Remember that some adverbs have the same form as adjectives.**

hard
He is working ~~hardly~~ at his new job.

Editing Task

Find and correct seven more mistakes in this conversation about studying.

well
Marisa I didn't do ~~good~~ on the test today!

Sam Did you study hardly last night?

Marisa I tried, but it was so loud in the library. How about you?

Sam I didn't do good, either. I studied, but I didn't sleep pretty well.

5 **Marisa** And the test seemed easy.

Sam But it wasn't. It was too hard!

Marisa Well, what happened? We took carefully notes.

Sam And we listened good in class.

Marisa Maybe we didn't study careful enough.

10 **Sam** I'm suddenly getting nervous!

Marisa Why?

Sam Well, we don't have a pretty long time before the next test!

5 Academic Writing

Argumentative Writing

Brainstorm > Organize > Write > Edit

In Unit 13, you looked at an essay, learned how to develop strong arguments, and brainstormed ideas for the prompt below. In this unit (14), you will learn about the structure of an argumentative essay, and you will start organizing and writing your essay.

> *Do you agree or disagree with the following statement? "The fashion industry is harmful to society and the environment." Use reasons and examples to support your answer.*

Introductory Paragraph in an Argumentative Essay

The introductory paragraph of an argumentative essay describes an issue with different viewpoints. It ends with a thesis statement, which shows the writer's position and the reasons that will follow in the body paragraphs. The following are examples of argumentative thesis statements.

Some people argue that bilingual education is a waste of money, but I believe that it is beneficial to a country economically and culturally.

The fashion industry has a negative influence on young people's body image and can cause serious problems like depression and eating disorders.

Exercise 5.1 Applying the Skill

Read the introductory paragraph below. Work with a partner. Ask and answer the questions.

The world's consumption of fashion is huge. To give just one example, the United States alone imported almost 122 billion dollars' worth of textiles in 2014. As consumption has risen, prices have fallen. Today, a hand-finished shirt may cost as little as five dollars. To make clothes at these low prices, companies have to keep costs down. They use offshore production to do this. Large multinational companies outsource their production to developing countries like Egypt or Cambodia, where workers are paid much less than in developed countries. Supporters of outsourcing claim that it helps local economies, but I believe it is harmful for two main reasons.

1 What issue does the writer describe?
2 How many sentences does the writer use to describe the issue?
3 What is the writer's position on the issue? Underline the thesis statement.
4 How many body paragraphs will there probably be in the essay?

Body Paragraphs in an Argumentative Essay

Two or more body paragraphs follow the introductory paragraph in an argumentative essay. The body paragraphs help the readers understand and hopefully convince them to agree with the writer's point of view. Each body paragraph has a topic sentence that introduces one of the reasons for the point of view in the thesis statement.

Exercise 5.2 Applying the Skill

Read the body paragraph below about the positive social aspects of fashion among young people. Work with a partner. Ask and answer the questions.

Fashion is important to teenagers because it allows them to develop their independence through self-expression. According to psychologist Dr. Stephanie Newman, by making their own choices in fashion, they develop their self-identity. Fashion is one way that teens find their own social circle and establish their relationships with similar people. For example, the Australian shoe brand Uggs became very popular a few years ago. Rebellion against teachers and parents is another way for teens to establish their independence, and fashions that parents do not like is one way to rebel.

1 Underline the topic sentence. What three reasons does the writer give to support it?
2 Cross out any evidence that does not support the topic sentence.
3 Is the writer's argument convincing? Why or why not?

My Writing

Exercise 5.3 Planning Your Introductory and Body Paragraphs

Look at the writing prompt on page 184. Complete the tasks below. Use the chart you completed in My Writing in Unit 13 to help you.

1 Write an introductory paragraph for your argumentative essay.

2 Write a topic sentence for each body paragraph that supports your thesis.

Using Adverbs of Degree

Adverbs make language more descriptive and accurate. Writers use adverbs of degree to make verbs or adjectives stronger or weaker, and to express opinions. For example:

Majoring in a foreign language has become **fairly** popular in the U.S. as students realize how useful it can be. Speaking a foreign language well is **extremely** impressive.

Latin has remained **somewhat** popular in certain high schools.

In some Northern European countries, young people speak English **amazingly** well.

Remember to use more formal adverbs of degree in academic writing.

Exercise 5.4 Applying the Skill

Review your introductory paragraph and topic sentences. Add at least two adverbs of degree to make your writing more descriptive and accurate.

15 Prepositions

Food on the Table

1 Grammar in the Real World

ACADEMIC WRITING

Argumentative writing

A Where did the food you ate today come from? Read the article about how food is produced and sometimes wasted. Where are three places that food goes before it reaches our plates?

B Comprehension Check **Answer the questions.**

1 How much food did Americans throw away in 2018? Is this food safe to eat?
2 According to the article, why do farmers throw away food?
3 Why do processing plants throw away food?
4 What are food banks?
5 Why is it better to buy food from local farmers?

C Notice **Find the sentences in the article and complete them.**

1 __________ 2016, 41.2 million people __________ the United States could not afford to eat every day.
2 Our food has often traveled hundreds of miles __________ farms __________ our plates.
3 __________ the farm, food usually goes __________ a processing plant.
4 Trucks take it __________ the country to warehouses, distribution centers, and supermarkets.

Look at the words you wrote in the blanks. Which words show time? Which show place? Which show movement?

From
Plow
to **Plate**
(and Sometimes to the Trash)

[1]**processing:** the preparation, change, or treatment of food with chemicals to make it last longer

[2]**warehouse, distribution center:** large building used for storing goods

In 2016, 41.2 million people in the United States struggled with hunger. **In** 2018, a study found that Americans throw out 150,000 tons of food a day, or about a pound per person. Most of the wasted food is fruit, vegetables, dairy, and meat. Most of this food is perfectly good and
5 safe to eat. Why do we waste this food? How can we waste less of it?

Our food has often traveled hundreds of miles **from** farms **to** our plates. **At** every step of this journey, people throw away food. **On** farms, farmers throw away food that is the wrong size, shape, or color. **From** the farm, food usually goes to a processing[1] plant. **At** the
10 processing plant, workers clean it, package it, and sometimes cook it or add chemicals. They also throw away food they cannot transport or sell. Then food leaves the plant. Trucks take it **across** the country to warehouses, distribution centers,[2] and supermarkets. All of these places throw away food that people do not buy.

15 **After** this long process, we buy the food and store it **in** our refrigerators. Sometimes we forget it, or we buy too much. Then we throw it away, too. Restaurants also throw away food that we do not order or eat.

We can waste less food. Supermarkets and restaurants can give
20 unused food to food banks – groups that distribute food to poor and hungry people. **At** the supermarket, we can ask ourselves, "Do I really need to buy this? Will I use this food right away?" We can also buy food **from** local farmers. This food does not go **through** processing plants, so there is less waste.

2 Prepositions of Place and Time

Grammar Presentation

Prepositions can show place and time.	People often have too much food **on** the table. **In** 2018, a study found that Americans throw out 150,000 tons of food a day, or about a pound per person.

2.1 Prepositions of Place

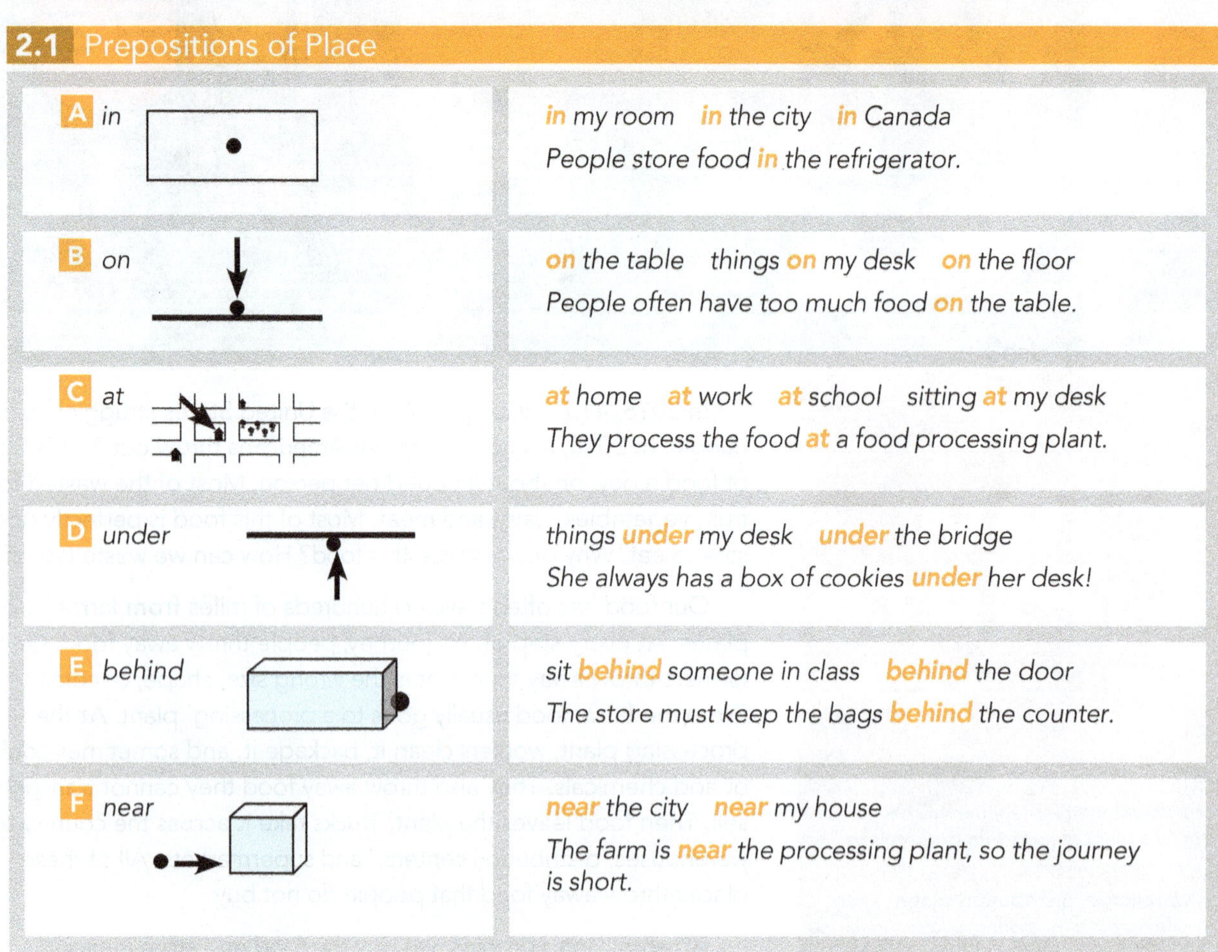

A *in*

in my room   ***in*** the city   ***in*** Canada
People store food ***in*** the refrigerator.

B *on*

on the table   things ***on*** my desk   ***on*** the floor
People often have too much food ***on*** the table.

C *at*

at home   ***at*** work   ***at*** school   sitting ***at*** my desk
They process the food ***at*** a food processing plant.

D *under*

things ***under*** my desk   ***under*** the bridge
She always has a box of cookies ***under*** her desk!

E *behind*

sit ***behind*** someone in class   ***behind*** the door
The store must keep the bags ***behind*** the counter.

F *near*

near the city   ***near*** my house
The farm is ***near*** the processing plant, so the journey is short.

2.2 Prepositions of Time

A Use prepositions of time to say when events happen.

Use *at* for clock times and with *night*.

*The trucks arrive **at** noon every day with fresh food.*
*We often go out **at** night.*

Use *in* for parts of the day (except *night*), months, seasons, and years.

***In** the spring, the farmers plant new crops.*
*The trucks arrive at the plant **in** the morning.*

Use *on* for dates and special days.

*People often have barbecues and picnics **on** July 4.*

B In sentences that include two different times . . .
use *before* to refer to the earlier time.

*I need to go grocery shopping **before** dinner. (First is grocery shopping, then dinner.)*

use *after* to refer to the later time.

***After** breakfast, we do the dishes. (First is breakfast, then the dishes.)*

C Use *during* to refer to the time that something is in progress.

*The food loses freshness **during** its journey to supermarkets.*

food loses freshness

journey

D Use *for* to say how long something takes or lasts.

*The food stays at the distribution center **for** three days.*

Day 1   Day 2   Day 3

Use *since* to refer to the time from a point in the past up to now.

***Since** June, the farm has sold 120 tons of fruit.*

June   now

2.3 Prepositional Phrases

A prepositional phrase is a preposition followed by an object of a preposition. The object must be a noun phrase or a verb in the *-ing* form.

PREP.   OBJECT OF PREP.
*They put the food **in the refrigerator**.*

PREP.   OBJECT OF PREP.
*The fruit is **on the counter**.*

PREP. OBJECT OF PREP.
*We need fresh water **for drinking**.*

Exercise 2.1 Prepositions of Place and Time

A Complete the magazine article. Circle the correct prepositions.

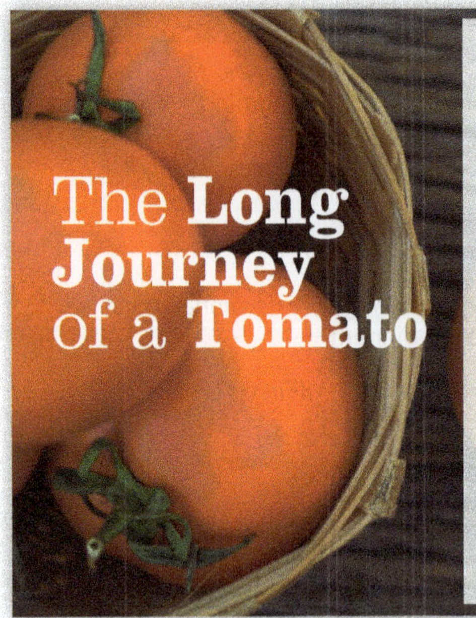

__On / At__ (1) Monday, July 13, Jeff Green picked the tomatoes at his farm in Florida. The next day, a truck arrived. It took the tomatoes to a processing plant __near / in__ (2) Jeff's farm. The plant was about five miles away. The tomatoes were there for three days. __At / During__ (3) that time, workers checked them, washed them, and put them __at / in__ (4) plastic containers. __In / On__ (5) July 17, the tomatoes went on trucks. The trucks took them to a distribution center 300 miles away. __After / Before__ (6) that, the tomatoes went to a supermarket in New Jersey. Ana Luz bought them, took them home, and put them in her refrigerator. __After / Before__ (7) that, the tomatoes sat __in / on__ (8) the supermarket shelf __for / since__ (9) two days. It was Friday, July 24. Ana did not know that her "fresh" tomatoes were 11 days old.

B Pair Work Write answers to the questions below. Use prepositions. Then ask and answer the questions with a partner.

1 A When did Jeff Green pick tomatoes on his farm?

  B *On Monday, July 13.*

2 A Where did a truck take the tomatoes?

  B ___________________________________

3 A Where was the processing plant?

  B ___________________________________

4 A How long were the tomatoes at the processing plant?

  B ___________________________________

5 A Where did the processing plant workers put the tomatoes?

  B ___________________________________

6 A Where did the tomatoes sit for two days?

  B ___________________________________

Exercise 2.2 Prepositions of Place

A Look at the picture and complete the answers. Use the prepositions in the box. You will use some prepositions more than once.

at	behind	in	on	under

1 A Where is the box of oranges? **B** It's ___*on*___ the floor.

2 A Where are the paper bags? **B** They're _________ the checkout stand.

3 A Where are the cartons of milk? **B** They're _________ the checkout stand.

4 A Where are the cartons of juice? **B** They're _________ the refrigerator case.

5 A Where are the bananas? **B** They're _________ the melons.

6 A Where is the cashier standing? **B** She's _________ the checkout stand.

7 A Where is the water? **B** It's _________ the shelf _________ the refrigerator case.

8 A Where are the tomatoes? **B** They're _________ a box _________ the floor.

9 A Where are the apples? **B** They're _________ the bananas.

B Over to You Answer these questions in complete sentences. Use a preposition from the box in A. Then compare your answers with a partner.

1 Where are you right now?

____

2 Who is sitting behind you right now?

____

3 Who is sitting near you?

____

4 What is on your desk?

____

3 Prepositions of Direction and Manner

Grammar Presentation

Prepositions can show direction and manner (a way of doing something).	The food goes **from** the processing plant **to** the supermarket. (direction: from X → Y) She prepares the food **with** fresh ingredients. (manner: how she prepares the food)

3.1 Prepositions of Direction and Movement

Use these prepositions to show how people and things move.

from		through	The food passes **through** two factories before it gets to the stores.
to	The food goes **from** the distribution center **to** the supermarket.	over	Farmers fly **over** their crops to spray them.
into	They throw old food **into** the trash.	around	Food often travels **around** the world before it gets to our homes.
across	Trucks transport the food **across** the United States.		

3.2 Prepositions of Manner and Logical Relationships

A With shows what people use to do something.	They treat the food **with** chemicals.
B For shows the purpose, intention, or goal of something.	They create meals **for** vegetarians.
C About refers to the topic of something.	The report is **about** food waste in the United States.

3.2 Prepositions of Manner and Logical Relationships *(continued)*

D *As* refers to the role or job of a person or thing.	*He works **as** a truck driver for a food processing company.*
E *Of* shows a close relationship, such as possession, identity, or being a part of something.	*People in the United States waste about a pound **of** food each per day.* *Most **of** this food is perfectly good to eat.*
F *Between* refers to the space that separates two people, things, or numbers.	*Families waste **between** 25 percent and 33 percent of the food that they buy.*

3.3 Using Prepositions with Noun Phrases and Pronouns

A You can use prepositions before noun phrases and pronouns. Use the object form of personal pronouns (*me, him, us*).	*__On__ my birthday, I had a special meal. Some friends cooked it **for** __me__.*
B You can use prepositions with *Wh-* questions (questions that start with *who, what, which,* etc.).	*__Who__ do I send this fruit basket **to**?*

 **DATA FROM THE REAL WORLD**

Research shows that the 20 most common prepositions in writing and speaking are:

about	around	at	between	during	from	into	on	since	to
after	as	before	by	for	in	of	over	through	with

Grammar Application

Exercise 3.1 Prepositions of Direction and Movement

A A teacher is taking a group of students on a tour of a local supermarket. Complete the conversation. Use the prepositions in the box.

across	around	from	into	over	through	~~to~~	to

Ms. Ross OK, everyone, let's go __*to*__ (1) the fruit and vegetable section. Now, can anyone tell me: Where do these peaches come ______________ (2) ?

Claire Let's see. Georgia.

Ms. Ross Right. And we're in Oregon. They came a long way. They traveled right ______________ (3) the United States, from the South to the Northwest.

Rob But peaches from Georgia are the best. I flew ______________ (4) Georgia once and saw some fruit farms from the air. Do you think these peaches came ______________ (5) Oregon by air?

Ms. Ross They probably came by truck. Workers put them ______________ (6) boxes and put the boxes into refrigerated trucks. Then they probably passed ______________ (7) a couple of factories and warehouses, too. Now, let's look at these beans. Where are they from?

Julia Kenya.

Ms. Ross Correct. A lot of these fruits and vegetables probably traveled ______________ (8) the world before they got here.

Exercise 3.2 Pronunciation Focus

Some common prepositions have two pronunciations: a strong form and a weak form.

	Strong Form	Weak Form
at	/æt/	/ət/
for	/fɔːr/	/fər/
from	/frʌm/ (or /frɑm/)	/frəm/
of	/ʌv/ (or /ɑv/)	/əv/
to	/tuː/	/tə/

Use the weak form in informal conversation, when you speak quickly and naturally.

*Let's go **to** the supermarket.*
*These tomatoes are **from** Florida.*

Use the strong form:
- when you speak formally, slowly, and carefully
- when you need to stress the preposition
- when the preposition is at the end of the sentence
- with *to* when the next sound is a vowel sound

*Welcome **to** this presentation of my work.*
*I was driving **to** the store, not **from** the store.*
*Where do these peaches come **from**?*
*Let's go **to a** farmers' market.*

A Listen to the questions and answers and repeat them.

1 **A** Are they from California? **B** No.

2 **A** So, where are they from? **B** From Georgia.

3 **A** Is that a box of apples? **B** No, it's a box of tomatoes.

4 **A** I'll see you at the restaurant. **B** No, let's go to the cafeteria.

5 **A** Who is this peach for? **B** It's for you. Enjoy!

6 **A** Are you going to the supermarket today? **B** No, we're going to a farmers' market.

B Pair Work Now practice asking and answering the questions in A with a partner.

Exercise 3.3 Prepositions of Place, Manner, and Logical Relationships

A Listen to the presentation and complete it with the prepositions that you hear.

Good morning. My talk today is _**about**_ merchandising. Supermarkets position
(1)
items carefully. They place things ___________________ refrigerator
(2)
cases, ___________________ shelves, and even ___________________
(3)   (4)
the checkout stand. This is called *merchandising*.

Merchandising helps supermarkets sell more items to people
in the store. For example, they put candy ___________________ other
(5)
food items, so children ask for the candy when their parents are
buying other things. Supermarkets also place certain items near the
floor. They put them ___________________ a place that children can see easily. For
(6)
example, they put items children want ___________________ the lower shelves. And
(7)
have you ever noticed kitchen gadgets ___________________ the food items on the
(8)
shelves? This is another example of merchandising.

Supermarkets also place items like magazines at the checkout stands. People
see them when they are waiting in line and put them ___________________ their carts.
(9)
In addition, research shows that people buy more cold items, for example juice or
cheese, when the refrigerated shelves are open. That's because they can see what is
___________________ them.
(10)
So, next time you're waiting in line ___________________ the checkout stand, ask
(11)
yourself, "Why did I buy this? Was it because I needed it, or just because I saw it?"
Even ___________________ careful shoppers, we all sometimes put things we don't
(12)
need in our carts.

B Pair Work When you go to a supermarket, what do you notice?
Discuss your ideas with a partner. Talk about these things:

- the prices of things

- information about ingredients, or what is in things

- information about where food comes from

- any other things that you notice or look for

A *The first things I notice are the products at the ends of the aisles. What about you?*
B *I usually look for what's on sale.*

4 Phrasal Prepositions and Prepositions After Adjectives

Grammar Presentation

Some prepositions consist of more than one word. These are called *phrasal prepositions*. Many adjectives have particular prepositions that follow them.	*Wei was standing **in front of** me at the checkout stand.* *Are you **good at** shopping for the best prices?*

4.1 Using Phrasal Prepositions

You can use phrasal prepositions just like one-word prepositions, before noun phrases and pronouns. Use the object form of personal pronouns (*me, him, us*).	*The organic food store is **next to** the bank on Ginsberg Street.* *My teacher was standing **in front of** me at the supermarket checkout yesterday.*

 **DATA FROM THE REAL WORLD**

Research shows that these are the most common phrasal prepositions in speaking and writing.

Phrasal Prepositions	Meaning	
as well as	means "and" or "also"	Restaurants, *as well as* supermarkets, throw away tons of food every year.
because of	tells you the reason	The food loses its freshness *because of* the long journey from the plow to the plate.
close to	means "near"	I live *close to* a small store.
in front of		At the checkout stand, do you look at what the person *in front of* you is buying?
instead of	means "A, not B"	Nowadays, I shop at a farmers' market *instead of* a big supermarket. (I shop at farmers' markets, not big supermarkets.)
next to		The tea is *next to* the coffee on the supermarket shelf.
out of		When the food comes *out of* the processing plant, it goes to a distribution center.
outside of		Do you buy food that is produced *outside of* the United States?
such as	means "for example"	The supermarket places products *such as* candy and toys on the lower shelves.
up to		Take the elevator *up to* the second floor, and you will see the books about food and nutrition.

4.2 Using Adjectives with Prepositions

A You can use adjectives with prepositions before nouns, noun phrases, and pronouns. Use the object form of personal pronouns (*me, him, us*).

The cafeteria was **full of** <u>students</u>.

Junk food is **bad for** <u>people's health</u>.

I was **surprised by** <u>the article about wasted food</u>.

Frozen food is **separate from** <u>the fresh fruit in the</u> supermarket.

I'm **worried about** <u>the chemicals used in food</u>.

Fresh vegetables are **good for** <u>us</u>.

He looks sick. Is anything **wrong with** <u>him</u>?

B You can use adjectives with prepositions without a noun or pronoun in sentences with a Wh- word *(who, what, which, etc.)*.

*What are the high food prices **due to**?*

*Which games are the kids **excited about**?*

*Who is the supermarket manager **responsible for**?*

DATA FROM THE REAL WORLD

These are the most common adjectives used with prepositions.

Adjectives	Preposition	
aware	of	Many people are not **aware of** the cost of transporting food.
full		Farmers' markets are **full of** fresh, local produce.
different	from	The tomatoes from my friend's garden were **different from** the supermarket tomatoes.
separate		Restaurants keep produce **separate from** meat and poultry.
due	to	High food prices this year are **due to** bad weather.
similar		The price of local fruit is sometimes **similar to** the price of imported fruit.
familiar	with	Are you **familiar with** this type of merchandising?
wrong		There's something **wrong with** these peaches. They're hard and dry.
good	at	Are you **good at** math? Can you add up these prices?
surprised		I was **surprised at** the amount of food we waste.
interested	in	I'm not **interested in** the quality of the food. I just want to eat.
responsible	for	Who is **responsible for** the quality of food in the student cafeteria?
good		Cooking at home is **good for** you.
worried	about	I'm **worried about** all the chemicals that they use to treat food.
excited		We're **excited about** the new restaurant in town.

Grammar Application

Complete the sentences. Use the words in the box.

because	close	instead	~~outside~~	outside	such	well	well

1 Many types of food come from places __*outside*__ of our own country or region.

2 Items _______________ as exotic fruits often travel across continents to supermarkets.

3 Transportation costs, as _______________ as production costs, are very high.

4 Buying food from farms ______________________ of our own country or region means food travels farther.

5 ______________________ of these factors, food prices are high.

6 Nowadays, many people prefer to buy local food ______________________ of food from other countries.

7 They prefer to buy food from farms that are in or ______________________ to their own region or state.

8 If you go to a local store or market ______________________ of a store that is a long way from your home, you are saving gas, as ______________________ as helping your neighborhood economy.

Exercise 4.2 More Phrasal Prepositions

Look at the pictures. Complete the statements. Use the words in the box.

as well as	close to	~~next to~~	out of
because of	in front of	next to	outside of

1 In picture 1, Lisa is sitting **_next to_** Diego.

2 Ali is sitting ______________________ Blanca.

3 Chelsea is sitting ______________________ Anne.

4 Anne isn't sitting ______________________ Blanca.

5 In picture 2, the traffic is going slowly ______________________ the snow.

6 There are trucks ______________________ cars on the highway.

7 The traffic is going ______________________ the city.

8 The highway is ______________________ the city.

A Complete the questionnaire about shopping. Write the missing prepositions.

Shopping Behavior

1 When you are in a supermarket, are you aware _____*of*_____ different package sizes?

Are you more likely to buy a larger package than a smaller package of something?

2 At a supermarket, what do you get excited __________ ?

3 Are you ever surprised __________ how much your grocery bill is at the checkout?

4 Do you only buy things that are good __________ you?

5 Is your supermarket cart often full __________ things you don't really need?

6 Do you buy books, clothes, and food all in one store, or do you prefer

bookstores and clothing stores that are separate __________ supermarkets?

7 When you spend too much at the supermarket, do you think it is due

__________ your choices, or is it the fault of the supermarket?

8 Do you think there is anything wrong __________ the way people shop in

supermarkets? If yes, what?

B Pair Work Make your own questionnaire about shopping. Choose five questions from A.
Then add three questions of your own.

Shopping Behavior

1 ____

2 ____

3 ____

4 ____

5 ____

6 ____

7 ____

8 ____

9 ____

10 ____

C Pair Work Take turns asking and answering your questions.

D Group work Discuss your questions with other classmates.

Tell the class anything interesting you learn.
Ana, Luis, Roberto and I never buy things we don't really need. We all make a shopping list and only buy the things on it.

5 Avoid Common Mistakes ⚠

1 **Use *in*, not *at*, with large areas such as cities, states, and countries.**

in

There are thousands of farmers' markets ~~at~~ the United States.

2 **Use *on*, not *at* or *in*, for days and dates.**

on

I always do my grocery shopping ~~in~~ Saturdays.

3 **Use *for*, not *during* or *since*, to refer to how long something takes or lasts.**

for

The food stays at the processing plant ~~since~~ two or three days.

4 **Use the correct preposition after an adjective.**

in

I am interested ~~on~~ ways to save money on food.

Editing Task

Find and correct six more mistakes in this article about the problem of wasting food.

in

Meg Handford lives ~~at~~ a small town in Oregon. She read about food processing and distribution. She was worried on the amount of gas people use to transport food from farms to supermarkets and from supermarkets to homes. She thought it was bad to the environment, so she decided to do something about it.

5   Meg wanted to make things better. She thought, "Maybe people can share shopping trips." So in July 2014, Meg set up Food Pool.

Food Pool is like a car pool. In a car pool, neighbors and colleagues travel to work together in one car instead of two or three. With Food Pool, neighbors go to the supermarket or a farmers' market together. They do this in Saturdays or other free days.

10   Meg started a website. She was surprised at the number of interested people. Soon her inbox was full in e-mails. Now there are more than 50 families at her area that share the trip to the supermarket. Food Pool has been running since five years and is growing every year.

6 Academic Writing

Argumentative Writing

Brainstorm > Organize > **Write** > **Edit**

In Unit 14, you looked at the relationship between the introductory and body paragraphs of an argumentative essay, and how to use adverbs to improve writing. In this unit (15), you are going to learn about cohesion, and then complete, revise, and edit your essay for the prompt below.

Do you agree or disagree with the following statement? "The fashion industry is harmful to society and the environment." Use reasons and examples to support your answer.

Writing with Cohesion

Cohesion refers to the way writers connect ideas within sentences, between different sentences, and between paragraphs. When writing is cohesive, it is clear and easy to follow. Writers use several techniques to make writing cohesive:

1 Transitions between sentences or between ideas

Serving fancy food from other countries has become fashionable. **As a result**, more stores are selling food that is imported instead of local food.

2 Repetition of nouns or use of synonyms

The best **fruits and vegetables** are often at local farmers' markets. Buying **produce** from local vendors usually means it is fresher than at the grocery store.

3 Pronouns that refer back to nouns in previous sentences

Farmers work incredibly hard to grow produce or raise animals for others to eat. **They** also have a lot of risk due to weather and disease.

4 *This / that / these / those* to refer back to earlier nouns or ideas

Many stores now give produce to food banks instead of throwing it away when it's not perfect. **This** means that more people are fed and less food is wasted.

Exercise 6.1 Applying the Skill

Work with a partner. Read the paragraph from an argumentative essay about vegetarian diets. Find an example of each cohesive technique. Write the correct number next to each example.

A vegetarian diet is a healthier option than a meat-based diet. Studies have consistently revealed that people who eat a plant-based diet experience less heart disease, cancer, or diabetes. The World Cancer Research Fund has shown that there is a direct link between these diseases and a meat-based diet. Vegetarians also tend to have a healthier weight. By contrast, obesity is more common among meat eaters. It shouldn't be surprising then that vegetarians or those who eat small amounts of meat live longer. A number of studies have shown that they live between 4 and 7 years longer than non-vegetarians. This suggests that a vegetarian lifestyle is a healthier lifestyle.

My Writing

Exercise 6.2 Writing Your First Draft

Write your essay. Use the plan below and your My Writing work in Units 13 and 14.

Introductory paragraph	• Introduce the topic and give background information about it. • In the thesis statement, state your position and the arguments you will use to support it.
Body paragraphs	• Give argument 1 with supporting reasons and evidence. • Give argument 2 with supporting reasons and evidence.
Concluding paragraph	• Restate your thesis and summarize your arguments. Use different words. • Make a final statement to convince your reader to agree with you.

Exercise 6.3 Revising Your Ideas

1 Work with a partner. Use the questions below to give feedback on your partner's essay.
   • Which of your partner's ideas seem strongest to you?
   • Which of your partner's ideas need to be explained more clearly?
   • What could your partner add or remove to make the essay stronger and easier to understand?
   • Do you agree or disagree with your partner's point of view? Why or why not?

2 Use the feedback from your partner to revise your essay.

Exercise 6.4 Editing Your Writing

Use the checklist to review and edit your essay.

Did you answer the writing prompt completely?	
Did you include a description and background of the issue in the introductory paragraph?	
Did you include a thesis statement that gives your position and main arguments?	
Did you include reasons and evidence to develop strong arguments?	
Did you restate your position and summarize your arguments in the concluding paragraph?	
Did you use a variety of techniques to make your writing cohesive?	

Exercise 6.5 Editing Your Grammar

Use the checklist to review and edit the grammar in your essay.

Did you use descriptive adjectives and adverbs of degree to make your writing clearer and more accurate?	
Did you use prepositions correctly?	
Did you avoid the common mistakes in the charts on pages 169, 183, and 203?	

Exercise 6.6 Writing Your Final Draft

Apply the feedback and edits from Exercises 6.3 to 6.5 to write the final draft of your essay.

Appendices

1 Capitalization and Punctuation Rules

Capitalize	Examples
1. The first letter of the first word of a sentence	*Today is a great day.*
2. The pronoun *I*	*After class, I want to go to the movies.*
3. Names of people	*Simon Bolivar, Joseph Chung*
4. Names of buildings, streets, geographic locations, and organizations	*Taj Mahal, Main Street, Mt. Everest, United Nations*
5. Titles of people	*Dr., Mr., Mrs., Ms.*
6. Days, months, and holidays	*Tuesday, April, Valentine's Day*
7. Names of courses or classes	*Biology 101, English Composition II*
8. Titles of books, movies, and plays	*Crime and Punishment, Avatar, Hamlet*
9. States, countries, languages, and nationalities	*California, Mexico, Spanish, South Korean, Canadian*
10. Names of religions	*Hinduism, Catholicism, Islam, Judaism*

Punctuation	Examples
1. Use a period (.) at the end of a sentence.	*I think I can pass this class.*
2. Use a question mark (?) at the end of a question.	*Why do you want to buy a car?*
3. Use an exclamation point (!) to show strong emotion (e.g., surprise, anger, shock).	*Wait! I'm not ready yet.* *I can't believe it!*
4. Use an apostrophe (') for possessive nouns. Add 's for singular nouns. Add s' for plural nouns. Add ' or 's for nouns that end in -s. Add 's for irregular plural nouns. Use an apostrophe (') for contractions.	*That's Sue's umbrella.* *Those are the students' books.* *It is Wes' house. It is Wes's house.* *Bring me the children's shoes.* *I'll be back next week. He can't drive a car.*

1 Capitalization and Punctuation Rules (*Continued*)

Punctuation	Examples
5. Use a comma (,): between words in a series of three or more items. (Place and before the last item.) after a time clause when it begins a sentence. after a prepositional phrase when it begins a sentence. after an adverb clause when it begins a sentence. before and, or, but, and so to connect two or more main clauses.	*I like fish, chicken, turkey, **and** mashed potatoes.* ***Before** I play soccer, I do my stretching exercises.* ***Next to** my house, there's a beautiful little park.* ***Because** she got a job, she was able to get her own apartment.* *You can watch TV, **but** I have to study for a test.*

2 Stative (Non-Action) Verbs

Stative verbs do not describe actions. They describe states or situations. Stative verbs are not usually used in the present progressive, even if we are talking about right now. Some are occasionally used in the present progressive, but often with a different meaning.

Research shows that the 25 most common stative verbs in spoken and written English are:

agree	dislike	hope	love	see
believe	expect	hurt	need	seem
care (about)	hate	know	notice	think
cost	have	like	own	understand
disagree	hear	look like	prefer	want

Other stative verbs are:

be	feel	matter	recognize	sound
belong	forgive	mean	remember	taste
concern	look	owe	smell	weigh
deserve				

Using the present progressive of these verbs sometimes changes the meaning to an action.

*Can you **see** the red car?*   (= use your eyes to be aware of something)

*I**'m seeing** an old friend tomorrow.*   (= meeting someone)

*I **think** you're right.*   (= believe)

*Dina **is thinking** of taking a vacation soon.*   (= considering)

*I **have** two sisters.*   (= be related to)

*We**'re having** eggs for breakfast.*   (= eating)

Irregular Verbs

Base Form	Simple Past	Past Participle	Base Form	Simple Past	Past Participle
be	was / were	been	keep	kept	kept
become	became	become	know	knew	known
begin	began	begun	leave	left	left
bite	bit	bitten	lose	lost	lost
blow	blew	blown	make	made	made
break	broke	broken	meet	met	met
bring	brought	brought	pay	paid	paid
build	built	built	put	put	put
buy	bought	bought	read	read [red]*	read [red]*
catch	caught	caught	ride	rode	ridden
choose	chose	chosen	run	ran	run
come	came	come	say	said	said
cost	cost	cost	see	saw	seen
cut	cut	cut	sell	sold	sold
do	did	done	send	sent	sent
draw	drew	drawn	set	set	set
drink	drank	drunk	shake	shook	shaken
drive	drove	driven	show	showed	shown
eat	ate	eaten	shut	shut	shut
fall	fell	fallen	sing	sang	sung
feed	fed	fed	sit	sat	sat
feel	felt	felt	sleep	slept	slept
fight	fought	fought	speak	spoke	spoken
find	found	found	spend	spent	spent
fly	flew	flown	stand	stood	stood
forget	forgot	forgotten	steal	stole	stolen
forgive	forgave	forgiven	swim	swam	swum
get	got	gotten	take	took	taken
give	gave	given	teach	taught	taught
go	went	gone	tell	told	told
grow	grew	grown	think	thought	thought
have	had	had	throw	threw	thrown
hear	heard	heard	understand	understood	understood
hide	hid	hidden	wake	woke	woken
hit	hit	hit	wear	wore	worn
hold	held	held	win	won	won
hurt	hurt	hurt	write	wrote	written

*pronunciation

4 Spelling Rules for Verbs Ending in *-ing*

1. For verbs ending in a vowel-consonant combination, repeat the consonant before adding *-ing*.
   get → *getting*   *swim* → *swimming*

2. However, if the verb has more than one syllable, repeat the consonant only if the final syllable is stressed.
   beGIN → *beginning*   BUT   *HAPpen* → *happening (no doubling of consonant)*

3. For verbs ending in a silent *e*, drop the *e* before adding *-ing*.
   move → *moving*   *drive* → *driving*

   For *be* and *see*, don't <u>drop</u> the *e* because it is not silent.
   be → *being*   *see* → *seeing*

   For verbs ending in *-ie*, change *ie* to *y* before adding *-ing*.
   die → *dying*   *lie* → *lying*

Verbs that end in *-ing* are also called *gerunds* when they are used as nouns. The same spelling rules above apply to gerunds as well.

5 Spelling Rules for Regular Verbs in the Simple Past

1. To form the simple past of regular verbs, add *-ed* to the base form of the verb.
   work → *worked*   *wash* → *washed*

2. For regular verbs that end in *-e*, add *-d* only.
   live → *lived*   *like* → *liked*

3. For regular verbs ending in a consonant + *-y*, change *y* to *i* and add *-ed*.
   study → *studied*   *hurry* → *hurried*

4. For regular verbs that end in a vowel + *-y*, add *-ed*.
   stay → *stayed*   *enjoy* → *enjoyed*

5. For regular verbs that end in a vowel-consonant combination, repeat the consonant before adding *-ed*. Exception: Do not double the last consonant for verbs that end with *-w*, *-x*, or *-y*.
   stop → *stopped*   *plan* → *planned*   BUT   *fix* → *fixed*

6. However, if the verb has more than one syllable, repeat the consonant only if the final syllable is stressed.
   preFER → *preferred*   BUT   *Visit* → *visited (no doubling of consonant)*

6 Verbs + Gerunds and Infinitives

<table>
<tr><td colspan="2">Verbs Followed by a Gerund Only</td></tr>
<tr><td>admit</td><td>keep (= continue)</td></tr>
<tr><td>avoid</td><td>mind (= object to)</td></tr>
<tr><td>consider</td><td>miss</td></tr>
<tr><td>delay</td><td>postpone</td></tr>
<tr><td>deny</td><td>practice</td></tr>
<tr><td>discuss</td><td>quit</td></tr>
<tr><td>enjoy</td><td>recall (= remember)</td></tr>
<tr><td>finish</td><td>risk</td></tr>
<tr><td>imagine</td><td>suggest</td></tr>
<tr><td>involve</td><td>understand</td></tr>
</table>

<table>
<tr><td colspan="3">Verbs Followed by an Infinitive Only</td></tr>
<tr><td>afford</td><td>hope</td><td>pretend</td></tr>
<tr><td>agree</td><td>intend</td><td>promise</td></tr>
<tr><td>arrange</td><td>learn</td><td>refuse</td></tr>
<tr><td>attempt</td><td>manage</td><td>seem</td></tr>
<tr><td>decide</td><td>need</td><td>tend (= be likely)</td></tr>
<tr><td>deserve</td><td>offer</td><td>threaten</td></tr>
<tr><td>expect</td><td>plan</td><td>volunteer</td></tr>
<tr><td>fail</td><td>prepare</td><td>want</td></tr>
<tr><td>help</td><td></td><td></td></tr>
</table>

<table>
<tr><td colspan="3">Verbs Followed by a Gerund or an Infinitive</td></tr>
<tr><td>begin</td><td>like</td><td>start</td></tr>
<tr><td>continue</td><td>love</td><td>stop*</td></tr>
<tr><td>forget*</td><td>prefer</td><td>try*</td></tr>
<tr><td>hate</td><td>remember*</td><td></td></tr>
</table>

*The meanings of these verbs are different when they are followed by a gerund or an infinitive. See Unit 28.

7 Verb and Preposition Combinations

Verb + *about*
- ask about
- complain about
- talk about
- think about
- worry about

Verb + *against*
- advise against
- decide against

Verb + *at*
- look at
- smile at

Verb + *for*
- apologize for
- ask for
- look for
- pay for
- wait for

Verb + *in*
- believe in
- succeed in

Verb + *of*
- approve of
- dream of
- think of

Verb + *on*
- count on
- decide on
- depend on
- insist on
- plan on
- rely on

Verb + *to*
- admit to
- belong to
- listen to
- look forward to
- talk to

Verb + *with*
- agree with
- argue with
- bother with
- deal with

8 Adjective and Preposition Combinations

Adjective + *of*
afraid of
ashamed of
aware of
careful of
full of
sick of
tired of

Adjective + *by*
amazed by
bored by
surprised by

Adjective + *at*
amazed at
angry at
bad at
good at
surprised at

Adjective + *from*
different from
separate from

Adjective + *with*
bored with
familiar with
satisfied with
wrong with

Adjective + *in*
interested in

Adjective + *for*
bad for
good for
responsible for

Adjective + *about*
concerned about
excited about
happy about
nervous about
pleased about
sad about
sorry about
surprised about
upset about
worried about

Adjective + *to*
similar to

Modal Verbs and Modal-like Expressions

Most modals have multiple meanings.

Function	Modal Verb or Modal-like Expression	Time	Example
Ability / Possibility	can	present, future	I **can** speak three languages. I **can** help you tomorrow.
	could	present, past	She **could** play an excellent game of tennis when she was young.
	be able to	past, present, future	I **won't be able to** help you tomorrow. I'**m not able to** help you today.
Permission less formal more formal	can could	present, future	Yes, you **can** watch TV now. You **could** give me your answer next week.
	may	present, future	You **may** leave now.
Requests less formal	can will	present, future	**Can** you stop that noise now? **Will** you please visit me tonight?
more formal	could would	present, future	**Could** you turn off your cell phone please? **Would** you please come for your interview this afternoon?
Offers	can could may will	present, future	I **can** help you paint your room. I **could** drive you to work next week. **May** I carry that for you? We**'ll** help you find your wallet.
Invitations	would you like	present, future	**Would you like** to come to my graduation tomorrow?
Advice less strong	ought to should	present, future	You really **ought to** save your money. She **shouldn't** go to school today.
stronger	had better	present, future	They **had better** be very careful in the park tomorrow.
Suggestions	could might want to	present, future	He **could** take a train instead of the bus. You **might want to** wait until next month.

Function	Modal Verb or Modal-like Expression	Time	Example
Preferences	*would like* *would prefer* *would rather*	present, future	*I **would like** to take a trip next year.* *We **would prefer** to go on a cruise.* *They **would rather** eat at home than in a restaurant.*
Necessity less formal	*have / has to* *need to*	past, present, future	*We **had to** cancel our date at the last minute.* *She **needs to** quit her stressful job.*
more formal	*have / has got to* *must*	past, present, future present, future	*They**'ve got to** study harder if they want to pass.* *You **must** be more serious about your future.*
Lack of Necessity	*don't / doesn't have to* *don't / doesn't need to*	past, present, future	*I **didn't have to** renew my driver's license.* *You **don't need to** worry about your brother.*
Prohibition	*can't* *must not* *may not*	present, future	*You **can't** attend tonight without an invitation.* *You **must not** fish without a license.* *You **may not** board the plane before going through security.*
Speculation / Probability	*could* *may* *might* *should*	present, future	*He **could** be late because he missed his train.* *I **may** stay home.* *It **might** rain later because I see dark clouds.* *We **should** probably leave now.*
	must	present only	*She **must** be sick because she didn't come to work today.*

10 Adjectives: Order Before Nouns

When you use two (or more) adjectives before a noun, use the order in the chart below.

Opinion	Size	Quality	Age	Shape	Color	Origin	Material	Nouns as Adjectives
beautiful	big	cold	ancient	rectangular	black	American	cotton	computer
comfortable	fat	free	new	round	blue	Canadian	glass	evening
delicious	huge	heavy	old	square	gold	Chinese	leather	rose
expensive	large	hot	young	triangular	green	European	metal	safety
interesting	long	safe			orange	Japanese	paper	software
nice	short				purple	Mexican	plastic	summer
pretty	small				red	Peruvian	stone	training
reasonable	tall				silver	Thai	wooden	
special	thin				yellow		woolen	
ugly	wide				white			

Examples:

I bought a beautiful, new, purple and gold Indian scarf.

There is a tall, young woman sitting next to that handsome man.

We're going to learn an interesting, new software program.

The museum has expensive glass jewelry.

11 Conditionals

The **factual conditional** describes general truths, habits, and things that happen routinely. The simple present is used in both clauses. You can use modals in the result clause, too.

IF CLAUSE   RESULT CLAUSE

If you use the highway, the drive is much faster.   (general truth)

If you enter before 11:00 a.m., you can get a discount.   (general truth)

Use the imperative in the result clause to give instructions or commands.

If you don't like the oranges, give them to me.   (command)

The **future conditional** describes things that will happen under certain conditions in the future. The simple present is used in the *if* clause and a future form is used in the result clause. You can use modals in the result clause, too.

IF CLAUSE   RESULT CLAUSE

If it rains tomorrow, they're going to cancel the game.

If I finish my homework early, I'll go to the movies.

If she works hard, she could get a promotion.

You can begin a conditional sentence with the *if* clause or the result clause. It doesn't change the meaning. Use a comma between the two clauses if you begin your sentence with the *if* clause.

RESULT CLAUSE | IF CLAUSE

They're going to cancel the game if it rains tomorrow.

IF CLAUSE | RESULT CLAUSE

If it rains tomorrow, they're going to cancel the game.

12 Phrasal Verbs: Transitive and Intransitive

Transitive (Separable) Phrasal Verbs

Phrasal Verb	Meaning	Phrasal Verb	Meaning
add up	add together, combine	*give up*	quit
blow up	explode	*hang up*	end a phone call
bring back	return something or someone	*help out*	assist someone
bring up	(1) raise a child, (2) introduce a topic	*lay off*	lose a job, end employment
build up	accumulate	*leave on*	keep on (a light, clothing, jewelry)
call back	return a phone call	*let in*	allow someone to enter
call off	cancel	*look over*	examine
cheer up	make someone happy	*look up*	find information
clear up	resolve a problem or situation, explain	*make up*	create or invent (a story, a lie)
do over	do again	*pass out*	distribute (paper, a test, material, homework)
figure out	find an answer, understand	*pay back*	repay money
fill in	write in blank spaces	*pay off*	repay completely
fill out	complete an application or form	*pick up*	(1) go get someone or something, (2) lift
find out	look for or seek information, learn	*point out*	call attention to something
give away	donate, give for free	*put away*	(1) save for the future, (2) put in the correct place
give back	return		

Transitive (Separable) Phrasal Verbs *(continued)*

Phrasal Verb	Meaning	Phrasal Verb	Meaning
put back	return something to its usual place	*talk over*	discuss
put off	delay, postpone	*think over*	consider
put out	(1) extinguish, stop the burning of a fire or cigarette, (2) place outside	*throw away / throw out*	get rid of something; discard
put together	assemble	*try on*	put on clothing to see if it fits
set up	(1) arrange, (2) plan, (3) build	*turn down*	(1) lower the volume, (2) reject
shut off / turn off	stop (a machine, a light, a TV)	*turn on*	start (a machine, a light, a TV)
sort out	(1) organize, (2) solve	*turn up*	increase the volume
straighten up	(1) make something look neat, (2) stand tall	*wake up*	stop sleeping
take back	return something	*work out*	(1) solve, (2) calculate
take out	(1) remove, (2) obtain something officially	*write down*	write on paper

Intransitive (Inseparable) Phrasal Verbs

Phrasal Verb	Meaning	Phrasal Verb	Meaning
break down	(1) stop working, (2) lose control	*fall down*	fall to the ground
break up	end a relationship, separate	*fool around*	act playfully
come back	return	*get ahead*	succeed, make progress
come from	originate	*get along*	have a good relationship
come on	(1) hurry, (2) start	*get over*	recover from an illness or a shock
dress up	put on nice or formal clothes	*get up*	arise from bed
drop in	visit without advance notice	*give up*	stop
drop out	quit (school, a race, a club)	*go ahead*	start or continue
eat out	eat in a restaurant	*go away*	leave; go to another place

Phrasal Verb	Meaning	Phrasal Verb	Meaning
go on	continue	*run out*	(1) leave, (2) be completely used
go out	not stay home	*set in*	begin and continue for a long time
go up	rise, go higher	*show up*	appear
grow up	become an adult	*sign up*	register for a class or event
hang on	(1) wait, (2) keep going	*sit down*	sit; take a seat
hold on	(1) wait, (2) persist	*slip up*	make a mistake
look into	investigate	*speak up*	talk louder
look out	be careful	*stand up*	stand; rise
make up	end a disagreement	*stay up*	remain awake
move in (to)	(1) take your things to a new home, (2) begin living somewhere	*take off*	(1) leave on an airplane, (2) grow; be successful
move out (of)	leave a place you live in	*watch out*	be careful
run into	meet someone by chance or unexpectedly	*work out*	(1) exercise, (2) go as planned

13 Adjectives and Adverbs: Comparative and Superlative Forms

		Adjective	Comparative	Superlative
1	**One-Syllable Adjectives**			
	a Add -*er* and -*est* to one syllable adjectives.	cheap high large long new old small strong tall	cheaper higher larger longer newer older smaller stronger taller	the cheapest the highest the largest the longest the newest the oldest the smallest the strongest the tallest
	b For one-syllable adjectives that end in a vowel + consonant, double the final consonant and add -*er* or -*est*.	big hot sad thin	bigger hotter sadder thinner	the biggest the hottest the saddest the thinnest
	Do not double the consonant w.	low	lower	the lowest

		Adjective	Comparative	Superlative
2	**Two-Syllable Adjectives**			
a	Add *more* or *most* to most adjectives.	boring	more boring	the most boring
		famous	more famous	the most famous
		handsome	more handsome	the most handsome
		patient	more patient	the most patient
b	Some two-syllable adjectives have two forms.	friendly	friendlier	the friendliest
			more friendly	the most friendly
		narrow	narrower	the narrowest
			more narrow	the most narrow
		simple	simpler	the simplest
			more simple	the most simple
		strict	stricter	the strictest
			more strict	the most strict
		quiet	quieter	the quietest
			more quiet	the most quiet
c	Remove the -y and add *-ier* or *-iest* to two-syllable adjectives ending in -y.	angry	angrier	the angriest
		easy	easier	the easiest
		friendly	friendlier	the friendliest
		happy	happier	the happiest
		lucky	luckier	the luckiest
		pretty	prettier	the prettiest
		silly	sillier	the silliest
3	**Three or More Syllable Adjectives** Add *more* or *most* to adjectives with three or more syllables.	beautiful	more beautiful	the most beautiful
		comfortable	more comfortable	the most comfortable
		creative	more creative	the most creative
		difficult	more difficult	the most difficult
		enjoyable	more enjoyable	the most enjoyable
		expensive	more expensive	the most expensive
		important	more important	the most important
		independent	more independent	the most independent
		relaxing	more relaxing	the most relaxing
		responsible	more responsible	the most responsible
		serious	more serious	the most serious
4	**Irregular Adjectives** Some adjectives have irregular forms.	bad	worse	the worst
		far	farther / further	the farthest / the furthest
		good	better	the best

Adjectives and Adverbs: Comparative and Superlative Forms *(continued)*

		Adjective	Comparative	Superlative
5	**-*ly* Adverbs** Most adverbs end in -*ly*. Add *more* or *most*. People usually only use *the* with superlative adverbs in formal writing and speaking.	dangerously patiently quickly quietly slowly	more dangerously more patiently more quickly more quietly more slowly	(the) most dangerously (the) most patiently (the) most quickly (the) most quietly (the) most slowly
6	**One-Syllable Adverbs** A few adverbs do not end in -*ly*. Add -*er* and -*est* to these adverbs.	fast hard	faster harder	(the) fastest (the) hardest
7	**Irregular Adverbs** Some adverbs have irregular forms.	badly far well	worse farther / further better	(the) worst (the) farthest / furthest (the) best

Glossary of Grammar Terms

action verb a verb that describes an action.

*I **eat** breakfast every day.*

*They **ran** in the 5K race.*

adjective a word that describes or modifies a noun.

*That's a **beautiful** hat.*

adjective clause see **relative clause**.

adverb a word that describes or modifies a verb, another adverb, or an adjective. Adverbs often end in *-ly*.

*Please walk **faster** but **carefully**.*

adverb clause a clause that shows how ideas are connected. Adverb clauses begin with conjunctions such as *because*, *since*, *although*, and *even though*.

***Although it is not a holiday**, workers have the day off.*

adverb of degree an adverb that makes other adverbs or adjectives stronger or weaker.

*The test was **extremely** difficult.   They are **kind of** busy today.*

adverb of manner an adverb that describes how an action happens.

*He has **suddenly** left the room.*

adverb of time an adverb that describes when something happens.

*She'll get up **later**.*

article the words *a / an* and *the*. An article introduces or identifies a noun.

*I bought **a** new MP3 player. **The** price was reasonable.*

auxiliary verb (also called **helping verb**) a verb that is used before a main verb in a sentence. *Do, have,* and *be* can act as auxiliary verbs.

***Does** he want to go to the library later?   **Have** you received the package?*

base form of the verb the form of a verb without any endings (*-s* or *-ed*) or *to*.

come   go   take

clause a group of words that has a subject and a verb. There are two types of clauses: **main clauses** and **dependent clauses** (*see* dependent clause). A sentence can have more than one clause.

MAIN CLAUSE   DEPENDENT CLAUSE   MAIN CLAUSE

I woke up when I heard the noise. It was scary.

common noun a word for a person, place, or thing. A common noun is not capitalized.

mother   building   fruit

comparative the form of an adjective or adverb that shows how two people, places, or things are different.

*My daughter is **older than** my son.* (adjective)

*She does her work **more quickly** than he does.* (adverb)

conjunction a word such as *and, but, so, or,* and *yet* which connects single words, phrases, or clauses.

*We finished all our work, **so** we left early.*

consonant a sound represented in writing by these letters of the alphabet: *b, c, d, f, g, h, j, k, l, m, n, p, q, r, s, t, v, w, x, y,* and *z*.

count noun refers to a person, place, or thing you can count. Count nouns have a plural form.

*There are three **banks** on Oak Street.*

definite article *the* is a definite article. Use *the* with a person, place, or thing that is familiar to you and your listener. Also, use *the* when the noun is unique – there is only one (*the sun, the moon, the Internet*).

The *movie we saw last week was very good.*

The *Earth is round.*

dependent clause a clause that cannot stand alone. Some kinds of dependent clauses are adverb clauses, relative clauses, and time clauses.

***After we return from the trip**, I'm going to need to relax.*

determiner a word that comes before a noun to limit its meaning in some way. Some common determiners are *some, a little, a lot, a few, this, that, these, those, his, a, an, the, much,* and *many*.

These *computers have **a lot** of parts.*

*Please give me **my** book.*

direct object the person or thing that receives the action of the verb.

*The teacher gave the students **a test**.*

factual conditional describes something that is generally true in a certain situation. The *if* clause describes the condition and is in the simple present. The result clause is in the simple present as well.

If *it's late, I don't stay online for a long time.*

formal a style of writing or speech used when you don't know the other person very well or where it's not appropriate to show familiarity, such as in business, a job interview, speaking to a stranger, or speaking to an older person who you respect.

Good evening. I'd like to speak with Ms. Smith. Is she available?

future a verb form that describes a time that hasn't come yet. It is expressed in English by *will, be going to,* and present tense.

*I**'ll meet** you tomorrow.*

*I**'m going to visit** my uncle and aunt next weekend.*

future conditional describes something that will happen under certain conditions in the future. The *if* clause describes the condition and is in the simple present. The result clause uses a future form of the verb.

If *I do well on this final exam, I**'ll get** an A for the course.*

gerund the *-ing* form of a verb that is used as a noun. It can be the subject or object in a sentence or the object of a preposition.

*We suggested **waiting** and **going** another day.*

*Salsa **dancing** is a lot of fun.*

*I look forward to **meeting** you.*

habitual past a verb form that describes repeated past actions, habits, and conditions using *used to* or *would*.

*Before we had the Internet, we **used to** go to the library a lot.*

*Before there was refrigeration, people **would** use ice to keep food cool.*

helping verb *see* **auxiliary verb**.

imperative a type of clause that tells people to do something. It gives instructions, directions to a place, and advice. The verb is in the base form.

***Listen** to the conversation.*

***Don't open** your books.*

indefinite article *a / an* are the indefinite articles. Use *a / an* with a singular person, place, or thing when you and your listener are not familiar with it, or when the specific name of it is not important. Use *a* with consonant sounds. Use *an* with vowel sounds.

*She's going to see **a** doctor today.   I had **an** egg for breakfast.*

indirect object the person or thing that receives the direct object.

*The teacher gave **the students** a test.*

infinitive *to* + the base form of a verb.

*I need **to get** home early tonight.*

infinitive of purpose *in order* + infinitive expresses a purpose. It answers the question *why*. If the meaning is clear, it is not necessary to use *in order*.

*People are fighting **(in order) to change** unfair laws.*

informal a style of speaking or writing to friends, family, and children.

Hey, there. Nice to see you again.

information question (also called **Wh- question**) begins with a *wh-* word *(who, what, when, where, which, why, how, how much)*. To answer this type of question, you need to provide information rather than answer *yes* or *no*.

inseparable phrasal verb a phrasal verb that cannot be separated. The verb and its particle always stay together.

*My car **broke down** yesterday.*

intransitive verb a verb that does not need an object. It is often followed by an expression of time, place, or manner.

*The flight **arrived** at 5:30 p.m.*

irregular adjective an adjective that does not change its form in the usual way. For example, you do not make the comparative form by adding *-er*.

good ➡ *better*

irregular adverb an adverb that does not change its form in the usual way. For example, you do not make the comparative form by adding *-er*.

badly ➡ *worse*

irregular verb a verb that does not change its form in the usual way. For example, it does not form the simple past with *-d* or *-ed*. It has its own special form.

go → *went*   *ride* → *rode*   *hit* → *hit*

main clause (also called **independent clause**) a clause that can be used alone as a complete sentence.

After I get back from my trip, ***I'm going to relax***.

main verb a verb that functions alone in a clause and can have an auxiliary verb.

*They **had** a meeting last week.*

*They have **had** many meetings this month.*

measurement word a word or phrase that shows the amount of something. Measurement words can be singular or plural.

*I bought **a box** of cereal, and Sonia bought **five pounds** of apples.*

modal a verb such as *can, could, have to, may, might, must, should, will*, and *would*. It modifies the main verb to show such things as ability, permission, possibility, advice, obligation, necessity, or lack of necessity.

*It **might** rain later today.*

*You **should** study harder if you want to pass this course.*

non-action verb *see* **stative verb**.

noncount noun refers to ideas and things that you cannot count. Noncount nouns use a singular verb and do not have a plural form.

*Do you download **music**?*

noun a word for a person, place, or thing. There are common nouns and proper nouns (*see* **common noun, proper noun**).

COMMON NOUN   PROPER NOUN

*I stayed in a **hotel** on my trip to New York.*   *I stayed in the **Pennsylvania Hotel**.*

object pronoun replaces a noun in the object position.

*Sara loves exercise classes. She takes **them** three times a week.*

particle a small word like *down, in, off, on, out*, or *up*. These words (which can also be prepositions) are used with verbs to form **two-word verbs** or **phrasal verbs**. The meaning of a phrasal verb often has a different meaning from the meaning of the individual words in it.

past participle a verb form that can be regular (base form + *-ed*) or irregular. It is used to form the present perfect and the passive. It can also be an adjective.

*I've **studied** English for five years.*

past progressive a verb form that describes events or situations in progress at a time in the past. The emphasis is on the action.

*They **were watching** TV when I arrived.*

phrasal verb (also called a **two-word verb**) consists of a verb + a particle. There are two kinds of phrasal verbs: separable and inseparable (*see* **particle, inseparable phrasal verb, separable phrasal verb**).

VERB + PARTICLE

*They **came back** from vacation today.* (inseparable)

*Please **put** your cell phone **away**.* (separable)

plural noun a noun that refers to more than one person, place, or thing.

students   women   roads

possessive adjective *see* **possessive determiner.**

possessive determiner (also called **possessive adjective**) a determiner that shows possession (*my, your, his, her, its, our,* and *their*).

possessive pronoun replaces a possessive determiner + singular or plural noun. The possessive pronoun agrees with the noun that it replaces.

*My exercise class is at night. **Hers** is on the weekend.*   (hers = her exercise class)

preposition a word such as *to, at, for, with, below, in, on, next to,* or *above* that goes before a noun or pronoun to show location, time, direction, or a close relationship between two people or things. A preposition may go before a gerund as well.

*I'm **in** the supermarket **next to** our favorite restaurant.*

*The idea **of** love has inspired many poets.*

present perfect a verb form that describes past events or situations that are still important in the present, actions that happened once or repeatedly at an indefinite time before now, and to give the number of times something happened up to now.

*Lately scientists **have discovered** medicines in the Amazon.*

*I've **been** to the Amazon twice.*

present perfect progressive a verb form that describes something that started in the past, usually continues in the present, and may continue in the future.

*He **hasn't been working** since last May.*

present progressive a verb form that describes an action or situation that is in progress now or around the present time. It is also used to indicate a fixed arrangement in the near future.

*What **are** you **doing** right now?*

*I'm **leaving** for Spain next week.*

pronoun a word that replaces a noun or noun phrase. Some examples are *I, we, him, hers,* and *it* (see **object pronoun, subject pronoun, relative pronoun, possessive pronoun, reciprocal pronoun, reflexive pronoun**).

proper noun a noun that is the name of a particular person, place, idea, or thing. It is capitalized.

***Central Park** is in **New York City**.*

punctuation mark a symbol used in writing such as a period (.), a comma (,), a question mark (?), or an exclamation point (!).

quantifier Some quantifiers are *much, many, some, any, a lot, plenty,* and *enough.*

reciprocal pronoun a pronoun *(each other, one another)* that shows that two or more people give *and* receive the same action or have the same relationship.

*Mari and I have the same challenges. We help **each other**.*   (I help Mari and Mari helps me.)

reflexive pronoun a pronoun *(myself, yourself, himself, herself, ourselves, yourselves, themselves)* which shows that the object of the sentence is the same as the subject.

*I taught **myself** to speak Japanese.*

regular verb a verb that changes its form in the usual way.

    live ➞ live**s**

    wash ➞ wash**ed**

relative clause (also known as **adjective clause**) defines, describes, identifies, or gives more information about a noun. It begins with a relative pronoun such as *who, that, which, whose,* or *whom.* Like all clauses, a relative clause has both a subject and a verb. It can describe the subject or the object of a sentence.

    *People **who have sleep problems** can join the study.* (subject relative clause)

    *There are many diseases **that viruses cause**.* (object relative clause)

relative pronoun a pronoun *(who, which, that, whose, whom)* that connects a noun phrase to a relative clause.

    *People **who** have sleep problems can join the study.*

    *There are many diseases **that** viruses cause.*

sentence a complete thought or idea that has a subject and a main verb. In writing, it begins with a capital letter and has a punctuation mark at the end (. ? !). In an imperative sentence, the subject (*you*) is not usually stated.

    This sentence is a complete thought.   Open your books.

separable phrasal verb a phrasal verb that can be separated. This means that an object can go before or after the particle.

    ***Write down** your expenses.*

    ***Write** your expenses **down**.*

simple past a verb form that describes completed actions or events that happened at a definite time in the past.

    *They **grew up** in Washington, D.C.*

    *They **attended** Howard University and **graduated** in 2019.*

simple present a verb form that describes things that regularly happen, such as habits and routines (usual and regular activities). It also describes facts and general truths.

    *I **play** games online every night.* (routine)

    *The average person **spends** 13 hours a week online.* (fact)

singular noun a noun that refers to only one person, place, or thing.

    *He is my best **friend**.*

statement a sentence that gives information.

    Today is Thursday.

stative verb (also called **non-action verb**) describes a state or situation, not an action. It is usually in the simple form of the present or past.

    *I **remember** your friend.*

subject the person or thing that performs the action of a verb.

    ***People** use new words and expressions every day.*

subject pronoun replaces a noun in the subject position.

    *Sara and I are friends. **We** work at the same company.*

superlative the form of an adjective or adverb that compares one person, place, or thing to others in a group.

*This storm was **the most dangerous** one of the season.* (adjective)

*That group worked **most effectively** after the disaster.* (adverb)

syllable a group of letters that has one vowel sound and that you say as a single unit.

There is one syllable in the word lunch *and two syllables in the word* breakfast. (Break *is one syllable and* fast *is another syllable.*)

tense the form of a verb that shows past or present time.

*They **worked** yesterday.* (simple past)

*They **work** every day.* (simple present)

third-person singular refers to *he, she,* and *it* or a singular noun. In the simple present, the third-person singular form ends in *-s* or *-es.*

***It looks** warm and sunny today.*   ***He washes** the laundry on Saturdays.*

time clause a clause that shows the order of events and begins with a time word such as *before, after, when, while,* or *as soon as.*

***Before** there were freezers, people needed ice to make frozen desserts.*

time expression a phrase that functions as an adverb of time. It tells when something happens, happened, or will happen.

*I graduated **in 2010**.*   *She's going to visit her aunt and uncle **next summer**.*

transitive verb a verb that needs an object. The object completes the meaning of the verb.

*She **wears** perfume.*

two-word verb see **phrasal verb**.

verb a word that describes an action or a state.

*Alex **wears** jeans and a T-shirt to school. Alex **is** a student.*

vowel a sound represented in writing by these letters of the alphabet: *a, e, i, o,* and *u.*

Wh- question see **information question**.

Yes / No question begins with a form of *be* or an auxiliary verb. You can answer such a question with *yes* or *no.*

*"**Are** they going to the movies?"*   *""**No**, they're not."*

*"**Can** you give me some help?"*   *"**Yes**, I can."*

Index

a / an, 85, 93, 118–19, 123
  before adjectives, 162
  for generalizations, definitions, 104
ability, with *can / could + not*, 246–47, A7
about, 113, 193, 198, 314, 316, A5, A6
adjectives, 162–63, A9
  for ages, lengths of time, 163, 169
  comparative, 338–40, 347, A12–A14
  ending in *-ed*, 165, 169
  ending in *-ful*, 169
  ending in *-ing*, 165–66
  patterns of, 165–69
  placement of, 166
  prepositions that follow, 196–98, 201
  superlative, 352–54, 357, A12–A14
adverbs, 183
  adverb clauses, 420–21, 425
  of certainty, 218, 223
  comparative, 338–40, 347, A14
  of degree, 179–81
  of frequency, 6, 7, 45
  of manner, 176–77
  with present perfect, 138–39, 148
  with present perfect progressive, 151
  superlative, 352–53, 357, A14

advice, 276–77, 283
  with *should / ought to / had better*, 276–77, A7
a few, 90
after, 10–11, 58, 60, 189
  in future time clauses, 232–33, 237
ago, 45, 128
a little, 89–90
a lot of, 89–90, 104
already, 138
although, 420–21, 425
always, 6–7, 45
  almost always, 6–7
  with imperatives, 32, 39
and, 362, 366, 379, 416–18, 425
any, 90
anything, 166
articles, 100–01, 104
  definite / indefinite, 100–01
as, 193
as . . . as, 343–45, 347
as soon as, 10, 58
  in future time clauses, 233
as well as, 197
at, 188–89, 198, 201, 316, A5, A6
  as time expression, 73
  at the moment, 19
away, 330
back, 326–28, 329
bad, 353, 357

be, 4, 18–19, 63, 155, A3
  adjectives after, 162, 165
  with adverbs of manner, 177
  agreement with nouns, 51, 211
  + gerunds, 376–77, 379
  + infinitives, 379
  + *not*, 4, 15, 18
  in past progressive, 79
  with present progressive, 25
  simple past of, 50–51
be able to
  for ability, 250–52, 255, A7
  for possibility, 250, 252, A7
  after other verbs, 254
because, 420–21, 425
  because of, 197
before, 10–11, 58, 67, 189
  in future time clauses, 232–33
be going to, 206–08, 216, 222–24, 226
  for future possibility, 304
but, 416–18, 424
by
  + gerund, 376
  + reflexive pronoun, 111
can
  with adverbs of manner, 177
  can / could
    in conversation, 252
    for offers, 266–68, 271, A7
    for permission, 262–64, 271, A7
    for requests, 266–67, A7

can/could + not
    for ability, possibility, 246–47
    cannot, 255
    for future possibility, 303–05
    for present possibility, 300–02
certainly, 193, 223, 263, 267
certainty, 193, 223
close to, 197
conditional clauses, 15, 236–38, A9–A10
conjunctions, 416–18, 420
contractions, 5, 18–20, 124, 150–51, 206
    of *has*, 289
    mustn't, 300
    of *will (not)*, 219
    of *would*, 64, 293
could, 280–81, A7
    + *not*, 281, 283
    for future probability, 303–04, A8
    for present probability, 300–02, A8
count nouns, 84–85, 90, 93, 100
    with adjectives, 162
    in generalizations, 104
definitely, 219, 223
determiners, 85, 89–90, 93
    possessive 110–11
did/didn't/did not, 45–46
    with base form of verbs, 53
    with *use to*, 61, 67
do/does, 5, 15, A3
    do you mind if, 262–64
    do you want to, 270
    with *have/need to*, 289–90, A8
    + *not*, 4, 15, 32, 39
down, 326–28, 333
during, 189, 201
each other, 111
enough, 90, 180

-er ending for comparative adjectives and adverbs, 339–40, 347, A12–A14
ever, 6–7, 125, 138, 145
everybody/everyone, 35, 330
factual conditionals, 10, A9
for, 113, 117, A5, A6
    as a preposition, 189, 193, 198, 201, 314, 316
    with present perfect, 142–43, 145
    with present perfect progressive, 151, 157
frequency expressions, 7
from, 192, 198, 314, A6
future
    with *be going to*, 206–08, 211, 222–24, 226
    conditionals, 236–38
    possibility, 303–05, 307, A8
    with present progressive, 206–08, 222–24
    with simple present, 206–08
    time clauses, 232–33, 237–38
    with *will*, 218–19, 222–24, 226
generalizations, 104, 105
gerunds, 362–63, 365–66, 369, 376–77, 383, A5
good, 176, 183, 353, 357
had better, 276–78, 283, A7
hardly ever, 6–7
has, 124–25, 150–51, A8
    + *not*, 124, 150–51
    for present perfect progressive, 157
    still before, 138
have, 124–25, 150–51, A3, A8
    with adverbs of manner, 177
    have (got) to, 288–90, A8
    + *not*, 124, 150–51
    for present perfect progressive, 157
    still before, 138

how
    how long, 60, 142, 150
    how often, 7, 62, 125, 251
if, 10–11
    clauses for future conditions, 237–38, 241, A7–A8
    clauses with imperatives, 32
imperatives, 32–33
    with *let's/let's not/let us*, 36–37
    negative, 38
    with subject pronouns, 35
    with time clauses, 37
in, 188–89, 197, 326, 353, A5, A6
    for past progressive, 73
    for simple past, 45
infinitives, 283, 292, 362–63, 365–66, 369, A5
    after *be/in order/it*, 379
in front of, 197
-ing form of verbs, 18–19, 25, 283, A4
    as nouns (gerunds), 362–63, A4
    as objects of a preposition, 189
    for past progressive, 72–73
    for present perfect progressive, 150–51
in order + infinitives, 379
instead of, 197
into, 192
intransitive verbs, 312–13, 319
    phrasal verbs, 326–27, 330, A11–A12
isn't/aren't, 5, 18–19
it + infinitive sentences, 379, 383
just, 37, 138
last, 45, 73, 128
lately, 138, 151
less, 339, 343
let's, 36–38
like, 22, 155
likely, 218, 219

look, 162, 177

-*ly* endings, 176–77, A14

make + object, 166

many, 90, 93

may
  may (not) for future possibility, 303–05, 307, A8
  for offers, 266–67, 271, A7
  for permission, 262–64, 271, A7
  for present possibility, 300–01, A8

maybe, 223, 277, 307

measurement words, 89, 92

might
  for future possibility, 303–05, 307, A8
  might want to, 280–81, A7
    + *not*, 281, 283
  for present possibility, 300–02, A8

more, 339–40, 347

most, 104

much, 90, 93

must (not), 288–90, A8
  for present possibility, 300–02, A8

near, 188

necessity, 295, A8
  have (got) to, need to, must, 288–90, A8

need to, 288–90, A8

never, 6–7, 45
  in affirmative statements, 145
  with imperatives, 32, 39
  before past participles, 138

next to, 197

no, 39, 263, 267–68
  no one, 330

noncount nouns, 84–86, 93, 100–01
  with determiners, 89–90, 93
  in generalizations, 104, 105
  with measurement words, 91
  with *there was*, 51, 53
  with *there wasn't*, 51

not, 6, 15, 293, 362, 417
  not a lot, 89
  not any, 89
  not as . . . as, 343–45
  not ever, 138
  not much, 89

nothing, 166, 330

nouns, 51, 84, 115, 162
  as adjectives, 162, A9
  for age and time, 163
  articles with, 100–01, 105
  count, 84–85, 90, 93, 100
  noncount, 84–86, 93, 100–01, 105, 354
  noun phrases, 189, 196–97
  placement of, 100–01, 166
  plural, 85, 100–01, 104, 105, 111, 354
  prepositions before, 197
  pronouns as replacement for, 110–11
  singular, 100–01, 111

objects, 110, 115
  combinations with verbs, prepositions, and, 314
  direct, 115, 117, 119
  indirect, 115, 117, 119
  object position, 110
  object pronouns, 110–11, 119, 329–30, 333, 409
  object relative clauses, 402–04, 406, 409
  of prepositions, 189, 197
  of transitive verbs, 312–13, 319, 329–30

of, 193, 198, 354, A5, A6
  of course, 263, 267

off, 326–27, 330–31

offers, 267–68
  with *can / could / may / will*, 267–68, A7

often, 6–7, 45

on, 188–89, 201, 316, 326–28, A5
  as time expression, 73

once, 233

one / ones, 111
  one another, 111
  one of the, 354

or, 293, 362, 366, 416

ought to, 276–78, A7

out, 326–28, 330–31
  out of, 197

outside of, 197

particles, 326–27, 329–30, 333

past participles, 124–25, 131, A3
  already before, 138

past progressive, 72–73
  contrasted with simple past, 76–77
  information questions in, 79
  with time clauses, 76–77
  use of, 79

perhaps, 223, 277

permission, 262–64, A8

phrasal verbs, 326–28, 329–31, A10–A12

plural nouns
  with *there were*, 51, 53
  with *there weren't*, 51

possibility with *can / could* + *not*, 247

possibly, 219, 223

predictions
  using *be going to*, 222
  using *will*, 218, 222, 226
  prefer, 293

preferences
  with *would like*, 292–93, A8
  with *would prefer / rather*, 292–93, A8

prepositions
  after adjectives, 196–98, 201, A6
  combinations with verbs, objects, and, 314, A5
  of direction, 192
  gerunds as objects of, 376–77, 383
  of manner, 192–93

with noun phrases and
pronouns, 193
with objects, 115, 117
phrasal, 196–97
of place, 188–89
prepositional phrases, 189, 314
pronunciation of, 193
with reflexive pronouns, 113
of time, 188–89
verbs with specific, 316–17
with *Wh-* questions, 193
in writing and speaking, 193
present perfect, 124–25, 131,
154–55
adverbs with, 138–39, 148
contrasted with present prefect
progressive, 154–55, 157
contrasted with simple past,
128–29
with *for*, 142–43
with *since*, 142
with stative verbs, 157
present perfect progressive,
150–51, 154–55
contrasted with present perfect,
154–55, 157
with *for/since*, 151
present probability, 300–02, A8
present progressive, 18–20, 21–22,
25, A2
contrasted with simple present,
21–22
for future events, 206–08,
222–24
probably, 218–19, 223, 277
prohibition
can't, 289, A8
must (not), 288–90, A8
pronouns, 4, 110–11
object, 110–11, 115, 117, 193,
196–97, 409
object relative, 402–03
order of adjectives and, 166
possessive, 110–11, 353
prepositions before, 197

reciprocal, 110–11
reflexive, 110–11, 113
subject, 110–11
subject relative, 388–89, 395,
403
pronunciation of *got/has/have to*,
289
quantifiers, 104
questions
already in, 138
determiners with noncount
nouns in, 90
about future possibility, 304–05
prepositions with *Wh-*, 193
with *should*, 277
with *why don't/doesn't/not*,
281
yet in, 138
rarely, 6, 45
really, 277
recently
with present perfect, 138
with present perfect
progressive, 151
relative clauses
object, 402–04, 406, 409
subject, 388–89, 392, 395, 403
requests, 90, 266–67, A7
with *can/could/will/would*,
266–67, 271, A7
with *do you want to*, 270
for permission, 262–64
's not/'re not, 4, 18
seem, 162, 177
should
with adverbs of manner, 177
to give advice, 276–78, A7
should (not) for future
probability, 303–05, 307
should (not) for present
probability, 300–01, A8
simple past, 44, A3, A4
of *be*, 50–51

contrasted with past
progressive, 76
contrasted with present perfect,
128–29
-ed endings for, 48, A4
with main/time clauses, 77
use of, 45, 53, 131
verbs before using *would*, 63
simple present, 4, 21–22, 25
contrasted with present
progressive, 21–22
contrasted with simple past, 53
in future clauses, 233, 237–38
in future conditional clauses,
237–38, 241
for future events, 206–08
questions, 7
statements, 6–7
since, 189, 201, 420–21
with present perfect, 142, 148
with present perfect
progressive, 151, 157
singular nouns
with *there was*, 51, 53
with *there wasn't*, 51
so, 416–17, 421
some, 85, 90–91, 100, 104
some of the, 354
somebody, 35
someone, 35, 330
something, 113, 166, 330
sometimes, 6–7, 15, 45
stative
meaning, 25
verbs, 21–22, 64, 155, 157, A2
still, 142–43
subjects, 110
gerunds as, 376, 379, 383
subject position, 110
subject pronouns, 110–11, 117,
124–25, 150–51, 206–07,
218–19

subject relative clauses, 388–90,
     392, 395, 403
such as, 197
suggestions
     with *could, might, why
          don't/ not*, 280–81, A7
     negative, 281, 283
than, 338–40, 347
that, 85
     as object relative pronoun,
          402–04, 409
     as subject relative pronoun,
          388–90, 395
     that would be great, 268
the, 85, 100–01, 103
     in generalizations, 104, 105
     the + -(i)est, 353–54
     the least/most, 353–54, 357
there was/were, 50–51, 53
this, 85
     for time expressions, 19, 128,
          151
though, 421, 425
     even though, 420–21, 425
time clauses, 10–11, 15
     answering questions with, 60,
          237
     future, 232–33, 241
     imperatives with, 32, 39
     need for subject in, 67
     for order of past events, 58–59
     with past progressive, 76–77,
          79
     placement of, 58
     in questions, 77
     with simple past, 76–77
     with *when/ while*, 76
time expressions, 7, 19
     with past progressive, 73
     with present perfect
          progressive, 151
     with simple past, 45, 53
     with *would*, 63
time words, 232–33, 237

to, 113, 115, 117, 192, 193, 198,
     314, 316, A5, A6
     + base form of verbs, 362, 369
too, 180
     too many, 90, 93
     too much, 90
transitive verbs, 312–13, 318–19
     phrasal verbs, 329–31, A10– A11
try + gerund/infinitive, 366
until, 59–60
     in future time clauses, 233
up, 326–28, 330–31, 333
     up to, 197
use to, 61–62, 67
used to, 61–64, 67
verbs
     action of, 115
     with adverbs, 176–77
     auxiliary, 177
     combinations with objects,
          prepositions, and, 314, A5
     followed by gerunds/infinitives,
          362–63, 365–66, 369, A5
     irregular simple past, 44, 124, A3
     linking, 162, 177
     main, 177
     with objects, 117–18
     prepositions for, 119
     regular simple past, 44–45, A4
     singular, with noncount nouns,
          85
     with specific prepositions,
          316–19
     used with the present perfect,
          126
was(n't)/were(n't), 50–51, 72–73
Wh- words, 6, 19
     with *be able to*, 251
     with *be going to*, 207, 211
     with *can/ could*, 247
     in future conditional questions,
          237
     with *have/ need to*, 289
     + *is/ are*, 19
     with past progressive, 73

prepositions with, 193, 197
with present perfect, 125
with present perfect
     progressive, 151
with simple past, 45, 51
with *use to*, 62
with *will*, 219
with *would*, 63
with *would like, would prefer,
     would rather*, 293
what, 193, 197, 237
     with *should*, 277
     what time, 7, 60
when, 7, 10, 15
     to answer questions about time,
          60
     in future time clauses, 232–33,
          237–38, 241
     with past progressive, 76–77
     with *should*, 277
     to show time something started,
          58
     with simple past, 45, 77
where, 15
which, 193, 197
     as object relative pronoun,
          402–04, 409
     as subject relative pronoun,
          388–90, 395
while, 10, 76–77
who, as subject relative pronoun,
     388–90, 395
     with *should*, 277
     who/ whom as object relative
          pronoun, 402–04, 409
whose, 392, 395, 403, 406, 409
why
     why doesn't/ don't, 280–81
     + *not*, 280–81, 283
will (not), 218–19, 222–24, 226, 237,
     241
     for ability, 251
     for offers, 267–68, 271, A7
     will for future possibility, 304
     will for requests, 266–67, 271, A7

with, 192, 314, 316, A6
would, 61–63, 226
    would like, 292–93, 295, A8
    would prefer/rather, 292–94,
       295, A8
    for requests, 266–67, 271, A7
writing
    academic, 36, 281
       adverb clauses in, 425
       as . . . as in, 344
       comparatives in, 339–40, 347
       conjunctions in, 425
       transitive phrasal verbs in,
         331
       was not/were not in, 50
       which in, 403
       will/be going to in, 223
    formal, 19, 46
       adverbs of degree in, 180
       with *be unable to*, 252
       with *must*, 289
       past progressive in, 73
       present perfect in, 155
       since in, 422
       that/which/who in, 389
       with *will (not)*, 219
    informal
       didn't in, 46
       imperatives in, 33
       past progressive in, 73
       that/who in, 389, 403
       Wh- words + *is* in, 19
       will (not) in, 219
yet, 138, 416, 417

Art Credits

Acknowledgements

The authors and publishers acknowledge the following sources of copyright material and are grateful for the permissions granted. While every effort has been made, it has not always been possible to identify the sources of all the material used, or to trace all copyright holders. If any omissions are brought to our notice, we will be happy to include the appropriate acknowledgements on reprinting and in the next update to the digital edition, as applicable.

Key: U = Unit.

Photography

All the photos are sourced from Getty Images.

U1: Antonio_Diaz/iStock/Getty Images Plus; Wavebreak Media; JGI/Tom Grill; Dolgachov/iStock/ Getty Images Plus; Jacoblund/iStock/Getty Images Plus; **U2:** Lilechka75/iStock/Getty Images Plus; JGI/ Tom Grill; Ariel Skelley/DigitalVision; Aldomurillo/ iStock/Getty Images Plus; Handout; Detlev van Ravenswaay/Picture Press; **U3:** M-imagephotography/ iStock/Getty Images Plus; Dstarky/iStock/Getty Images Plus; Dstarky/iStock/Getty Images Plus; Fuse/ Corbis; Clerkenwell/Vetta; Gareth Brown/Cultura; Jeff Greenough; CARLOS CLARIVAN/Science Photo Library; **U4:** Ralph Orlowski; AFP; Jean Baptiste Lacroix/WireImage; Michael Ochs Archives; A'Lelia Bundles/Madam Walker Family Archives/Washington, D.C; Stocktrek/Photodisc; **U5:** Vincenzo Assenza/ EyeEm; Bettmann; Jenifoto/iStock/Getty Images Plus; Mimi Haddon/Photodisc; gremlin/iStock/ Getty Images Plus; **U6:** AFP; Marvin E. Newman/ Photographer's Choice; Klaus Vedfelt/Taxi; Shannon Fagan/The Image Bank; Ajr_images/iStock/Getty Images Plus; Mauro_Repossini/iStock/Getty Images Plus; Otto Greule Jr; Warren Faidley/Corbis; NASA/ Handout/Hulton Archive; Judy Bellah/Lonely Planet Images; **U7:** Corbis/VCG; MistikaS/iStock/Getty Images Plus; Alexandr Dubovitskiy/iStock/Getty Images Plus; Zak00/DigitalVision Vectors; Zak00/ DigitalVision Vectors; Joern Pollex; John B. Carnett/ Popular Science; VCG/Visual China Group; **U8:** Ezra Bailey/Taxi; Tom Werner/DigitalVision; **U9:** Geber86/ E+; PeopleImages/E+; Stocknroll/E+; Hoxton/Ryan Lees; Hero Images; **U10:** Ariel Skelley/Photodisc; Georgette Douwma/Photographer's Choice; Zubin Shroff/The Image Bank; Encyclopaedia Britannica/ Universal Images Group; Barcroft; Wolfgang Poelzer/WaterFrame; Universal History Archive; Sarah Peters/Moment; Suefeldberg/iStock/Getty Images Plus; **U11:** Peter Chadwick LRPS/Moment Open; Dndavis/iStock/Getty Images Plus; AFP; Vm/ iStock/Getty Images Plus; Westend61; Sarkophoto/ iStock/Getty Images Plus; **U12:** Westend61; Yuji Kotani/Taxi Japan; Brittak/iStock/Getty Images Plus Unrelease; Jose Luis Pelaez Inc/DigitalVision; Masuti/ iStock/Getty Images Plus; Coral_Brunner/iStock/ Getty Images Plus; **U13:** Maximilian Stock Ltd/The Image Bank; DigitalVision; Steve Cole/The Image Bank; Juice Images/Cultura; KHALED DESOUKI/ AFP; **U14:** Monkeybusinessimages/iStock/Getty Images Plus; Luckyraccoon/iStock/Getty Images Plus; **U15:** Roberto Machado Noa/LightRocket; VisionsofAmerica/Joe Sohm/DigitalVision; Elena_ Danileiko/iStock/Getty Images Plus; Peter Dazeley/ Photographer's Choice; Sawitree Pamee/EyeEm; MATTHIASRABBIONE/iStock/Getty Images Plus;

Illustrations

Ben Hasler; Ed Fotheringham; Maria Rabinky; Monika Roe; Rob Schuster; Oxford Designers & Illustrators.

Audio

Audio production by John Marshall Media

Typeset

Q2A Media Services Pvt. Ltd